Books by Robert Ackart

Spirited Cooking

SPIRITED

New York   1984   Atheneum

Robert Ackart

COOKING

An Introduction to Wines in the Kitchen

TITLE PAGE DRAWING BY MARJORIE ZAUM

Library of Congress Cataloging in Publication Data

Ackart, Robert C.
    Spirited cooking.

    Includes index.
    1. Cookery (Wine)   2. Cookery (Liquors)   I.   Title.
TX726.A24   1984   641.6'22   84-45059
ISBN 0-689-11471-0

Copyright © 1984 by Robert Ackart
All rights reserved
Published simultaneously in Canada by McClelland and Stewart Ltd.
Composition by Heritage Printers, Inc.,
Charlotte, North Carolina
Manufactured by Haddon Craftsmen, Scranton, Pennsylvania
Designed by Kathleen Carey
First Edition

*For Lola Wilson Hayes
and Lynne Esther Trichter*

Introduction

For several years I have wanted to write a book on cooking with wine and spirits (and, by extension, with beer, which is commonly used in Flemish countries). I have wanted to write the book because I feel there is an elegance about such cooking. One may, if one wishes, refer to *boeuf bourguignon* and *coq au vin* as "stews"—which, indeed, they are—but stews fit for kings, if not for the gods, made so by the use of wine as the braising liquid. Again, to cite arbitrarily from among desserts, what is more festive than a handsomely turned out charlotte russe made with liqueur, or a shimmering chilled ginger soufflé laced with rum?

Cooking with wine and spirits raises the most prosaic recipe to a tempting level of refinement. The dish at once becomes glamorous. It is also better-tasting, for the wine or liquor imparts flavor to whatever ingredients it complements.

Cooking with wine and spirits is fun, because once the dish is range- or oven-ready, these magic elixirs do the work for you, bringing out and binding together the flavors of all the ingredients.

Cooking with wine and spirits is also reasonably economical. True, wine and spirits are not cheap, but their cost is more than offset by the fact that in using them you are able to create very special fare. Tender and tempting meat dishes, for example, may be made with less expensive cuts; vegetables take on added zest; desserts become more delectable.

Do not, however, be misled by that ignominious handle "cooking wine," which is merely cheap wine of negligible quality, and will reveal itself as such in your completed recipe. I do not suggest, of course, that you cook with wines of rare vintage; but the quality of the wine you choose will be reflected in the finished dish, tasting smooth and mellow rather than sharp or bitter, faults that no amount of additional seasoning can disguise.

Do not be put off by having invested in a bottle of wine for a recipe that calls for only two cupfuls. Store the rest in the refrigerator, to use later in another recipe; wine keeps very well for a month if properly chilled. Or enjoy a glass of the leftover wine with the completed dish. Many of our domestic wines are admirable for use at table and in the kitchen. They are, by and large, less expensive than imported wines, more readily available, and equal to their European counterparts at producing palatable foods in the kitchen and warm sociability at table.

Certain foods lend themselves more naturally than others to preparation with wine or spirits. Because long, slow cooking brings out their full flavor, soups, meats, poultry, certain baked goods, and many sauces respond ideally to the use of wine and spirits. Many desserts are also improved by their use. No menu category, however, is omitted. Fish, for instance, which cooks very rapidly, is enhanced when prepared with wine. Many vegetables, too, are transformed (for the better) by being cooked in wine. I do not believe I ever really tasted cabbage until I braised it in white wine.

Here, I would add a word of caution: In cooking with wine and spirits, more is not necessarily better. These recipes are quite specific in stating the amount of wine and spirits to be used.

In preparing these recipes, I held as my one paramount criterion that the wine or spirit (or beer) be an *essential* ingredient of the dish. For example, if some dish called for two tablespoons of rum as a flavoring agent only—and another seasoning might as well have been used—I did not consider the rum integral to the completed dish, and so did not include it. Even with this self-imposed limitation, I had to pare down the possible choices to arrive at the more than 250 recipes included.

Please note the subtitle of the book: *An Introduction to Wines in the Kitchen*. I have not attempted to write "the complete book of wine cookery." Can such a book exist? I doubt it, for the variations in cooking with wine and spirits are almost limitless. *Spirited Cooking* aims to present a sampling of the possibilities open to you for the use of wine in cooking. As you will see in the Lexicon of Wines and Spirits (page 337), their number is limited and their choice dictated by their general availability at average—not highly specialized—wine and spirits shops. The emphasis throughout the book is on the ease and creativity of cooking with wines and spirits, and the consequent pleasure it will afford you in the kitchen and at table.

No cookbook is the work of its author alone; recipes contributed, the comments and criticisms of friends, and other influences and ideas affect the final product. For all this help, the cookbook writer is grateful. For this reason, I want to thank Jinx Hufnagel for suggesting the subject of this book; one night as we were dining together, she said casually, "Why don't you write about cooking with wines?" And the idea, having been planted, took root. I want to thank, too, Jacqueline Pery, Director of Foreign Relations, and Simone Cointat, author, both of SOPEXA, the Paris-based agency working toward worldwide use of French wines and foodstuffs; the recipes supplied by these friends are an important addition to the book. In America, SOPEXA is represented by Food and Wines from France, Inc.; I am grateful to Mary Lyons, Director of Public Relations, for putting me in touch with her colleagues in Paris. To the French writer Marianne Andrau I am happily beholden for having enjoyed at her home in St. Cloud many recipes from her native Gascony that are included here.

Robert Ackart

Katonah, New York
1984

Author's Note

In many of the recipes, two wines or spirits are suggested, one imported and one domestic. Because of the national character of many recipes, the imported wines or spirits are listed first throughout. All the dishes, however, may be made successfully with domestic wines or spirits, often with a saving in cost.

To give you examples of how the listings work: the recipe for Boeuf Bourguignon (page 49) calls for "1 bottle dry red Burgundy (recommended: Mâcon [imported] *or* Gamay Beaujolais [domestic])." Again, the recipe for Broccoli or Cauliflower, Roman Style (page 205) calls for "2 cups dry white wine (recommended: Soave [imported] *or* Chablis [domestic])."

When a single wine is listed ("recommended: Beaujolais"), either imported or domestic wine of that type may be used; the choice is yours.

Contents

Spirited Cooking

A Lexicon of
Terms Used in This Book

I hope you will read this section of the book, for I feel it will make pleasanter and easier your adventure in cooking with wine and spirits.

First, a few general remarks.

The length of time needed to prepare the dish and the length of time needed to cook it are suggested at the start of each recipe. The preparation time is approximate; it will vary with the expertise of the cook, and includes peeling, chopping, and other readying of ingredients. It is assumed that, whenever possible, two or three steps in the preparation will be undertaken simultaneously. The cooking time refers to the period needed to finish the dish. The suggestion "At *this point you may stop and continue later*" is included when recipes may be made in either one session or, if preferred, two; it is omitted when the recipe is more effectively prepared in a single period. If a recipe is oven-cooked, the temperature setting is indicated at the outset, so that your oven will be ready when you need it. Ingredients are listed in order of use, and for cooks who (like me) arrange their spice shelves alphabetically, herbs and seasonings are listed in that way.

Now for the terms that follow: The subjects are entered alphabetically and cross-referenced when necessary. The entries give definitions for terms used in the recipes—*beurre manié* and *roux*, for example, expressions that we have adopted from foreign cuisines. Many entries deal with "how to"—how to defat dishes or to prepare seasoned flour, for example.

3

ALMONDS, TOASTED: Spread the almonds evenly on a baking sheet. Bake them in a 350° oven, turning occasionally with a spatula, for about 12 minutes, or until they are a rich golden brown. Allow them to cool and "dry" before proceeding with your recipe.

BÉCHAMEL: A basic butter-flour-and-milk sauce (page 259), made from a roux (see page 6) to which milk and seasonings are added; the mixture is cooked and stirred until thickened and smooth. A velouté is made in the same way, with meat, poultry, or fish stock used in place of the milk.

BEURRE MANIÉ: A mixture of softened butter and flour, most often in equal quantities, blended to a smooth paste and stirred into a simmering liquid as a thickening agent.

BLANCH: To blanch meat or vegetables is to plunge them briefly into boiling water, after which they are refreshed in cold water. Blanching gives firmness to veal and preserves the whiteness of certain flesh (veal and sweetbreads, for example).

BOUQUET GARNI: A selection of herbs and/or spices loosely tied together in cheesecloth and simmered with other ingredients to give added flavor. The cheesecloth bag facilitates discarding the seasonings once they are used, and also prevents the herbs from coloring or flecking the liquid. Bouquets garnis can (and should) be largely a product of your imagination, but to start you off, here are two that I find useful. I: 2 bay leaves, 2 whole cloves, 1 peeled and split garlic clove, 8 parsley sprigs, 6 peppercorns, ½ teaspoon dried thyme. II: 2 bay leaves, 3 celery tops with leaves, ½ teaspoon dried marjoram, 4 parsley sprigs, 1 teaspoon dried sage, 1 teaspoon dried summer savory. One can always add rosemary leaves, and a piece of lemon or orange zest lends a delightful nuance.

BUTTER: Sweet (unsalted) every time! Why? Because wine and spirits bring out flavors, just as salt does. And just as you will need less salt in these recipes than you probably use ordinarily, you will find that sweet butter gives a richer taste than you might have imagined, and does not add salt to the dish.

CHEESE, GRATED: These days, when many people have food processors to take the drudgery out of various kitchen chores, we really should allow ourselves the luxury of fresh-grated (actually, fresh-ground) Parmesan and other similar cheeses. Use the steel blade, and drop the cheese, cut into about ¾-inch cubes, into the container, one piece at a time. If you have no food processor, you probably have a strong elbow, and hand-grated cheese is not really so arduous to prepare. In both cases, fresh-prepared cheese tastes nothing like the store-prepared or packaged product—it is infinitely better.

DEFATTING : To defat a casserole-prepared recipe, make the dish 24 hours in advance of serving it. Refrigerate it overnight, and the following day remove the fat, which will have solidified. This step is particularly helpful in such dishes as Boeuf Bourguignon (page 49), which cannot be made without creating a layer of fat on the top of the casserole.

To defat canned chicken broth, refrigerate the can overnight. The following day the solidified fat will strain out as you pour the chilled broth through a fine sieve.

FLAME : To warm, ignite, and pour over food brandy or other fortified wine. Doing so adds flavor—to Cherries Jubilee (page 228), for example. It not only adds flavor to uncooked meat, but also helps to seal in the juices and tenderize the flesh.

HERBS : Dried herbs are used unless fresh ones are specifically suggested. A word of caution, however: Dried herbs lose their savor when kept for long periods. It is best to buy them in small quantities and replace unused portions after six months.

JULIENNE : A French culinary term meaning fine-cut vegetables, meats, or fruit rinds. Julienne of carrots, for example, are pieces about the size of a wooden matchstick; julienne of ham is cut about half as thick as a lead pencil; and fruit zest (the outer, oily part of the skin of a lemon or orange) is very fine indeed, about 3/32 inch (but you do not have to measure).

MUSHROOMS, TO PREPARE FOR USE IN COOKED DISHES : Trim and cut the mushrooms as the recipe directs. In a saucepan, combine 2 tablespoons each water, strained fresh lemon juice, and butter. Heat the mixture, and when the butter is melted, add the mushrooms, tossing them gently with a rubber spatula to coat them well. Cover the pan and cook them over moderate heat for 5 minutes. Add them, together with their liquid, to the recipe; or, if you prefer, drain them and reserve the liquid for mushroom soup (which is what I do).

ONIONS, **WHITE, TO PEEL**: Cut a thin bit off the bulb end of the onions; leave the root end intact. Drop the onions into briskly boiling water for 1 minute; do not cover. Drain them, and refresh them in cold water. The skins will slip off easily when you pinch the root end.

ROUX: Equal quantities of flour and fat (usually butter); the butter is heated and the flour added to it; the mixture is cooked over gentle heat to eliminate the graininess of the flour and its mealy taste. Roux is used as a thickening agent in sauces and soups (see Béchamel Sauce, page 259). If desired, the flour may be cooked in the butter until it darkens, thus lending color to the sauce.

SALTING: As I suggest from time to time throughout the book, wines and liquors bring out food flavors. For this reason, you will need less salt in these recipes than you may be acustomed to using. Unless specifically directed to add salt elsewhere in the preparation of the dish, season the recipe to taste with salt only when it is completed.

SEASONED **FLOUR**: Dredging meats in seasoned flour before browning them is one way to seal in meat essences, and at the same time to begin the sauce for the dish, for the flour thickens the cooking liquid as the meat is tenderized. Combine in a wax paper bag ⅔ cup of flour, 1 teaspoon salt, and ½ teaspoon white pepper (which will not speckle the sauce); shake the bag to blend the ingredients. A few pieces at a time, shake the meat or chicken in the bag, and proceed to brown it. Add a little of the remaining seasoned flour when making the sauce.

SOUPS, **FREEZING**: Soups freeze very well; however, frozen soups tend to separate when thawed. They are easily brought to their original consistency by being whirled, about 2 cups at a time, in the container of a blender. Once blended, the soup may be heated or chilled, depending upon your preference.

THICKENED **CREAM**: In France, crème fraîche, a thick cream with the consistency of our sour cream (although the two are unrelated) and a slightly nutty taste, is used plain on hot desserts or as a topping, as we use whipped cream, and as an enrichment for sauces. It is available in this country, imported by specialty food shops in large metropolitan centers, and it is expensive. You may, however, make your own thickened cream (I do not call it crème fraîche, because it is not) by combining in a jar with a tight-fitting lid 1 cup heavy cream and 1 tablespoon buttermilk. Shake the jar vigorously for a minute or two and allow the mixture to stand, refrigerated, overnight. The following day, the cream will have thickened and its flavor will be somewhat richer. If you like, use it in recipes calling for thickened cream. Regular heavy cream, two days old, will yield equally satisfying results.

VEGETABLES, COOKING OF: A list of "don'ts." Don't overcook vegetables. Don't oversalt the water in which they are cooked. (If possible, use no salt at all, but season them when done.) Don't drown them; cook them rapidly in as small an amount of liquid as possible. Rewards: more flavor, greater crispness, and more of their nutrients preserved.

ZEST: The outermost rind of citrus fruits, which contains the flavorful oils. To remove the zest, use a vegetable peeler; avoid including any of the white part of the skin, which is bitter. The zest of limes, lemons, and oranges gives a concentrated flavor of the fruit and can be used in various ways to enhance many recipes.

Soups and Appetizers

Soups

In the following selection of recipes, I have tried to include as many different kinds of soup as possible. My problem lay in deciding which to exclude, for the number of soups enhanced by wine and spirits is indeed large. I hope that you will find among these recipes soups to fit almost every need or whim: elegant cream soups, hearty one-dish-meal soups, thin-and-light soups, soups made of meat or fish or fruit or vegetables. Fish and fruit soups lend themselves particularly well to the use of wine and spirits—perhaps that is why there are several recipes in each of these categories. Fruit soups, incidentally, may be served as dessert; I sometimes use them for this purpose, and find that my fellow diners enjoy them as an unusual and refreshing end to the meal.

Apple Soup

6 TO 8 SERVINGS
PREPARATION AND COOKING: ABOUT 45 MINUTES
REFRIGERATES; FREEZES

    5 large tart apples, peeled and cored
    2½ cups chicken stock or 2 (10½-ounce) cans of defatted
        chicken broth
    1 bay leaf

In a saucepan, combine the apple peel and cores, the chicken stock, and the bay leaf. Bring the liquid to the boil, reduce the heat, and simmer the mixture, covered, for 15 minutes. Strain it; reserve the liquid and discard the residue.

Prepared apples, chopped coarse	1 medium onion, peeled and chopped coarse
2½ cups dry red wine (recommended: Beaujolais)	Zest of 1 small lemon
	2 bay leaves
	½ teaspoon salt

In a large saucepan, combine these six ingredients. Bring the liquid to the boil, reduce the heat, and simmer the apples, covered, for 20 minutes, or until they are very soft. Discard the lemon zest and bay leaves; allow the mixture to cool somewhat. In the container of a food processor or blender, whirl the mixture, 2 cups at a time, until it is smooth. Return it to the saucepan.

⅓ cup sugar
2 tablespoons cornstarch

Sift together the sugar and cornstarch and add the mixture to the contents of the sauceplan. Bring the purée just to the boil, stirring constantly until it is thickened and smooth.

Reserved stock
Strained juice of 1 small lemon
Sour cream

Stir in the stock and lemon juice. If the soup is to be served hot, bring it to serving temperature; if it is to be served chilled, allow it to cool and then refrigerate it for at least 3 hours. Garnish each portion with a spoonful of sour cream.

Chilled Cream of Apricot Soup

6 SERVINGS
PREPARATION AND COOKING: ABOUT 40 MINUTES
CHILLING TIME: 4 HOURS
REFRIGERATES; FREEZES

1 (11-ounce) package
    tenderized dried apricots
1 (3-inch) piece cinnamon
    stick
4 cloves
Zest of 1 small lemon
2 cups chicken stock

or 1 (10½-ounce) can of
    defatted chicken broth
    plus water to equal
    2 cups
1 cup dry white wine
    (recommended:
    Riesling)

In a large saucepan, combine these six ingredients. Bring the liquid to the boil, reduce the heat, and simmer the apricots, covered, for 20 minutes. Allow the mixture to cool.

Remove the cinnamon stick, cloves, and lemon zest. In the container of a food processor or blender, whirl the mixture, about 2 cups at a time, until it is smooth. Transfer it to a serving bowl.

At this point you may stop and continue later.

Strained juice of 1 small lemon
½ cup heavy cream, scalded
Sugar

Salt
Fine-chopped fresh mint

Into the soup, stir first the lemon juice and then the cream. Season it to taste with sugar and salt. Chill it for at least 4 hours. Serve the soup garnished with a sprinkling of mint.

Avocado Soup

6 SERVINGS
PREPARATION AND COOKING: ABOUT 20 MINUTES
REFRIGERATES; FREEZES

2 large ripe avocados, peeled, seeded, and chopped coarse
1 cup chicken stock or 1 (10½-ounce) can of defatted
    chicken broth

In the container of a food processor or blender, combine the avocado and stock; whirl until the mixture is smooth. Transfer it to a mixing bowl.

2 cups cream (light or heavy, depending upon the degree of richness you desire)
1 cup dry white wine (recommended: Chablis)

Strained juice of ½ lemon
Salt
A few grains of cayenne pepper

To the contents of the mixing bowl, gradually add the cream, stirring to blend the mixture. Stir in the wine and lemon juice. Season the soup to taste with salt and cayenne pepper. Transfer it to the top of a double boiler or to a serving bowl. If you wish to serve it hot, bring it to serving temperature over simmering water; if you wish to serve it chilled, refrigerate it for 4 hours.

Beer Soup (ALSACE)

6 SERVINGS
PREPARATION: ABOUT 25 MINUTES
COOKING: 30 MINUTES
REFRIGERATES; FREEZES

3 tablespoons butter
1 garlic clove, peeled and chopped fine
2 medium onions, peeled and chopped fine

1 tablespoon paprika (preferably sweet Hungarian)
1 cup dry bread crumbs

In a large saucepan, heat the butter and in it cook the garlic and onion until translucent. Stir in the paprika and then the bread crumbs.

1¼ cups stale beer (recommended: Pilsner) or 1 (12-ounce) can domestic beer
3 cups beef or chicken stock or 2 (10½-ounce) cans beef bouillon or chicken broth, plus water to equal 3 cups

Into the contents of the saucepan, stir the beer and stock. Bring the liquid to the boil, reduce the heat, and simmer the soup, covered, for 30 minutes.

Salt
Fresh-ground pepper
¼ cup fine-chopped parsley
Fresh-grated hard cheese (recommend: Sapsago)

Season the soup to taste with salt and pepper; stir in the parsley. Offer the grated cheese separately.

Variation:

Follow the first two steps of the recipe as written. In step three, omit the parsley and substitute a generous grating of nutmeg. At the time of serving, stir in ¼ cup heavy cream.

Black Bean Soup (UNITED STATES)

6 TO 8 SERVINGS
PREPARATION: ABOUT 30 MINUTES
COOKING: 2½ HOURS
REFRIGERATES; FREEZES

The traditional American recipe is given distinctive zest by the addition of bourbon whiskey. If desired, the whiskey may be omitted and ½ cup of Madeira or dry sherry stirred into the soup at the time of serving.

1 pound black beans, rinsed
8 cups water

In a soup kettle, combine the beans and water. Bring the liquid to the boil and, over high heat, cook the beans, uncovered, for 10 minutes. Away from the heat, allow them to stand, covered, for 1 hour.

Ham bone
2 large carrots, scraped and
    chopped coarse
2 medium celery ribs, with the
    leaves, chopped coarse
2 large onions, peeled and
    chopped coarse
Bouquet garni (page 4)
1 cup bourbon whiskey

To the contents of the kettle, add these ingredients. Return the liquid to the boil, reduce the heat, and simmer the mixture, covered, for 2½ hours, or until the beans are very tender. Discard the ham bone and bouquet garni.

At this point you may stop and continue later.

In the container of a food processor or blender, whirl the soup, about 2 cups at a time, until it is smooth. If the final purée is not of the consistency you desire (it may be quite thick), add a little water.

> **Salt**
> **Fresh-ground pepper**
> **Paper-thin lemon slices**
> **Fine-chopped parsley**

Season the soup to taste with salt and pepper. Bring it to serving temperature and offer it in heated dishes, garnished with a floating lemon slice sprinkled with parsley.

Dried Bean Soup (NETHERLANDS)

6 TO 8 SERVINGS
PREPARATION: ABOUT 35 MINUTES
COOKING: 2 HOURS
REFRIGERATES; FREEZES

> **1 cup dried white beans of your choice**
> **3 (12 ounce) cans stale beer**
> **3½ cups water**

In a soup kettle, combine the beans, beer, and water. Bring the liquid to the boil and cook the beans over high heat for 10 minutes. Remove the kettle from the heat and allow it to stand, covered, for 1 hour.

> **2 bay leaves**
> **5 cloves**
> **6 peppercorns**

Tie the seasonings in cheesecloth and add them to the contents of the kettle. Return the liquid to the boil, reduce the heat, and simmer the beans, covered, for 1 hour, or until they are tender. Discard the cheesecloth bag. Allow the mixture to cool somewhat.

At this point you may stop and continue later.

In the container of a food processor or blender, whirl the beans with their liquid, about 2 cups at a time, until they are reduced to a smooth purée. Return the purée to the soup kettle.

4 tablespoons butter
2 large carrots, scraped and
  sliced
2 large celery ribs, with the
  leaves, chopped
2 medium leeks (white part
  only), rinsed and sliced

2 medium onions, peeled
  and chopped
Worcestershire sauce
Salt
Fresh-ground pepper

In a skillet, heat the butter and in it cook the vegetables, stirring, until the onion is translucent. Add them to the contents of the kettle. Simmer the soup, covered, for 1 hour. Season it to taste with Worcestershire sauce, salt, and pepper. (If you like, thin the soup by adding a little water.)

Borsch

8 TO 10 SERVINGS
PREPARATION: ABOUT 30 MINUTES
COOKING: 1½ HOURS
REFRIGERATES

The beer gives the soup a pleasantly nutty flavor.

3 cups beef stock or canned
  beef bouillon
3 cups stale beer
4 medium beets, scraped and
  grated
1½ cups shredded cabbage

1 medium carrot, scraped
  and diced
1 cup fine-chopped celery
1 medium onion, peeled
  and chopped fine

In a soup kettle, combine these seven ingredients. Bring the liquid to the boil, reduce the heat, and simmer the vegetables, covered, for 1½ hours.

1 tablespoon red wine vinegar
2 teaspoons sugar
Salt

Fresh-ground pepper
Sour cream

Stir in the vinegar. Season the soup with the sugar and with salt and pepper. Serve it garnished with sour cream.

Variation:

For a heartier soup, add 4 medium potatoes, peeled and diced, for the final 20 minutes of cooking.

Bouillabaisse

8 TO 10 SERVINGS
PREPARATION: ABOUT 45 MINUTES
COOKING: 40 MINUTES
REFRIGERATES

This soup is not from France—indeed, a Frenchman would say it is not at all a bouillabaisse. He would be right. The recipe is my approximation, given American ingredients, of the celebrated fish stew from Marseilles. I admit its lack of authenticity, but hope you will enjoy it nonetheless.

> ½ cup fine olive oil
> 4 large garlic cloves, peeled and chopped fine
> 4 medium onions, peeled and chopped
> 1 (6-ounce) can of tomato paste

In a soup kettle, heat the oil and in it cook the garlic and onion until they are just golden. Stir in the tomato paste and cook the mixture, stirring, for 5 minutes.

> 2 bay leaves
> Zest of 1 medium orange
> 2 generous pinches of saffron
> ½ teaspoon dried thyme
> 2 teaspoons sugar
> 3 cups fish stock plus 1
>   (8-ounce) bottle of clam

> juice or 4 (8-ounce)
>   bottles of clam juice
> 2 cups dry white wine
>   (recommended: Chablis)
> Salt, if needed
> Fresh-ground pepper

Into the contents of the kettle, stir the seasonings. Add the stock and wine. Bring the mixture to the boil, reduce the heat, and simmer it, covered, for 30 minutes. Season the broth to taste with salt and pepper.

At this point you may stop and continue later.

> 3 pounds assorted lean white-fleshed fish fillets, cut into
>   bite-size pieces (cod, flounder, haddock, halibut,
>   ocean perch, scrod, turbot)
> ½ cup chopped parsley
> Toasted rounds of French bread
> Rouille (page 301) (optional)

Bring the broth to a rapid boil. Add the fish. Return the soup to the boil and cook the fish, uncovered, for 10 minutes; do not overcook it. Stir in the parsley. Serve the soup over the toasted bread. Offer the rouille separately.

Cream of Brussels Sprouts Soup

6 SERVINGS
PREPARATION AND COOKING: ABOUT 30 MINUTES
REFRIGERATES; FREEZES

> 4 tablespoons butter
> 2 medium onions, peeled and chopped
> ¼ cup Pernod

In a large saucepan, heat the butter and in it cook the onion until translucent. Warm the Pernod in a small pan, ignite it, and pour it over the onion.

> 2 tablespoons flour
> 1½ cups dry white wine (recommended: Chablis)
> 1 cup chicken stock or 1 (10½-ounce) can of defatted chicken
>   broth

Into the onion, stir the flour. Over gentle heat, cook the mixture for a few minutes. Gradually add the wine and stock, stirring constantly until the mixture is thickened and smooth.

> 1 quart Brussels sprouts, trimmed, rinsed, and chopped coarse
> 1 bay leaf

To the contents of the saucepan, add the Brussels sprouts and bay leaf. Simmer the mixture, covered, for 15 minutes. Remove the bay leaf. Allow the mixture to cool somewhat.

At this point you may stop and continue later.

In the container of a food processor or blender, whirl the mixture, about 2 cups at a time, until it is smooth.

> 1 cup light cream, scalded
> Salt
> Fresh-ground white pepper

Stir the cream into the purée. Bring the soup to serving temperature and season it to taste with salt and pepper.

Cream of Cauliflower Soup

6 TO 8 SERVINGS

PREPARATION AND COOKING: ABOUT 40 MINUTES

REFRIGERATES; FREEZES

> 1 large head of cauliflower, chopped coarse
> 4 cups chicken stock or canned chicken broth
> Strained juice of 1 medium lemon

In a large saucepan, combine the cauliflower, 2 cups of the stock, and the lemon juice. Bring the liquid to the boil and cook the cauliflower, covered, for 15 minutes, or until it is very tender.

> 4 tablespoons butter   4 tablespoons flour
> 2 medium celery ribs, chopped   Remaining chicken stock
> 1 small onion, peeled and   ¼ cup Pernod
>   chopped

In a second saucepan, heat the butter and in it cook the celery and onion, covered, until they are tender. Stir in the flour and, over gentle heat, cook the mixture for a few minutes. Add the chicken stock and Pernod, stirring constantly until the mixture is thickened and smooth.

Combine the cauliflower and its liquid with the onion mixture. In the container of a food processor or blender, whirl the soup, 2 cups at a time, until it is smooth.

At this point you may stop and continue later.

> 2 cups light cream, scalded
> Salt
> Fresh-ground white pepper
> ¼ cup fine-chopped parsley

Into the hot purée, stir the cream. Season the soup to taste with salt and pepper and garnish it with parsley.

Chilled Cherry Soup (HUNGARY)

PREPARATION AND COOKING: ABOUT 30 MINUTES
CHILLING TIME: 4 HOURS
REFRIGERATES

This soup may also be served hot. If you prefer a smooth soup, whirl it, 2 cups at a time, in the container of a food processor or blender.

> 1 (1-pound) can of pitted sour cherries and their liquid
> 1 (1-pound) can of pitted sweet cherries and their liquid
> 1 (3-inch) piece cinnamon stick
> A pinch of powdered cloves
> 1 bottle of dry red wine (recommended: Cabernet Sauvignon)
> 1 cup water

In a large saucepan, combine these six ingredients. Bring the mixture to the boil, reduce the heat, and simmer it, covered, for 15 minutes. Discard the cinnamon stick.

> 2 tablespoons cornstarch
> Cold water
> Sugar
> Salt

Blend the cornstarch with a little water until the mixture is smooth. Add it to the contents of the saucepan, stirring constantly until the soup is somewhat thickened and smooth. Season it to taste with sugar and salt. Allow it to cool before chilling it for at least 4 hours.

Sour cream

Serve the soup in chilled plates. Offer the sour cream separately.

Cioppino

6 TO 8 LARGE SERVINGS
PREPARATION: ABOUT 30 MINUTES
COOKING: 10 MINUTES
REFRIGERATES

Cioppino, created by Portuguese fishermen living in California, is a robust fish stew, a one-dish meal when offered with a substantial bread.

½ cup olive oil
3 garlic cloves, peeled and chopped fine
2 large onions, peeled and chopped
1 medium green pepper, seeded and chopped
6 scallions (with as much of the green as is crisp), trimmed and chopped
1 (6-ounce) can of tomato paste
1 (29-ounce) can of Italian tomatoes

3 cups dry red wine (recommended: Zinfandel) or dry white wine (recommended: Riesling)
½ teaspoon dried basil
2 bay leaves
½ teaspoon dried oregano
½ cup chopped parsley
1½ teaspoons sugar
Salt
Fresh-ground pepper

In a soup kettle, heat the oil and in it cook the garlic, onion, pepper, and scallion until they are limp. Add the remaining ingredients except the salt and pepper; stir to blend the mixture well. Bring it to the boil, reduce the heat, and simmer it, covered, for 15 minutes. Season it to taste with salt and pepper.

At this point you may stop and continue later.

1½ pounds assorted lean white-fleshed fish, cut into bite-size
   pieces (cod, flounder, haddock, halibut, ocean perch,
   scrod, turbot)
½ pound raw shrimps, shelled and deveined
12 cherrystone clams or mussels, scrubbed under cold running
   water

Into the simmering broth, gently stir the fish. Cook it for 5 minutes. Add the shrimps and clams. Cook the stew for 5 minutes longer, or until the clams have just opened. Discard any that do not open. Transfer the cioppino to a heated tureen and offer it in warmed soup plates.

Variation:

Neither Portuguese nor Californian, but very good: Add ⅓ cup Pernod to the broth just before cooking the fish.

Fish Soup "La Guérite du Saint Amour" (FRANCE)

6 SERVINGS
PREPARATION: ABOUT 30 MINUTES
COOKING: 3 HOURS
REFRIGERATES; FREEZES

On the busy Boulevard Raspail in Paris, La Guérite du Saint Amour extends its warm welcome. The restaurant, named for a village in the Beaujolais, translates literally as "A Niche of Holy Love." It offers *spécialités périgordines* carefully prepared by Yves Azzi, the proprietor-chef, and attentively served by Martine, his wife. It is one of my favorite Paris retreats.

2 pounds *very* fresh lean-
   fleshed fish bones, heads,
   and trimmings
1 sole (or flounder), cleaned
1 pound lean-fleshed fish
   fillet, cut into small pieces
3 carrots, scraped and cut
   into ¼-inch rounds

1 medium celery rib,
   with the leaves,
   chopped coarse
3 leeks (with a little of
   the green part), rinsed
   and cut into ¼-inch
   rounds
1¼ cups red port

In a soup kettle, combine these seven ingredients and, over medium heat, bring to the boil.

> 2 tablespoons butter
> ½ pound raw medium shrimps, shelled and deveined (reserve the shells)

While the kettle is coming to the boil, in a skillet heat the butter and in it, over gentle heat, cook the shrimps, stirring, until they are just pink. Add them and their shells to the contents of the kettle. Reduce the heat to very low and simmer the mixture, covered, for 2 hours.

> ¾ bottle of dry Beaujolais (red or white)

In a saucepan, bring the wine to the boil, immediately reduce the heat to low, and simmer the wine, uncovered, for 20 minutes.

> 1 tablespoon sweet paprika (preferably Hungarian)
> 2 tablespoons tomato paste
> 1 large garlic clove, peeled and put through a press
>
> A few drops of Tabasco sauce
> Salt
> Fresh-ground pepper

Blend together the paprika and tomato paste. To the contents of the soup kettle, add the simmered Beaujolais, the garlic, the tomato paste mixture, and the Tabasco sauce. Continue to simmer the soup, covered, for 1 hour. Through a heavy sieve lined with cheesecloth, strain the mixture, pressing to extract all the liquid. (The cheesecloth is used to assure a boneless soup. When the residue is sufficiently cool to touch, form a bag of the cheesecloth and squeeze it firmly to extract any remaining liquid.) Season the soup to taste with salt and pepper.

> Rounds of well-toasted French bread
> Rouille (page 301)
> Fresh-grated Gruyère cheese

Bring the soup to serving temperature and offer it in heated bowls accompanied by the toast rounds, rouille, and grated cheese.

Creamed Fish Soup (FRANCE)

8 SERVINGS
PREPARATION AND COOKING: ABOUT 50 MINUTES
REFRIGERATES; FREEZES

Potage crème normande makes an especially elegant first course.

1 large celery rib, chopped	½ teaspoon dried thyme
2 medium onions, peeled and chopped	1½ cups dry white wine (recommended: Muscadet)
4 medium, ripe tomatoes, quartered	4½ cups fish stock *or* 4 (8-ounce) bottles of clam juice plus ½ cup water
1 pound lean white-fleshed fish fillet, cut into chunks	
2 bay leaves	
8 peppercorns	

In a soup kettle, combine these nine ingredients. Bring the liquid to the boil, reduce the heat, and simmer the mixture, covered, for 30 minutes. Strain it. Transfer the strained broth to a clean saucepan and reserve it. Discard the bay leaves, peppercorns, and tomato skins.

In the container of a food processor or blender, using a little of the strained broth if necessary, whirl the celery, onion, and fish until they are reduced to a smooth purée. Stir the purée into the reserved broth.

4 tablespoons softened butter
4 tablespoons flour

In a small mixing bowl, blend the butter and flour to make a beurre manié. Add it to the contents of the saucepan and bring the soup gently to the boil, stirring constantly until it is thickened and smooth.

At this point you may stop and continue later.

1 cup cream (heavy or light, depending upon the degree of richness you desire)	A grating of nutmeg Salt Fresh-ground white pepper Fine-chopped parsley

Bring the mixture to serving temperature, stir in the cream, and season the soup to taste with nutmeg, salt, and pepper. Serve it garnished with parsley.

Fresh Fruit Soup

6 SERVINGS
PREPARATION AND COOKING: ABOUT 35 MINUTES
CHILLING TIME: 4 HOURS
REFRIGERATES

1¼ cups dry red wine (recommended: Zinfandel)

1¼ cups dry white wine (recommended: Riesling)

1 tablespoon cornstarch

¾ cup sugar

1 teaspoon cinnamon

¼ teaspoon ground cloves

A few grains of salt

In a saucepan, combine the two wines. Sift together the cornstarch, sugar, cinnamon, cloves, and salt; stir the mixture into the wine. Bring the liquid to the boil, stirring; reduce the heat and simmer it, stirring constantly, for about 3 minutes, or until it is thickened and smooth.

½ cup strained fresh orange juice
Sugar, if desired

Off the heat, stir in the orange juice. Adjust the sugar to taste.

2½ cups peeled, seeded, and diced assorted fresh fruit of your choice (blueberries, cherries, grapes, peaches, pears, pineapple, plums, strawberries)
Thickened cream (page 6) *or* sour cream
Fine-chopped fresh mint leaves

Into the contents of the saucepan, stir the fruit. Allow the mixture to cool before refrigerating for at least 4 hours. Serve the soup in chilled plates, garnished with a spoonful of thickened cream and a sprinkling of mint.

Variation:

If desired, ¼ cup orange-flavored liqueur may be added to the wine mixture together with the orange juice.

Lamb Soup (GREECE)

6 TO 8 SERVINGS
PREPARATION: ABOUT 35 MINUTES
COOKING: 2 HOURS
REFRIGERATES; FREEZES

A recipe I enjoyed when plying a fifty-five-foot ketch through the Aegean Islands.

> 3 pounds breast of lamb
> 1 bottle dry red wine (recommended: Demestica or
>   Burgundy)
> 2 cups water

In a soup kettle, combine the lamb, wine, and water. Bring the liquid to the boil and skim the surface. Lower the heat and simmer the soup, covered, for 2 hours, or until the lamb is tender.

> ¼ cup olive oil
> 5 large onions, peeled and sliced thin
> 4 large ripe tomatoes, peeled, seeded, and chopped
> 2 tablespoons chopped fresh mint or 1 teaspoon dried mint

Meanwhile, in a skillet, heat the olive oil and in it cook the onion until golden. Add the tomatoes and mint and cook, stirring often, for 10 minutes. Add to the contents of the simmering kettle.

Remove the lamb. Cut the meat from the bones; chop and reserve it, well covered to keep it moist.

At this point you may stop and continue later.

Allow the broth to cool, refrigerate it overnight, and the following day remove the solidified fat.

> ⅓ to ½ cup orzo (rice-shaped pasta), depending upon how
>   thick you want the soup to be
> Reserved lamb
> Salt
> Fresh-ground pepper

Bring the broth to the boil, add the pasta, and cook it, stirring often, for 7 minutes, or until it is just tender. Reduce the heat, add the lamb, and heat it through. Season the soup to taste with salt and pepper.

Cream of Mushroom Soup

6 SERVINGS

PREPARATION AND COOKING: ABOUT 40 MINUTES

REFRIGERATES; FREEZES

4 tablespoons butter
1 pound mushrooms, trimmed and chopped coarse
2 shallots, peeled and chopped, or 3 scallions (white part only), trimmed and chopped

¼ cup dry sherry
3 tablespoons flour
2 cups chicken stock or canned chicken broth
1 cup dry white wine (recommended: Chablis)

In a large saucepan, heat the butter and in it cook the mushrooms and shallots, stirring, until they are limp. Add the sherry and continue to cook the mixture, stirring, for 3 minutes. Add the flour and then stir the mixture to blend it well. Gradually add the stock and wine, stirring constantly until the mixture is thickened and smooth. Simmer it, covered, for 20 minutes. Allow it to cool somewhat.

In the container of a food processor or blender, whirl the soup, 2 cups at a time, until it is smooth. Return it to the saucepan.

At this point you may stop and continue later.

1 cup heavy cream, scalded
Salt
Fresh-ground white pepper
Fine-chopped parsley

Stir in the cream. Bring the soup to serving temperature, season it to taste with salt and pepper, and serve it in heated cups, garnished with parsley.

Cream of Mussels Soup (Billi Bi) (FRANCE)

8 SERVINGS

PREPARATION AND COOKING: ABOUT 45 MINUTES

REFRIGERATES; FREEZES

"Billi Bi" was named by Maxim's in Paris for William B. Leeds, a wealthy American tin magnate who frequented the celebrated restaurant. Popular for its smooth, elegant flavor, this soup may be served hot or cold.

> 2 cups dry white wine (recommended: Muscadet *or* Muscat)
> 2 medium onions, peeled and chopped
> 6 shallots, peeled and chopped, or 6 scallions (white part
>   only), trimmed and chopped
> Bouquet garni (page 4)

In a soup kettle, combine these four ingredients. Bring the liquid to the boil, reduce the heat, and simmer the mixture, covered, for 10 minutes.

> 3 pounds fresh mussels, thoroughly scrubbed under cold
>   running water (discard any that are open)

To the contents of the soup kettle, add the mussels; increase the heat to high and steam them, tightly covered, for 5 to 8 minutes, or until they open. Discard any that do not open.

Away from the heat, using a slotted spoon, remove the mussels from the broth; discard the bouquet garni. Remove the mussels from their shells and discard the shells.

Through a sieve lined with cheesecloth, strain the broth. Add enough of it to the mussels just to cover them. Transfer the remaining broth to a large saucepan and bring it to the simmer.

> 4 tablespoons softened butter
> 4 tablespoons flour

In a small mixing bowl, blend the butter and flour to make a beurre manié. Add it to the simmering broth, stirring constantly until the liquid is thickened and smooth.

At this point you may stop and continue later.

1 cup heavy cream, scalded

2 cups fish stock *or* 2
   (8-ounce) bottles of
   clam juice

A generous pinch of saffron,
   softened for 10 minutes
   in ¼ cup boiling water

A few drops of Tabasco
   sauce

Salt

Reserved mussels

Fine-chopped parsley

Stir in the cream, fish stock, and saffron-water mixture. Season the soup to taste with Tabasco sauce and salt. Stir in the mussels and bring the soup to serving temperature, but do not allow it to cook (the mussels will toughen). Serve it hot, garnished with parsley; or, if you prefer, allow it to cool and then chill it for at least 4 hours.

Onion Soup (FRANCE)

8 TO 10 SERVINGS
PREPARATION: ABOUT 30 MINUTES
COOKING: 1 HOUR
REFRIGERATES

Not the traditional recipe, but one I have enjoyed at a private home in France.

4 tablespoons butter
2 tablespoons fine olive oil
2 pounds yellow onions, peeled and cut into ⅛-inch slices
3 tablespoons flour

In a soup kettle, heat the butter and oil. Add the onion and cook it, stirring often, until it is golden. Stir in the flour and continue to cook the mixture for 3 minutes.

5½ cups beef stock or 4 (10½-ounce) cans of beef bouillon
2½ cups dry white wine (recommended: Chablis)

Gradually add the stock, stirring to blend the mixture. Stir in the wine.

Bring the liquid to the boil, reduce the heat to low, and simmer the soup, covered, for 1 hour.

At this point you may stop and continue later.

Salt	Fine olive oil
Fresh-ground pepper	Fresh-grated cheese
Slices of French bread	(recommended:
(¼ inch thick)	Cantal)

Season the soup to taste with salt and pepper. On a baking sheet, toast the bread slices in a 300° oven for 20 minutes. Brush both sides with olive oil and bake them 10 minutes longer.

To serve the soup, arrange slices of the bread on the bottom of each warmed plate; over them sprinkle about 2 tablespoons of the cheese. Bring the soup to serving temperature and ladle it over the bread.

Variations:

You may use ½ cup brandy as part of the quantity of stock. Instead of the white wine you may use 2½ cups dry red wine (recommended: California Zinfandel) *or* 1½ cups red wine plus 1 cup port.

WHITE ONION SOUP: Peel 2 pounds small white onions (page 6) and dice 1 large celery rib; in 4 tablespoons butter, sauté the vegetables until the onions are faintly colored. In place of the beef stock, use chicken stock *or* 4 (10½-ounce) cans of defatted chicken broth. Bring the liquid to the boil, reduce the heat, and simmer the onions, uncovered, for 30 minutes, or until they are tender but still hold their shape. Thicken the soup with 2 tablespoons cornstarch mixed with a little cold water. Complete the recipe as above.

Oxtail Soup

6 TO 8 SERVINGS
PREPARATION: ABOUT 40 MINUTES
COOKING: 3 HOURS
REFRIGERATES; FREEZES

3 pounds oxtail, disjointed
¼ to ½ cup medium pearl
    barley (depending upon
    how thick you want
    the soup to be)
3 medium carrots, scraped
    and cut into ½-inch
    rounds
3 large celery ribs, with some
    of the leaves, chopped
2 large onions, peeled and
    sliced

½ cup coarse-chopped
    parsley
2 bay leaves
½ teaspoon dried thyme
2 teaspoons sugar
4 cups beef stock or 3
    (10½-ounce) cans of
    beef broth
4 cups hearty red
    wine (recommended:
    Zinfandel)

In a soup kettle, combine all of the ingredients. Bring the liquid to the boil, reduce the heat, and simmer the mixture, covered, for 3 hours, or until the meat falls from the bones. Remove the meat and return it to the kettle; discard the bones.

At this point you may stop and continue later. (Allow the soup to cool, refrigerate it overnight, and the following day remove the solidified fat.)

Salt
Fresh-ground pepper

Bring the soup to serving temperature and season it to taste with salt and pepper.

Parsley Broth

4 SERVINGS
PREPARATION AND COOKING: ABOUT 45 MINUTES
REFRIGERATES

In a book called *Le Menagier de Paris* (1393), written by a wealthy Frenchman for the enlightenment of his child bride, the author directs (in free translation): "Take parsley and fry it in butter, then pour boiling water over it, and boil it, and add salt, and serve your sops." A healthy broth, but not very appetizing. An English recipe of the same period suggests: "Take parsley and hyssop and sage and hack it small and boil it in wine and in water and a little powder of pepper and mess it forth." A combination of the two recipes yields a refreshing clear soup with which to begin a substantial dinner.

  4 tablespoons butter
  1 large bunch of parsley, rinsed and drained, the leaves
      removed and reserved, the stems tied in a bundle and
      bruised

In a large saucepan, heat the butter and in it cook the parsley leaves until they wilt and darken.

  1 cup chicken stock or 1
      (10½-ounce) can of
      chicken broth
  1½ cups dry white wine
      (recommended:
      Mosel or Chenin
      Blanc

  1½ cups water
  1 teaspoon rubbed sage,
      tied in cheesecloth
  Reserved parsley stems
  Salt
  Fresh-ground white pepper

To the contents of the saucepan, add the first five ingredients. Bring the liquid to the boil, reduce the heat, and simmer the mixture, covered, for 30 minutes. Discard the sage. Remove the parsley stems and, using a sieve, press into the contents of the saucepan the liquid they have absorbed. Season the broth to taste with salt and pepper.

Cream of Pea Soup

6 SERVINGS

PREPARATION AND COOKING: ABOUT 25 MINUTES

REFRIGERATES; FREEZES

The soup may be served hot or chilled, depending upon the season and your choice.

  1 (10-ounce) package frozen
      baby peas
  1 medium onion, peeled
      and chopped
  ¾ teaspoon salt

  ¼ teaspoon fresh-ground
      white pepper
  1 cup chicken stock or
      defatted canned
      chicken broth

In a saucepan, combine these five ingredients. Bring the liquid to the boil, reduce the heat, and simmer the peas, covered, for 12 minutes, or until they are very tender. Allow them to cool somewhat. In the container of a food processor or blender, whirl the mixture until it is smooth. Return it to the saucepan.

> 2 cups light cream or half-and-half
> ¼ cup Pernod
> Fine-chopped parsley

Into the contents of the saucepan, stir the cream. Bring the soup just barely to the boil. Add the Pernod, stirring to evaporate the alcohol. Serve the soup, hot or chilled, garnished with parsley.

Red Cabbage Soup (FRANCE)

6 TO 8 SERVINGS
PREPARATION: ABOUT 20 MINUTES
COOKING: 2 HOURS
REFRIGERATES

A substantial one-dish meal. If you prefer, water may be substituted for the stock.

> 3 tablespoons butter
> 3 large onions, peeled and sliced

In a soup kettle, heat the butter and in it cook the onion until golden.

> 3 medium carrots, scraped and grated
> 3 garlic cloves, peeled and chopped fine
> 3 medium potatoes, peeled and grated
> 1 small red cabbage, cored and shredded thin
>
> 3 small white turnips, scraped and grated
> 6 cups chicken stock or 4 (10½-ounce) cans of chicken broth plus water to equal 6 cups

To the contents of the kettle, add these six ingredients. Bring the liquid to the boil, reduce the heat, and simmer the mixture, covered, for 1¾ hours.

At this point you may stop and continue later.

> 2 cups dry red wine (recommended: Beaujolais)
> Salt
> Fresh-ground pepper
> Thickened cream (page 6) *or* sour cream

Into the simmering mixture, stir the wine, and continue to cook it, uncovered, for 15 minutes. Season the soup to taste with salt and pepper and serve it in heated bowls. Offer the thickened cream separately as a garnish.

Senegalese Soup (FRANCE)

6 SERVINGS
PREPARATION AND COOKING: ABOUT 30 MINUTES
CHILLING TIME: 4 HOURS
REFRIGERATES; FREEZES

Usually served chilled, the soup may, however, be offered hot. Heat it in the top of a double boiler over simmering water.

> 2 tablespoons butter
> 3 tart apples, peeled, cored, and chopped coarse
> 1 large onion, peeled and chopped

In a large saucepan, heat the butter and in it cook the apple and onion until the onion is translucent.

> 2 tablespoons flour
> 2 teaspoons curry powder (preferably sweet Madras)
> A pinch of cayenne pepper
>
> 4 cups chicken stock or 3 (10½-ounce) cans of chicken broth
> 1 cup dry white wine (recommended: Muscadet or Sauvignon Blanc)

Into the contents of the saucepan, stir the flour; over gentle heat, cook the mixture for a few minutes. Stir in the curry powder and cayenne pepper. Gradually add the stock and then the wine, stirring constantly until the mixture is smooth. Bring it to the boil, reduce the heat, and simmer it, covered, for 10 minutes, or until the apple is very tender. Allow the mixture to cool somewhat.

In the container of a food processor or blender, whirl the soup, 2 cups at a time, until it is smooth. Chill it for at least 4 hours.

> 1 cup light cream, chilled
> Salt
> Chopped chives

When ready to serve, stir in the cream. Adjust the seasoning to taste with salt, and garnish the soup with a sprinkling of chopped chives.

Variation:

If desired, 1 cup fine-diced cooked white chicken meat may be added with the cream—a very tasty addition.

Strawberry Soup (RUSSIA)

8 SERVINGS
PREPARATION AND COOKING: ABOUT 30 MINUTES
REFRIGERATES; FREEZES

Traditionally served hot, this soup, offered chilled, is an attractive warm-weather first course.

> 1 quart strawberries, hulled   1 cup sour cream
>   and rinsed   ½ cup superfine sugar
> 2 cups light, dry red wine   A few grains of salt
>   (recommended: claret)
>   or dry white wine
>   (recommended:
>   Chablis)

In the container of a food processor or blender, whirl these five ingredients, 2 cups at a time, until the mixture is smooth. Transfer it to a large saucepan.

> 3 cups cold water
> Sugar (optional)

Into the purée, blend the water. Over gentle heat, bring the soup to serving temperature, stirring to dissolve the sugar; do not let the soup boil. Add sugar to taste.

Tomato Soup (ITALY)

6 TO 8 SERVINGS
PREPARATION AND COOKING: ABOUT 1 HOUR
REFRIGERATES; FREEZES

> 4 tablespoons olive oil
> 2 large onions, peeled and chopped
> 4 tablespoons flour

In a large saucepan, heat the oil and in it cook the onion until translucent. Stir in the flour and cook over gentle heat for a few minutes.

> 2 pounds ripe tomatoes, quartered
> 2 teaspoons sugar
> 1 tablespoon fresh tarragon leaves or 1 teaspoon dried tarragon

Add the tomatoes, sugar, and tarragon. Over gentle heat, cook the tomatoes, covered, for 20 minutes, or until they are very tender; stir them often. Strain the mixture and discard the residue.

> 2 cups dry white wine (recommended: Soave or Chablis)
> 4 cups veal stock or 3 (10½-ounce) cans of defatted chicken
>   broth
> Salt
> Fresh-ground pepper

Add the wine and stock and simmer the soup, covered, for 20 minutes. Season it to taste with salt and pepper.

Variation:

CREAM OF GREEN TOMATO SOUP (inspired by the necessity of my doing something—anything—with green tomatoes or risk losing them to early frost): Follow step one of the preceding recipe as written; in step two, substitute green tomatoes for ripe ones and cook them with the onion-flour mixture, adding the wine from step three (green tomatoes have much less juice than red ones); double the quantity of sugar. Omit the wine in step three. Finally, stir in 1 cup heavy cream, scalded.

Tripe and Vegetable Soup (NICARAGUA)

8 SERVINGS
PREPARATION: ABOUT 30 MINUTES
COOKING: 3½ HOURS
REFRIGERATES; FREEZES

> 1 pound honeycomb tripe, cut into bite-size pieces
> 4 cups dry white wine (recommended: Chenin Blanc)
> 4 cups chicken stock or 3 (10½-ounce) cans of defatted
>   chicken broth

In a soup kettle, combine the tripe, wine, and stock. Bring the mixture to the boil, reduce the heat, and simmer the tripe, covered, for 3 hours, or until it is very tender. Strain the mixture into a second utensil; reserve the tripe.

At this point you may stop and continue later. (Allow the broth to cool, refrigerate it overnight, and the following day remove the solidified fat.)

> 1 cup (packed) shredded   2 medium green peppers,
>   cabbage   seeded and chopped
> 2 garlic cloves, peeled and   1 large potato, peeled and
>   put through a press   diced
> 2 medium onions, peeled   1 medium sweet potato,
>   and chopped   peeled and diced

Return the broth to the boil, add the vegetables, reduce the heat, and simmer them, covered, for 20 minutes, or until the potato is tender.

> Reserved tripe
> Salt
> Fresh-ground pepper
> Fine-chopped parsley

To the contents of the kettle, add the tripe. Season the soup to taste with salt and pepper, and serve it garnished with parsley.

Vegetable Soup with Red Wine

6 TO 8 SERVINGS
PREPARATION: ABOUT 30 MINUTES
COOKING: 1 HOUR
REFRIGERATES

3 large carrots, scraped and
    cut into julienne
2 large leeks (with a little
    of the green part),
    thoroughly rinsed under
    cold running water and
    cut into thin rounds
18 white onions, peeled
    (page 6)
2 medium white turnips,
    scraped and cut into
    julienne
Bouquet garni (page 4)
1 teaspoon sugar
1 bottle of hearty red wine
    (recommended:
    Burgundy)

In a soup kettle, combine these seven ingredients. Bring the mixture to the boil, reduce the heat, and simmer it, uncovered, for 30 minutes.

4 cups beef stock or 3 (10½-ounce) cans of beef bouillon

Add the stock and continue to simmer the soup 30 minutes longer. Discard the bouquet garni.

1½ tablespoons quick-cooking tapioca
Salt
Fresh-ground pepper

To the mixture, add the tapioca, stirring gently until the soup is somewhat thickened and smooth. Season it to taste with salt and pepper.

Appetizers and First-Course Dishes

Of the following recipes, the greater number are "sit-down" first courses, chosen for their ease of preparation and their lightness. I admit to being partial to the vegetable recipes, which are light and stimulate the appetite rather than slake it. In Chapter 6, "Vegetables and Side Dishes," you will find other vegetable dishes that can be served as first courses. In

Chapter 5, "Egg and Cheese Dishes," there are also recipes that may appeal to you as appetizers.

Avocado Cocktail Dip

YIELD: ABOUT 2 CUPS
PREPARATION: ABOUT 10 MINUTES
REFRIGERATES

2 large ripe avocados, peeled, seeded, and chopped coarse	Strained fresh lemon juice Salt A few drops of Tabasco sauce
¼ cup dark rum	
½ teaspoon sugar	Melba toast

In the container of a food processor equipped with the steel blade, combine the avocado and rum. Whirl them until the mixture is smooth. Season the dip with the sugar and, to taste, with lemon juice, salt, and Tabasco sauce. Transfer it to a serving dish and chill it. Offer it with melba toast.

Grated Carrots with Orange

6 SERVINGS
PREPARATION: ABOUT 20 MINUTES
CHILLING TIME: 3 HOURS
REFRIGERATES

This refreshing first course may also be served as a salad.

8 large carrots, trimmed and scraped	Strained juice of 3 large oranges
⅓ cup orange-flavored liqueur	Salt Fresh-ground white pepper

Into a mixing bowl, grate the carrots lengthwise. Warm the liqueur in a small pan, ignite it, and pour it over the carrots, stirring until the flame dies. Add the orange juice. Season the carrots to taste with salt and pepper, then chill the dish for at least 3 hours. Drain, and serve the carrots on a bed of salad greens.

Cheddar and Beer Spread

YIELD: ABOUT 2½ CUPS
PREPARATION: ABOUT 15 MINUTES (ALL INGREDIENTS SHOULD BE AT ROOM
  TEMPERATURE)
REFRIGERATES

A traditional cocktail snack from the southern United States.

2 medium garlic cloves, peeled and put through a press
2 cups (8 ounces) grated sharp Cheddar cheese
½ cup stale beer
A few drops of Tabasco sauce
½ teaspoon dry mustard
1 tablespoon Worcestershire sauce
Salt
Melba toast

In the container of a food processor equipped with the steel blade, combine all of the ingredients except the salt and melba toast. Whirl them until the mixture is smooth. Season it to taste with salt. Transfer the spread to a serving dish and offer it with melba toast.

Brandied Cheddar Cheese

YIELD: ABOUT 2 CUPS
PREPARATION: ABOUT 10 MINUTES (ALL INGREDIENTS SHOULD BE AT ROOM
  TEMPERATURE)
CHILLING TIME: 2 HOURS
REFRIGERATES

1 pound sharp Cheddar cheese, shredded coarse
3 tablespoons softened butter
½ cup brandy
¾ teaspoon sugar
A few drops of Tabasco sauce
Melba toast

In the container of a food processor equipped with the steel blade, combine all of the ingredients except the melba toast. Whirl them until the mixture is smooth. Transfer the spread to a serving dish and chill it, covered, for at least 2 hours. Offer it with melba toast.

Variation:

SHERRIED AMERICAN CHEESE: In place of the Cheddar, use 1 pound American cheese (my grandmother called it "store cheese"); with the Tabasco sauce, add ¾ teaspoon paprika. In place of the brandy, use ½ cup dry sherry. The other ingredients and the procedure remain the same as above.

Blue Cheese and Brandy Spread

YIELD: ABOUT 1½ CUPS
PREPARATION: ABOUT 15 MINUTES (ALL INGREDIENTS SHOULD BE AT ROOM TEMPERATURE)
REFRIGERATES

1 cup (4 ounces) crumbled blue cheese	½ teaspoon powdered thyme
1 (8-ounce) package of cream cheese	Salt Fresh-ground pepper
½ cup brandy	Melba toast
1½ tablespoons heavy cream	

In the container of a food processor equipped with the steel blade, combine all of the ingredients except salt, pepper and melba toast. Whirl them until the mixture is smooth. Season it to taste with salt and pepper. Transfer the spread to a serving bowl, cover it, and allow it to stand at room temperature for 1 hour so the flavors will meld. Offer it with melba toast.

Cheese Toasts

6 SERVINGS
PREPARATION: 15 MINUTES
COOKING: 10 MINUTES IN A 400° OVEN

½ cup dry white wine (recommended: Chablis)
6 slices firm white bread, with crusts removed

Pour the wine into a shallow dish. One at a time, lay the bread slices in the wine on one side only, and immediately remove them to a plate. Reserve the remaining wine.

1 egg
1½ cups (6 ounces) fresh-
    grated Gruyère cheese
Reserved wine

Fresh-grated nutmeg
Salt
Fresh-ground pepper

In a mixing bowl, beat the egg; stir in the cheese and wine. Season to taste with nutmeg, salt, and pepper. Arrange the mixture evenly over the dry side of each bread slice.

Softened butter

Generously butter a baking pan just large enough to accommodate the bread slices in a single layer. (The butter becomes an ingredient of the cheese toasts.) Arrange the bread, wine-dipped-side down, on the butter. Bake it at 400° for 10 minutes, or until the cheese is melted and golden. Serve the cheese toasts hot.

Eggs in Aspic

4 SERVINGS
PREPARATION: ABOUT 35 MINUTES
CHILLING TIME: 6 HOURS
REFRIGERATES

If you are daring, you may poach the eggs—the traditional way of cooking them for this recipe—but the dish will taste the same if you boil the eggs in the manner directed. They should, however, not be overcooked.

½ cup chicken stock *or*
    defatted canned
    chicken broth
¾ cup dry white wine
    (recommended:
    Chablis)

1 envelope unflavored
    gelatin, softened for
    5 minutes in ¼ cup dry
    white wine
1½ teaspoons dried
    tarragon
Sugar
Salt

In a saucepan, combine the stock and wine, bring the mixture to the boil, and add the gelatin and tarragon, stirring until the gelatin is dissolved. Let it sit off the heat, covered, for 30 minutes. Season it to taste with a little sugar and salt.

4 eggs

In boiling water, cook the eggs for 4 or 5 minutes. Refresh them under cold running water. Peel and reserve them.

¼ cup Madeira *or* Marsala
Reserved eggs
Fine-chopped parsley

Into the white wine mixture, stir the Madeira. In individual ramekins, arrange the eggs. Strain the liquid over each egg. Chill the ramekins for at least 6 hours, or until the gelatin is thoroughly set. To serve the eggs, unmold them onto chilled plates and garnish with parsley.

Braised Leeks

6 SERVINGS
PREPARATION: ABOUT 15 MINUTES
COOKING: 35 MINUTES (20 MINUTES IN A 400° OVEN)

This may also be served as a vegetable side dish.

6 large leeks (with a little of the green part), thoroughly rinsed
    under cold running water and trimmed
Lightly salted boiling water

Cook the leeks in the boiling water for 15 minutes. Drain them well and
arrange them in a buttered baking dish.

1½ tablespoons butter	3 tablespoons thickened
1½ tablespoons flour	cream (page 6) *or*
1¾ cups dry white wine	sour cream
(recommended: dry	Salt
sauterne)	Fresh-ground white pepper

In a saucepan, heat the butter and in it, over gentle heat, cook the flour
for a few minutes. Gradually add the wine, stirring constantly until the
mixture is thickened and smooth. Simmer it, uncovered, for 10 minutes.
Stir in the cream, and season the sauce to taste with salt and pepper.

At this point you may stop and continue later.

½ cup fresh-grated Parmesan cheese
Fine-chopped parsley

Over the leeks, evenly spoon the sauce. Sprinkle on the grated cheese.
Bake the leeks at 400° for 20 minutes, or until the cheese is melted and
golden. Garnish the dish with parsley.

Melon with Wine (SPAIN)

4 TO 6 SERVINGS
PREPARATION: ABOUT 10 MINUTES
CHILLING TIME: 3 HOURS

This refreshing Spanish conceit, and the variations that follow, enhance
the flavor of chilled melon, which may also be offered as a dessert.

1 large ripe Spanish or Persian melon *or* 2 medium-sized
    ripe cantaloupes
1 cup ruby port *or* sweet sherry *or* Madeira *or* Marsala

Cut out a plug from the stem end of the melon. Pour in the wine; replace the plug and refrigerate the melon for at least 3 hours. Remove the plug and drain the melon; strain and reserve the wine. Cut the melon into serving portions, discard the seeds, and pour some of the reserved wine over the melon slices.

Variations:

Alternatively, you may cut the melon into cubes or make melon balls (you should have about 3 cups), and macerate them, refrigerated, in any one of the wines suggested above. *Or . . .*

In a combination of ½ cup light rum, ⅓ cup dark brown sugar, and the strained juice of 1 lime; stir the mixture to dissolve the sugar. *Or . . .*

In a combination of 1 cup Sauternes and superfine granulated sugar to taste; stir the mixture to dissolve the sugar. *Or . . .*

In a combination of ½ cup orange-flavored liqueur and ½ cup dry white wine (recommended: Chablis) and superfine granulated sugar to taste; stir the mixture to dissolve the sugar.

If you use melon cubes or balls, garnish the dish with a few strawberries and coarse-chopped fresh mint leaves.

Mushrooms in Cream

6 SERVINGS
PREPARATION: ABOUT 30 MINUTES
REFRIGERATES

Suitable also as a main dish for luncheon or supper.

> 4 tablespoons butter
> 1½ pounds mushrooms, trimmed and quartered
> Salt
> Fresh-ground white pepper

In a large skillet, heat the butter and in it cook the mushrooms for 10 minutes, or until they are just limp. Season them to taste with salt and pepper.

3 tablespoons flour	½ cup fine-chopped
½ cup dry vermouth	parsley
1½ cups light cream	Salt
⅓ cup fresh-grated	Fresh-ground white pepper
Parmesan cheese	6 toast slices or patty shells

Sprinkle the flour over the mushrooms, stirring. Over gentle heat, cook the mixture for a few minutes. Stir in the vermouth. Gradually add the cream, stirring constantly until the mixture is thickened and smooth. Stir in the cheese and parsley. Season to taste with salt and pepper. Serve the mushrooms on toast or in patty shells.

Pork, Veal, and Ham Pâté (FRANCE)

8 TO 10 SERVINGS
PREPARATION: ABOUT 1 HOUR
COOKING: 1½ HOURS IN A 350° OVEN
REFRIGERATES

Terrine de porc, veau, et jambon, perhaps the classic *pâté de campagne,* is always a welcome first course. Offer it with a hearty crusty bread.

2 tablespoons butter	1 large garlic clove, peeled
2 medium onions, peeled and chopped fine	and put through a press
½ cup cognac *or* dry Madeira *or* dry sherry	¼ teaspoon ground allspice
¾ pound lean pork, ground very fine	¾ teaspoon crumbled dried thyme
½ pound pork fat, ground very fine	½ teaspoon sugar
¾ pound lean veal, ground very fine	1½ teaspoons salt
2 eggs, beaten	¼ teaspoon fresh-ground pepper

In a skillet, heat the butter and in it cook the onion until translucent; transfer it to a mixing bowl. To the skillet, add the cognac, bring it to the boil, and reduce it by half; add it to the mixing bowl. Into the onion-cognac mixture, mix until thoroughly blended the ground meats and fat, the eggs, and the seasonings.

½ pound lean veal, cut into ¼-inch strips	1 scallion (with some of the green part), chopped fine
3 canned truffles, chopped fine (optional)	¼ cup cognac
	Salt
	Fresh-ground pepper

In a mixing bowl, combine the first four ingredients. Season the mixture to taste with salt and pepper. Allow it to stand for 1 hour.

Remove the veal strips and strain the cognac, reserving the truffles. Stir the cognac into the pork-veal mixture.

½ pound fresh pork fat, ⅛ inch thick (or less), *or* salt pork, cut into pieces no thicker than ⅛ inch and blanched, *or* blanched bacon slices
½ pound boiled ham, cut into ¼-inch strips
2 bay leaves

With the pork fat, line one of two 9 × 5-inch loaf pans. (You will use the second pan later.) Reserve enough slices to cover the top of the pan. Add in an even layer one-third of the pork-veal mixture. Cover the layer with half of the veal and ham strips. Over them, arrange the truffles in two lengthwise rows. Repeat the layers of one-third of the pork-veal mixture and the remaining veal and strips. Finish with an even layer of the pork-veal mixture. Put the bay leaves on top and cover the whole with the remaining slices of pork fat. Cover the pan tightly with heavy-duty aluminum foil and set it in a pan of hot water reaching halfway up the mold. Bake the pâté at 350° for 1½ hours, or until it has shrunk away from the sides of the pan and the juices are clear (there should be no pinkness). Remove the foil. Place the second 9 × 5-inch pan, bottom-side down, on top of the pâté; weight it (canned goods are fine for this purpose), and allow the pâté to cool overnight at room temperature.

Unmold the pâté and serve it on a platter garnished with watercress, or slice it into individual portions. The pâté may be kept, tightly covered, in the refrigerator for several days; bring it to room temperature before serving.

Smoked Sausage in Wine Sauce (SWITZERLAND)

4 TO 6 SERVINGS
PREPARATION AND COOKING: ABOUT 20 MINUTES
REFRIGERATES

⅓ cup dry red wine (recommended: Zinfandel)
1 scallion (with as much of the green part as is crisp), trimmed and chopped fine

2 tablespoons Dijon-style mustard
¼ teaspoon dried thyme
½ teaspoon sugar
Salt
Fresh-ground pepper

In a saucepan, combine all the ingredients except the salt and pepper. Bring the mixture to the boil, reduce the heat, and simmer it, covered, for 5 minutes. Season it to taste with salt and pepper.

1 pound smoked sausage (such as cervelat or kielbasa), the skin removed, cut into ¼-inch rounds

To the wine mixture, add the sausage rounds. Simmer for 5 minutes, or until they are thoroughly heated. Serve the sausage with Hot Potato Salad (page 212).

Smoked Sturgeon in Ramekins

6 SERVINGS
PREPARATION: ABOUT 20 MINUTES
COOKING: 5 MINUTES IN A 400° OVEN
REFRIGERATES

6 tablespoons butter
3 scallions (white part only), trimmed and chopped fine
4 tablespoons flour
½ teaspoon ground celery seed
A grating of nutmeg
2 cups light cream

⅓ cup sherry *or* Madeira
¼ cup fine-chopped parsley
½ pound smoked sturgeon, diced
Salt
Fresh-ground white pepper
½ cup butter-toasted bread crumbs

In a skillet, heat the butter and in it cook the scallion until translucent. Stir in the flour and cook the mixture over gentle heat for a few minutes. Stir in the celery seed and nutmeg. Gradually add the cream, stirring constantly until the mixture is thickened and smooth. Stir in the sherry and parsley; do not allow the sauce to boil. Stir in the sturgeon. Season the mixture to taste with salt and pepper. Spoon it equally into six ramekins; top with a sprinkling of bread crumbs. Bake at 400° for 5 minutes, or until the crumbs are golden.

Meats and Game

Beef

The recipes, all variants on braised beef, have been chosen for their ease of preparation and attractive melding of flavors. We start with the French classic, *boeuf bourguignon*, and move on to its cousin, *boeuf à la mode*, with several variations. Recipes for ground beef, beef rolls, and beef fillet follow. An unusual beef stroganoff calls for sherry as a principal ingredient.

Boeuf Bourguignon (FRANCE)

6 SERVINGS
PREPARATION: ABOUT 30 MINUTES
MARINATION: OVERNIGHT
COOKING: 2½ HOURS IN A 350° OVEN
REFRIGERATES; FREEZES

The most celebrated of beef-and-red-wine dishes, beef Burgundy improves by being made a day in advance of serving, so that you can remove the solidified fat. The recipe is traditionally served with good French bread or boiled potatoes or buttered noodles.

1 bottle dry red Burgundy (recommended: Mâcon *or* Gamay Beaujolais)	½ teaspoon ground cloves A grating of nutmeg Bouquet garni (page 4)
2 carrots, chopped fine	3 pounds lean chuck,
2 onions, chopped fine	trimmed of fat and
½ teaspoon ground allspice	cut into 1½-inch cubes

Combine all the ingredients except the *bouquet garni* and the meat. In a stainless steel or crockery bowl, arrange the meat; add the bouquet garni and the marinade. Let the beef sit, covered, in the refrigerator overnight.

¼ pound salt pork, diced	18 small white onions,
Marinated beef	peeled (page 6)
⅓ cup brandy	4 tablespoons flour

In a large flameproof casserole, cook the salt pork until it is crisp and golden; remove it to absorbent paper and reserve it. Remove the beef from the marinade and dry it on absorbent paper. Strain and reserve the marinade and bouquet garni.

In the hot pork fat, brown the meat thoroughly on all sides. Remove it to a flat dish. In a small pan, warm the brandy; ignite it and pour it over the beef; allow it to burn itself out. Discard all but 4 tablespoons of the fat; in the remaining fat, brown the onions. Sprinkle them with the flour and stir them gently.

2 teaspoons sugar	Reserved salt pork
1 teaspoon salt	3 large carrots, scraped and
½ teaspoon fresh-ground pepper	cut into ½-inch rounds (optional)
Reserved bouquet garni	Reserved marinade
1 calf's foot, split (optional)	Beef stock *or* canned beef bouillon, as needed

Add to the casserole the beef and any juices that have accumulated; stir to mix the onions and beef. Sprinkle with the sugar, salt, and pepper. Tuck in the bouquet garni and the calf's foot; add the salt pork and carrots. Add the marinade and sufficient stock to cover. Bake the beef, covered, at 350° for 2½ hours, or until it is tender.

At this point you may stop and continue later. (Let the casserole cool, refrigerate it overnight, and the following day remove the solidified fat.)

½ pound mushrooms, trimmed, sliced, and prepared (page
    5)
⅓ cup fine-chopped parsley

Allow the casserole to return to room temperature. Add the mushrooms.
Bring the beef Burgundy to serving temperature, either over medium heat
or in a 350° oven. Remove and discard the bouquet garni. Serve directly
from the casserole.

Boeuf à la Mode (FRANCE)

6 SERVINGS
PREPARATION: ABOUT 35 MINUTES
MARINATION TIME: OVERNIGHT
COOKING: 2½ HOURS IN A 350° OVEN
REFRIGERATES; FREEZES

Boeuf à la mode, boeuf en daube, and *estouffade de boeuf*—they are so
similar that I group them under the one title *boeuf à la mode* (*"française"*
being understood). A *daube* is, indeed, a French cooking utensil; we
would call it a casserole, whereas *casserole* to a French cook means
saucepan, the casserole being called a *faitout.* It is very confusing! Not
confusing, however, is the tastiness of this dish, which bears a strong re-
semblance to the classic Boeuf Bourguignon (page 49). The principal dif-
ferences are the omission of mushrooms in *boeuf à la mode* and the fact
that it may be made with one piece of meat, if desired, while *boeuf
bourguignon* is always prepared with beef cut into cubes. The dish improves when made a day ahead of serving.

Bouquet garni (page 4)
3 pounds lean chuck or round, cut into 1½-inch cubes, *or* a
    single (about 4-pound) piece of chuck or round
1 bottle dry red wine (recommended: Mâcon or Cabernet
    Sauvignon)

Put the bouquet garni in a deep bowl; over it lay the beef; add the wine.
Allow the meat to marinate, covered and refrigerated, overnight.

¼ pound slab bacon, diced

In a flameproof casserole, cook the bacon until it is crisp and golden. Using a slotted spoon, remove it to absorbent paper and reserve it. Remove the beef from the marinade and dry it on absorbent paper. In the hot bacon fat, brown the meat well; remove and reserve it. Reserve the marinade.

3 large onions, peeled and sliced	Reserved beef
3 large carrots, scraped and cut into ½-inch rounds	Reserved bacon
	2 teaspoons sugar
4 tablespoons flour	1 teaspoon salt
Reserved bouquet garni	Reserved marinade
1 calf's foot or pig's foot, split (optional)	Beef stock or canned beef bouillon, as needed

In the remaining bacon fat, cook the onions until translucent. Stir in the carrots and then the flour; over gentle heat, cook the mixture, stirring, for a few minutes. Add the bouquet garni, the calf's foot, the beef, and the bacon. Sprinkle with the sugar and salt. Add the marinade. If necessary, add beef stock just to cover. Bake the beef, covered, at 350° for 2½ hours, or until it is tender.

At this point you may stop and continue later. (Allow the casserole to cool to room temperature, refrigerate it overnight, and the following day remove the solidified fat and the bouquet garni.)

Fine-chopped parsley

Allow the casserole to come to room temperature before heating it to serve, either on top of the stove or in a 350° oven. Garnish the dish generously with parsley. Serve it with buttered noodles, plain boiled potatoes, or rice.

Variations:

To the bouquet garni may be added 2 walnut-sized pieces of fresh ginger root, sliced, *or* a 3-inch piece of cinnamon stick.

Salt pork may be used in the place of the bacon.

The browned beef may be flamed with brandy.

In place of the wine, use 2 cups corn whiskey plus beef stock *or* bouillon to cover; *or* use 1 cup applejack and 1 cup cider, plus beef stock *or* bouillon to cover; in these instances, do not marinate the beef. (These variations are of American origin.)

In Flemish countries, a *carbonnade flammande* would be made with beer in place of wine. (For an English dish, you might use stout or dark ale.) Do not marinate the beef.

B OEUF EN D AUBE P ROVENÇAL : Add to the bouquet garni the zest of 1 medium orange and ½ teaspoon red pepper flakes; use olive oil to brown the meat and onions; add to the onion-carrot-flour mixture 3 ripe medium tomatoes, peeled, seeded, and chopped (or blend into the marinade a 6-ounce can of tomato paste); when heating the casserole to serving temperature, add 1 cup pitted ripe olives, sliced lengthwise, *or* 12 large tenderized pitted prunes, *or* 1 small eggplant, peeled, diced, soaked for 30 minutes in cold salted water, and drained.

H UNGARIAN G OULASH (M AGYAR G ULYÁS): Use dry white wine (recommended: Hungarian Tokay); in place of the bacon fat, use lard to brown the meat and wilt the onions (discard any excess fat following this step); if desired, flame the beef with slivovitz; omit the carrots; into the onions stir 2 tablespoons sweet Hungarian paprika, together with the flour. When heating the casserole to serving temperature, stir in 1 cup sour cream; do not allow the goulash to boil after the cream has been added. Serve with buttered noodles.

Irish Stew

6 SERVINGS
PREPARATION: ABOUT 25 MINUTES
COOKING: 2½ HOURS IN A 350° OVEN
REFRIGERATES; FREEZES

This simple dish from the Emerald Isle is easily made and very nourishing, thanks to the stout, which also gives a pleasant nutty flavor.

Seasoned flour (page 6)
3 pounds lean chuck, cut
    into 1½-inch cubes
4 tablespoons oil

¼ cup Irish whiskey
4 medium onions, peeled
    and cut into ¼-inch
    slices

Dredge the beef in the seasoned flour. Reserve 2 tablespoons of the flour. In a flameproof casserole, heat the oil and brown the meat, a few pieces at a time; as they are done, remove them to a flat baking pan. Warm the whiskey in a small saucepan, ignite it, and pour it over the meat; allow the flame to die. In the fat remaining in the pan, cook the onions until they are golden brown. Stir in the reserved flour and cook the mixture for a few minutes.

> 3 cups stout

Return the beef to the casserole, together with any accumulated juices. Add the stout. Bake the meat, covered, at 350° for 2½ hours, or until it is fork-tender. Serve the stew with new potatoes boiled in their skins.

Beef Patties in Wine Sauce

4 SERVINGS
PREPARATION: ABOUT 25 MINUTES
COOKING: 10 MINUTES
REFRIGERATES; FREEZES

> 2 tablespoons butter
> 1 medium onion, peeled and chopped fine
> 1 garlic clove, peeled and put through a press

In a skillet, heat the butter and in it cook the onion until translucent. Add the garlic and stir to blend.

> 1 pound ground round   ¾ teaspoon powdered
> ½ cup bread crumbs   coriander
> 1 egg, beaten   Salt
> ¼ cup fine-chopped parsley   Fresh-ground pepper

In a mixing bowl, combine the onion-garlic mixture and the first five ingredients listed above. Blend the mixture well; season it to taste with salt and pepper. Form the meat into 8 patties.

> 3 tablespoons butter

In the skillet, heat the butter and in it, over gentle heat, cook the beef patties for about 4 minutes on each side, or until they are lightly browned. Remove and reserve them.

At this point you may stop and continue later. (Cover the beef patties to keep them moist.)

1 small onion, peeled and
    chopped fine
1 tablespoon flour
2 teaspoons paprika
    (preferably sweet
    Hungarian)
½ teaspoon dried thyme
½ cup chicken stock or
    canned chicken broth

½ cup dry white wine
    (recommended:
    Chablis)
½ cup heavy cream or
    thickened cream
    (page 6)
Salt

In the butter remaining in the skillet, cook the onion until translucent. Add the flour and cook over gentle heat for a few minutes. Stir in the paprika and thyme. Add the chicken stock and wine and bring to the boil, stirring until the mixture is thickened and smooth. Add the cream. Return the beef patties to the skillet; spoon the sauce over them. Reduce the heat and simmer the dish, covered, for 10 minutes.

Beef Paupiettes

6 SERVINGS
PREPARATION: ABOUT 40 MINUTES
COOKING: 1½ HOURS (IN A 350° OVEN, IF DESIRED)
REFRIGERATES; FREEZES

The recipe may also be made with dry red wine in place of the beer.

12 slices beef round (each about 4 × 6 inches × ⅛ inch),
    pounded thin
Salt
Fresh-ground pepper

Season the beef slices to taste with salt and pepper. Set them aside while you make the stuffing.

6 slices thin-cut bacon, diced
1 large garlic clove, peeled
　　and chopped fine
6 medium mushrooms,
　　trimmed and chopped fine
1 medium onion, peeled
　　and chopped fine
2 cups soft bread crumbs

½ cup fresh-grated
　　Parmesan cheese
1 egg, beaten
¼ cup fine-chopped
　　parsley
Water, as needed
Salt
Fresh-ground pepper

In a skillet, cook the bacon until it is crisp and golden; with a slotted spoon, remove it to absorbent paper and reserve it. In the bacon fat, cook the garlic, mushrooms, and onion until they are limp. Remove the skillet from the heat and stir in the bread crumbs; allow the mixture to cool somewhat and then stir in the Parmesan cheese, egg, parsley, and reserved bacon. If necessary, add just sufficient water to bind the mixture. Season it to taste with salt and pepper.

Over one end of each piece of beef, evenly spoon about 2 tablespoons of stuffing. Roll each piece, starting at the stuffing end; tie the ends of each paupiette with kitchen twine, about 1 inch in.

Seasoned flour (page 6)
2 tablespoons butter
2 tablespoons oil

Dredge the beef rolls in the seasoned flour. In the skillet, heat the butter and oil. Brown the rolls, a few at a time, and remove them to absorbent paper. Reserve the fat in the skillet.

At this point you may stop and continue later.

2 tablespoons flour
1 cup beef stock *or* canned beef bouillon
1 (12-ounce) can of stale beer
3 tablespoons tomato paste

Into the fat remaining in the skillet, stir the flour; cook the mixture over gentle heat for a few minutes. Gradually add the beef stock and beer, stirring until the sauce is thickened and smooth. Blend in the tomato paste. Add the beef rolls and simmer them, covered, for 1½ hours. (Or arrange them in a single layer in a baking dish and pour the sauce over them; bake, covered, at 350° for 1½ hours.) Remove the string before serving the paupiettes.

Beef Stroganoff

6 SERVINGS
PREPARATION: ABOUT 40 MINUTES
COOKING: 15 MINUTES
REFRIGERATES; FREEZES

> 4 tablespoons butter
> 2 medium onions, peeled and chopped fine
> 1 large garlic clove, peeled and chopped fine

In a skillet, heat the butter and in it cook the onion and garlic until translucent.

> 2 pounds beef sirloin, cut into   1 cup beef stock *or*
>   thin strips about 2 inches   canned beef bouillon
>   long   1 cup dry sherry
> Seasoned flour (page 6)   2 teaspoons
>   Worcestershire sauce

Dredge the beef in the seasoned flour; shake off any excess. Add the floured meat to the skillet and cook it, stirring often, until it is lightly browned. Add the stock, sherry, and Worcestershire sauce, stirring constantly until the sauce is thickened and smooth. Reduce the heat and simmer the mixture, covered, for 10 minutes.

At this point you may stop and continue later.

> ½ pound mushrooms,   Salt
>   trimmed, sliced and   Fresh-ground white pepper
>   prepared (page 5)   Fine-chopped parsley
> 1 cup sour cream

Into the simmering contents of the skillet, stir the mushrooms and their liquid. Blend in the sour cream. Season the beef stroganoff to taste with salt and pepper. Transfer it to a heated serving dish and garnish it with parsley. Serve it with bulgur, buttered noodles, or rice.

Variation:

In place of the sherry, use 1 cup dry Madeira.

Braised Beef Fillet

6 SERVINGS
PREPARATION: ABOUT 30 MINUTES
COOKING: 1½ HOURS IN A 350° OVEN
REFRIGERATES; FREEZES

4 tablespoons butter	½ teaspoon dried thyme
1 (3-pound) beef fillet	Salt
2 medium onions, peeled and chopped fine	Fresh-ground pepper

In a flameproof casserole, heat the butter. Add the beef fillet, onion, and seasonings. Over medium-high heat, brown the fillet.

2 tablespoons flour
1 cup beef stock *or* canned beef bouillon
1 carrot, scraped and chopped fine
¼ pound smoked ham, chopped fine

Mix the flour with the beef stock until smooth. Add this, with the carrot and ham, to the casserole. Bake the fillet at 350°, for 1 hour, basting it often. Remove the fillet to a baking pan. Transfer the remaining contents of the casserole to a food processor or blender and whirl until the mixture is smooth.

At this point you may stop and continue later. (Cover the fillet to keep it moist.)

1 cup Marsala
¼ cup fine-chopped parsley

Blend the wine with the vegetable purée and pour it over the meat. Return the fillet to the 350° oven for 15 minutes; baste it with the sauce. Remove the fillet to a heated serving platter, garnish it with the parsley, and offer the sauce separately.

Beef Tenderloin in Cream Sauce (NORWAY)

6 SERVINGS
PREPARATION: ABOUT 10 MINUTES
COOKING: 15 MINUTES
REFRIGERATES; FREEZES

    12 juniper berries
    ½ teaspoon salt
    Fresh-ground pepper
    6 (about 6-ounce) thick-cut tenderloin steaks

In a small mixing bowl, combine the juniper berries, salt, and a grinding of pepper. Using the back of a spoon, blend the seasonings and crush the berries. Rub both sides of the steaks with the mixture.

    8 tablespoons butter
    ½ cup akvavit

In a large skillet, heat the butter and in it sauté the steaks, 3 minutes on each side; the steaks will be rare. Pour off the excess butter. Warm the akvavit in a small pan, ignite it, and pour it over the steaks. When the flame dies, remove the steaks to a serving dish and keep them warm.

    1½ cups heavy cream

Add the cream to the skillet and cook the sauce, stirring, over high heat for 4 or 5 minutes, or until it is reduced by half. To serve, spoon a little of the sauce onto each steak. Offer the remaining sauce separately.

A Casserole of Three Meats (Baekerhof) (ALSACE-LORRAINE)

6 SERVINGS
PREPARATION: ABOUT 30 MINUTES
COOKING: 2 HOURS IN A 350° OVEN (ABOUT 2½ HOURS IF YOU ADD THE
    OPTIONAL CUSTARD)
REFRIGERATES (IF YOU OMIT THE CUSTARD)

6 medium potatoes, peeled
   and cut into ¼-inch
   slices
1 pound lean chuck, cut
   into ¾-inch cubes
1 pound lean pork, cut
   into ¾-inch cubes
1 pound lean veal, cut
   into ¾-inch cubes

3 large onions, peeled and
   sliced
2 bay leaves
12 juniper berries
½ teaspoon dried thyme
Salt
Fresh-ground pepper

In a buttered casserole, arrange in layers half the potato slices, half the mixed meats, and half the onions. Add the bay leaves, juniper berries, and thyme; season to taste with salt and pepper. Repeat the layers, ending with onions; season again.

At this point you may stop and continue later.

1½ cups dry white wine (recommended: Sylvaner)
4 tablespoons softened butter
¼ cup fine-chopped parsley

Pour the wine over the contents of the casserole and dot with the butter. Cover the casserole tightly. (A sheet of heavy-duty aluminum foil placed under the lid is a good seal.) Bake in a 350° oven for 2 hours. Check at the end of 1½ hours to ascertain that there is still some wine; if necessary, add a little more. When the cooking is completed, the dish should be moist but with no excess liquid; if necessary, remove the cover and continue to cook the casserole until the liquid is just evaporated. You may serve the dish now, garnished with parsley, or add a custard:

3 eggs
1½ cups light cream
¼ cup fine-chopped
   parsley

Salt
Fresh-ground white pepper

Beat together the eggs and cream; add the parsley and season the mixture to taste with salt and pepper. Over the contents of the casserole, pour the custard. Reduce the heat to 325° and bake, uncovered, for 20 minutes, or until the custard is set.

Variation:

In Corsica there is a dish called *stufatu*, considerably more stalwart in flavor than *baekerhof*, but very good. In step one, omit the potatoes and add to the onions 3 garlic cloves, peeled and chopped fine; add to the seasonings 3 whole cloves. Add to the layers of meats and onions layers of 4 ripe tomatoes, peeled, seeded, and chopped. In place of white wine, use a dry red wine (recommended: Zinfandel). *Stufatu* will have some liquid because of the omission of the potatoes; reduce the liquid, if you wish, as suggested above. Omit the custard and serve the casserole garnished with parsley, accompanied by buttered macaroni tossed with ½ cup fresh-grated Gruyère cheese.

Lamb

Braised shoulder of lamb is followed by the traditional French *navarin d'agneau*. Then we move to Italy for lamb "hunter's style," to Spain for a sherry-based lamb dish, and finally come home to America and my kitchen for lamb with cherries and lamb shanks with vegetables and with fruit.

Lamb may be successfully braised with red, white, or rosé wine. It responds equally well to beef or chicken stock as a second cooking liquid. Although I make specific suggestions in the recipes, you should feel free to experiment on your own. By the way, flaming lamb (after browning it) with ¼ cup Pernod gives the dish a delicious extra flavor. Allow the flame to die before continuing with the recipe.

Because lamb is fatty, you may want to prepare these recipes a day in advance of serving in order to offer them fat-free. To do so, allow them to cool to room temperature, refrigerate them overnight, and the following day remove the solidified fat. This direction, given explicitly for several of the dishes, may be applied to all. In addition, using leaner cuts—the leg or shoulder—will considerably reduce the fat. Bite-size cubes from these cuts, thoroughly browned and then drained on absorbent paper for a minute or two, will yield a dish with so little fat that you can remove it by delicately touching the surface of the sauce with a paper towel.

Braised Shoulder of Lamb

6 SERVINGS
PREPARATION: ABOUT 30 MINUTES
MARINATION TIME: OVERNIGHT
COOKING: 2 HOURS, STARTING IN A 350° OVEN
REFRIGERATES; FREEZES

1 medium carrot, scraped and chopped fine	1½ teaspoons sugar
	2 teaspoons salt
4 medium garlic cloves, peeled and chopped	2 cups dry red wine (recommended: Beaujolais)
2 bay leaves, crumbled	
4 whole cloves	½ cup fine olive oil
1 teaspoon dried oregano	1 (4- to 5-pound) shoulder of lamb, boned, rolled, and tied
8 peppercorns, bruised	
1 teaspoon dried rosemary	
1 teaspoon dried tarragon	

In cheesecloth, loosely tie together the first eight ingredients to make a bouquet garni. In a saucepan, combine the bouquet garni, sugar, and salt; add the wine and olive oil. Bring the liquid to the boil, reduce the heat, and simmer the mixture, covered, for 5 minutes; allow it to cool. Arrange the lamb in a deep ceramic or stainless steel dish. Add the marinade and the bouquet garni. Refrigerate the lamb, covered, overnight.

2 large onions, peeled and chopped fine
1 medium green pepper, seeded and chopped fine

In a roasting pan with a cover, arrange the onion and pepper. Over them, lay the lamb. Add the marinade and the bouquet garni. Bake the lamb, covered, at 350° for 1 hour.

At this point you may stop and continue later. (To avoid overcooking the lamb, remove the roasting pan from the oven, but leave it covered.)

Set the oven at 300°.

4 tablespoons tomato paste
1 cup pitted ripe olives, sliced lengthwise
Fine-chopped parsley

Into the marinade, stir the tomato paste. Return the lamb to the oven and bake it 1 hour longer. Remove the meat to a warmed serving platter. Remove and discard the bouquet garni. Remove the fat from the pan gravy; add the olives to the sauce. Serve the lamb garnished with parsley; offer the sauce separately.

The dish may be cooked a day in advance of serving. Remove the lamb from the sauce and seal well with plastic wrap. Transfer the sauce to a small bowl to facilitate removal, the following day, of the solidified fat.

If desired, the sauce may be thickened with 2 teaspoons cornstarch mixed until smooth with a little cold water.

Ragout of Lamb (Navarin d'Agneau) (FRANCE)

6 SERVINGS
PREPARATION: ABOUT 40 MINUTES
COOKING: 1¼ HOURS IN A 350° OVEN
REFRIGERATES; FREEZES

Navarin is the French term for a ragout or stew of mutton (not lamb); because mutton is rarely found in the United States, I substitute lamb. When made with various vegetables, as this dish is, the recipe is titled even more elaborately: *navarin d'agneau à la printanière*. Despite its imposing handle, I believe you will find the dish fresh-tasting and satisfying.

3 pounds lean lamb, cut into 1½-inch cubes	Fresh-ground pepper
	2 tablespoons butter
Salt	2 tablespoons oil

Season the lamb to taste with salt and pepper. In a flameproof casserole, heat the butter and oil. Brown the lamb, a few pieces at a time; remove them and reserve.

2 garlic cloves, peeled and chopped fine	4 medium celery ribs, with some of the leaves, chopped
3 medium onions, peeled and chopped	3 medium white turnips, scraped and diced
4 medium carrots, scraped and cut into ½-inch rounds	

In the fat remaining in the casserole, cook the garlic and onion until transparent. Stir in the carrots, celery, and turnips.

Reserved lamb
1 **bay leaf**
1 **teaspoon dried thyme**
1 **teaspoon sugar**
1 **cup chicken stock** *or*
    defatted canned
    chicken broth

2 **cups dry red wine**
    (**recommended:**
    Mâcon *or* **Burgundy**)
1 (6-ounce) **can of tomato**
    paste

To the contents of the casserole, add the lamb and bay leaf; sprinkle with the thyme and sugar; add the chicken stock. Blend in the wine and tomato paste. Bake the lamb, covered, at 350° for 1 hour. Using a bulb baster, remove the fat from the surface of the liquid (see also the following instruction).

At this point you may stop and continue later. (Allow the casserole to cool to room temperature, refrigerate it overnight, and the following day remove the solidified fat. Allow the casserole to return to room temperature before continuing with the recipe.)

1 **cup green beans, cut into 1-inch lengths,** *or* 1 **cup green peas**
Beurre manié (page 4) **of 2½ tablespoons each softened**
    butter and flour (optional)
¼ **cup fine-chopped parsley**

Add the beans to the casserole. Bake the lamb, covered, 15 minutes longer, or until it is tender. Add the beurre manié, stirring over medium heat until the sauce is thickened and smooth. Garnish the navarin with parsley and offer it with boiled potatoes.

Hunter's Style Lamb (Abbacchio alla Cacciatora) (ITALY)

6 SERVINGS
PREPARATION: ABOUT 25 MINUTES
COOKING: 1 HOUR IN A 350° OVEN
REFRIGERATES; FREEZES

Abbacchio is the Roman word for suckling lamb, eaten chiefly at Easter time. *Alla cacciatora* refers to the way Italian hunters of an earlier time cooked venison; the seasonings, incidentally, are traditional. Originally the dish was made with wine about to go to vinegar—hence the wine vinegar that we use today.

4 tablespoons olive oil
3 pounds lean lamb, cut
    into 1-inch cubes
1 tablespoon flour
2 medium garlic cloves,
    peeled and put through
    a press
1½ teaspoons dried
    rosemary

½ teaspoon dried sage
½ cup white wine vinegar
¾ cup dry white wine
    (recommended:
    Soave *or* Chenin
    Blanc)
Salt
Fresh-ground pepper

In a flameproof casserole, heat the olive oil and in it brown the lamb, a few pieces at a time. When all the meat is browned, return it to the casserole. Over it, sprinkle the flour; add the garlic, rosemary, and sage. Over high heat, add the wine vinegar, stirring to deglaze the casserole. When the vinegar is considerably reduced, add the wine. Bake the casserole, covered, at 350° for 1 hour, or until the lamb is tender. Season it to taste with salt and pepper. Serve it with rice or buttered pasta.

Lamb Braised with Sherry (SPAIN)

6 SERVINGS
PREPARATION TIME: ABOUT 25 MINUTES
MARINATION TIME: 4 HOURS
COOKING: 1 HOUR IN A 350° OVEN
REFRIGERATES; FREEZES

3 pounds lean lamb, cut into 1½-inch cubes
Dry sherry
Water

Marinate the lamb for 4 hours in equal parts sherry and water to cover. Drain the lamb and dry it on absorbent paper. Discard the marinade.

2 teaspoons ground cumin	4 tablespoons olive oil
Salt	3 garlic cloves, peeled and
Fresh-ground pepper	split

Sprinkle the lamb with the cumin and season it to taste with salt and pepper. In a flameproof casserole, heat the olive oil and in it cook the garlic until it is barely golden; remove and reserve the garlic. In the hot oil, brown the lamb, a few pieces at a time, and set aside.

2 medium onions, peeled	1 teaspoon ground cumin
and chopped	Reserved lamb
1½ tablespoons flour	Reserved garlic

To the casserole, add the chopped onion, stirring until it is limp. Blend the flour and cumin and stir into the onion. Return the lamb to the casserole, together with any juices that have accumulated. Add the garlic, putting it through a press. Stir the contents of the casserole so it does not lie in layers.

At this point you may stop and continue later.

1 cup dry sherry, heated to boiling
¼ cup fine-chopped parsley

To the casserole, add the sherry. Bake the lamb, covered, at 350° for 1 hour, or until it is tender. Garnish it with parsley, and serve it with rice.

Lamb with Sour Cherries

6 SERVINGS
PREPARATION TIME: ABOUT 35 MINUTES
COOKING: 1 HOUR IN A 350° OVEN
REFRIGERATES

The contrast of sweet (the raisins and port wine) and sour (the cherries) makes this dish an unusual and elusive-tasting main course.

2 tablespoons butter
2 tablespoons oil
3 pounds lean lamb, cut into 1½-inch cubes

In a flameproof casserole, heat the butter and oil; brown the lamb, a few pieces at a time. Remove and reserve. Discard all but 2 tablespoons of the fat.

8 scallions (with as much
    of the green as is crisp),
    trimmed and cut into
    1-inch lengths
1½ teaspoons ground
    cardamom
1½ teaspoons salt
½ teaspoon fresh-ground
    white pepper

½ cup golden raisins
Liquid from 2 (1-pound)
    cans of pitted sour
    cherries (reserve the
    cherries)
1 cup chicken stock *or*
    defatted canned
    chicken broth
¾ cup ruby port

In the remaining fat, cook the scallions until they are barely limp. Replace the lamb and over it sprinkle the seasonings. Add the raisins and liquids. Bake the lamb, covered, at 350° for 1 hour, or until it is tender.

At this point you may stop and continue later.

1½ teaspoons cornstarch
¼ cup ruby port
Reserved cherries
¼ cup fine-chopped parsley

Blend the cornstarch and port until the mixture is smooth. Stir it into the simmering casserole. When the sauce is somewhat thickened, add the cherries and heat through. (This final step is made easier by top-of-the-stove cooking.) Garnish the dish with parsley and offer it with rice.

Braised Lamb with Orange (PUERTO RICO)

6 SERVINGS
PREPARATION: ABOUT 30 MINUTES
COOKING: 1 HOUR IN A 350° OVEN
REFRIGERATES; FREEZES

Light and fresh-tasting, an ideal hot dish for warm weather.

2 tablespoons butter

2 tablespoons oil

3 pounds lean lamb, cut
  into 1½-inch cubes

Salt

Fresh-ground pepper

In a flameproof casserole, heat the butter and oil. Brown the lamb, a few pieces at a time; remove and reserve each batch. Season them to taste with salt and pepper. Discard all but 2 tablespoons of the fat.

4 shallots, peeled and chopped
  fine, *or* 4 scallions (white
  part only), trimmed
  and chopped fine

1 cup dry white wine
  (recommended:
  Muscadet *or* Sauvignon Blanc)

¾ cup strained fresh orange
  juice

2 teaspoons cornstarch

¼ cup strained fresh lime
  juice

2 medium garlic cloves,
  peeled and chopped
  fine

Grated rind of 1 large
  orange

¼ cup golden raisins

1 bay leaf

1 teaspoon chili powder

¼ teaspoon ground cloves

In the remaining fat, cook the shallots until translucent. Add the wine and orange juice. Blend the cornstarch with the lime juice until the mixture is smooth; add it to the casserole, stirring until the sauce is thickened and smooth. Stir in the remaining ingredients. Replace the lamb and any juices that have accumulated. Spoon the sauce over the lamb.

At this point you may stop and continue later.

2 large navel oranges, peeled and segmented, the segments
  cleaned of all white pith and seeded

Fine-chopped parsley

Bake the lamb, covered, at 350° for 1 hour, or until it is tender. Add the orange segments and heat them through for 10 minutes. Garnish the dish with parsley and offer it with rice.

Braised Lamb (or Veal) Shanks with Vegetables

6 SERVINGS
PREPARATION: ABOUT 30 MINUTES
COOKING: 1½ HOURS IN A 325° OVEN
REFRIGERATES; FREEZES

> 6 lamb shanks
> Seasoned flour (page 6)
> 2 tablespoons butter
> 2 tablespoons oil

Dredge the lamb shanks in the seasoned flour; reserve any remaining flour. In a flameproof casserole, heat the butter and oil and brown the meat. Remove and reserve it.

> 2 medium onions, peeled and chopped
> 1 large garlic clove, peeled and chopped fine
> 2 tablespoons reserved seasoned flour
> Bouquet garni (page 4)

In the remaining fat, cook the onion and garlic until translucent. Stir in the reserved flour and cook the mixture over gentle heat for a few minutes. Add the bouquet garni and replace the lamb shanks.

At this point you may stop and continue later.

> 1 cup beef stock *or* canned beef bouillon
> 2 cups dry red wine (recommended: Zinfandel)
> 6 medium carrots, scraped and cut into ½-inch rounds
> 12 white onions, peeled (page 6)
> 3 medium white turnips, scraped and diced
> Fine-chopped parsley

Add the stock and wine to the casserole. Bake the dish, covered, at 325° for 1 hour. Gently stir in the vegetables. Re-cover and cook for 30 minutes more, or until the lamb is tender and the vegetables are tender-crisp. Discard the bouquet garni. Garnish the dish with parsley, and serve it with buttered noodles or boiled potatoes.

Variation:

LAMB (OR VEAL) SHANKS WITH FRUIT: Follow steps one and two as written. In place of beef stock, use chicken stock *or* defatted canned chicken broth; in place of red wine, use white wine (recommended: Chablis). Omit the vegetables and add the grated rind and strained juice of 1 medium lemon and a 3-inch piece of cinnamon stick. Cook the casserole as directed, adding for the final 30 minutes one or a combination of the following tenderized dried fruits: 24 apricot halves, 12 peach halves, 12 pear halves, 12 large prunes; *or* 1 cup golden raisins. Or use 2 cups fresh seedless grapes, halved lengthwise. Add them about 5 minutes before serving—just time enough to heat through.

Pork

Like lamb, pork accommodates itself happily to being cooked with red, white, or rosé wine. It also responds well to the addition of bruised juniper berries in such bouquets garnis as are called for. Fruit complements pork; in addition to the pork-and-fruit recipes, you may enjoy the zest of an orange in your bouquet garni. All of the recipes for braising pork may be made a day in advance of serving, cooled, chilled overnight in the refrigerator, and skimmed of any solidified fat the next day. (If you use lean pork, this step will not be necessary.)

Roasted Fresh Ham

6 TO 8 SERVINGS
PREPARATION: ABOUT 20 MINUTES
COOKING: 3¾ HOURS IN A 325° OVEN
REFRIGERATES

    1 (5-pound) fresh ham, with bone, trimmed of excess fat
    1 large garlic clove, peeled and sliced lengthwise
    Salt
    Fresh-ground pepper

Wipe the ham as dry as possible with absorbent paper. Rub it vigorously with the cut edges of the garlic, then with salt and pepper to taste.

2 medium carrots, scraped
   and chopped
2 medium celery ribs,
   with the leaves,
   chopped

4 medium onions, peeled
   and chopped
1 bay leaf
4 whole cloves
⅓ cup Pernod *or*
   anise-flavored liqueur

Over the bottom of a roasting pan, arrange the carrot, celery, and onion. Tie the bay leaf and cloves loosely in cheesecloth and add to the pan. On top of the vegetables, arrange the ham, fat side down. Warm the Pernod in a small saucepan, ignite it, and pour it over the meat; allow the flame to die.

1 cup chicken stock *or* canned chicken broth
1 cup dry white wine (recommended: Muscadet *or*
   Chenin Blanc)

Add the chicken stock and wine to the pan. Roast the ham, uncovered, at 325° for 1 hour; baste it frequently with the pan juices. Turn the meat so that the fat side is up and roast it, basting often (more wine may be added as needed), for 2¾ hours more. Transfer it to a heated serving platter and keep it warm.

Skim the fat from the pan juices; remove and discard the cheesecloth bag. In the container of a food processor or blender, whirl the vegetables and their liquid, 2 cups at a time (more chicken stock may be added if needed), until the mixture is smooth. Bring it to serving temperature in a saucepan, and offer it separately.

Variations:

Follow step one as written. In step two, to the contents of the cheesecloth bag add a 3-inch piece of cinnamon stick; in place of the Pernod, flame the ham with akvavit. In step three, in place of the chicken stock and white wine, use canned consommé and Madeira. (More Madeira may be added as needed for basting.) Complete the recipe as written.

Follow step one as written. In step two, flame the ham with Geneva (Dutch gin) or plain gin. In step three, in place of the white wine, use dry sherry in which you dissolve ¼ cup dark brown sugar. (More sherry may be added as needed for basting.) Complete the recipe as written.

Roasted Loin of Pork (FRANCE)

6 SERVINGS
PREPARATION: ABOUT 15 MINUTES
MARINATION TIME: 24 HOURS
COOKING: 2½ HOURS IN A 325° OVEN
REFRIGERATES

Although red wine is suggested, the dish may also be made with dry white or rosé wine.

> 1 bottle dry red wine (recommended: Mâcon *or* Burgundy)
> 1 cup red wine vinegar
> Bouquet garni (page 4), to which you add ¾ teaspoon cumin
>   seed, 1 peeled and chopped garlic clove, and 6 bruised
>   juniper berries
> 1 (3-pound) pork loin roast, boned and trimmed of excess fat

In a deep earthenware or stainless steel bowl, combine the wine, vinegar, and bouquet garni. Add the loin roast and marinate it, covered and refrigerated, for 24 hours.

Remove the meat from the marinade. Dry it thoroughly with absorbent paper and arrange it on a rack in a roasting pan. Bake the loin at 325° for 2½ hours, basting it often with the marinade.

> ½ cup thickened cream (page 6) *or* sour cream
> Fine-chopped parsley

Remove the meat to a heated serving platter. Skim the fat from the pan juices; blend in the cream. Garnish the roast with parsley and offer the sauce separately.

Pork Loin with Garlic (FRANCE)

6 SERVINGS
PREPARATION: ABOUT 20 MINUTES
COOKING: 2½ HOURS IN A 325° OVEN
REFRIGERATES; FREEZES

Surprisingly, the sauce tastes most delicately of garlic.

1 (about 4-pound) pork loin, boned, rolled, and tied	20 garlic cloves, peeled
	3 cups milk
Salt	⅓ cup anise-flavored
Fresh-ground pepper	liqueur
1 bay leaf	

Rub the pork loin with salt and pepper to taste. Arrange it in a flameproof covered casserole. Add the bay leaf and garlic. In a saucepan, bring the milk to the boil; pour it over the pork and bake the meat, covered, at 325° for 2¼ hours. Turn off the oven. Pour the liqueur over the pork, replace the cover, and allow the pork to rest in the oven for 10 minutes. Remove it to a heated serving platter.

Beurre manié (page 4) of 2 tablespoons each softened butter and flour

Strain the milk, reserving 2 cups of it; discard the remainder and the bay leaf. In the container of a food processor or blender, whirl the garlic with a little of the milk until the mixture is smooth. In a saucepan, combine the garlic purée and remaining reserved milk. Bring the mixture to the boil, add the beurre manié, and stir the sauce until it is thickened and smooth. Offer it separately.

Variation:

From Portugal: Marinate the pork overnight in 1 bottle of dry white wine and 1 cup white wine vinegar, to which you add a bouquet garni (page 4) and the garlic cloves. The following day, bake the pork in its marinade, as suggested above. Remove the meat to a heated serving platter; discard the bouquet garni. Strain the marinade, retaining 2 cups. In the container of a food processor or blender, whirl the garlic with a little of the marinade until the mixture is smooth. Add the garlic purée to the remaining reserved marinade; bring the mixture to the boil and thicken it with the beurre manié. Offer the sauce separately.

Braised Pork with Dried Fruit

6 SERVINGS
PREPARATION: ABOUT 30 MINUTES
COOKING: 2 HOURS IN A 350° OVEN
REFRIGERATES

> 2 tablespoons butter
> 2 tablespoons oil
> 2½ pounds shoulder of pork, cut into 1½-inch cubes

In a flameproof casserole, heat the butter and oil. Brown the pork, a few pieces at a time, removing them as they are done.

> 1 garlic clove, peeled and
>   chopped fine
> 3 medium onions, peeled
>   and chopped
> 1 teaspoon dried dill
> 1 teaspoon chopped fresh
>   mint *or* ½ teaspoon
>   dried mint

> 1 teaspoon sugar
> Salt
> Fresh-ground pepper
> 2 cups dry red wine
>   (recommended:
>   Beaujolais)

In the remaining fat, cook the garlic and onion until translucent. Replace the pork and add the dill, mint, and sugar; season to taste with salt and pepper. Stir to mix the ingredients. Add the wine. Bake the casserole, covered, at 350° for 1½ hours.

At this point you may stop and continue later.

> 24 tenderized dried apricot halves *or* tenderized pitted
>   prunes *or* a combination of the two

Add the fruit and continue to bake the pork, covered, 30 minutes longer.

> 2 teaspoons cornstarch, blended until smooth with ¼ cup
>   water
> Fine-chopped parsley

Add the cornstarch, stirring gently until the sauce is thickened. Garnish the dish with parsley.

Variations:

From Sweden: Roll a 4-pound boned loin of pork with 12 tenderized pitted prunes and 1 apple, peeled, cored, and chopped; season the pork to taste with salt and pepper; tie the roll securely. In the casserole, brown the meat, as suggested above. Discard all remaining fat. Add 1 cup dry white wine (recommended: Chablis) and 1 cup heavy cream. Bake the meat as suggested for 2 hours. Remove it to a warmed serving platter. Over high heat, reduce the sauce to 1½ cups. Stir in 1 tablespoon red currant jelly and thicken the sauce, if desired, with 1 teaspoon cornstarch blended until smooth with a little cold water. Garnish the pork with parsley and offer the sauce separately.

PORK PAUPIETTES WITH PRUNES: In 2 cups dry red wine, cook 18 tenderized pitted prunes for 10 minutes. Drain and reserve them and the wine. On each of 6 pork cutlets pounded flat with a meat hammer, spread a slice of boiled ham. On the ham, arrange 2 tenderized pitted prunes (*not* those you have cooked). Roll and tie the cutlets. Dredge them in seasoned flour (page 6), and brown them in a combination of butter and oil, as suggested above. Arrange them in a skillet and add a bouquet garni (page 4) and the reserved wine. Simmer the paupiettes, covered, for 40 minutes. Add the reserved prunes and cook the dish 10 minutes longer. Remove the rolls to a warmed serving platter. Over high heat, reduce the sauce to 1½ cups and stir in 4 tablespoons thickened cream (page 6) *or* sour cream and 2 tablespoons currant jelly; do not allow the sauce to boil. Pour the sauce over the paupiettes and garnish the dish with parsley.

Ragout of Pork (FRANCE)

6 SERVINGS
PREPARATION: ABOUT 35 MINUTES
COOKING: 2 HOURS IN A 350° OVEN
REFRIGERATES; FREEZES

This dish is really a *porc bourguignon*—less celebrated than its cousin, *boeuf bourguignon,* but utilizing the same ingredients and yielding a very tasty main course.

> ¼ pound salt pork, diced
> 3 pounds shoulder of pork, cut into 1½-inch cubes
> ⅓ cup brandy

In a flameproof casserole, cook the salt pork until it is crisp and golden. With a slotted spoon, remove it to absorbent paper and reserve it. In the pork fat, brown the meat, a few pieces at a time; remove them to a flat pan. Warm the brandy in a small saucepan, ignite it, and pour it over the pork; allow the flame to die out.

> 24 white onions, peeled (page 6)
> 1 large garlic clove, peeled and chopped fine
> 2 shallots, peeled and chopped fine, *or* 2 scallions, trimmed
>   and chopped fine

In the remaining fat, glaze the onions; remove and reserve them. Discard all but 2 tablespoons of the fat and in it cook the garlic and shallots until they are translucent.

> 4 tablespoons flour   Bouquet garni (page 4)
> 1 bottle dry red wine   Reserved pork
>   (recommended: Reserved salt pork
>   Beaujolais)   Reserved onions
> Salt

Stir the flour into the shallots; over gentle heat, cook the mixture, stirring, for a few minutes. Gradually add the wine, stirring constantly until the sauce is thickened and smooth. Season it to taste with salt. Add the bouquet garni and the pork, salt pork, and onions. Bake the casserole, covered, at 350° for 2 hours, or until the meat is tender. Remove and discard the bouquet garni.

At this point you may stop and continue later.

> ½ pound mushrooms, trimmed, sliced, and prepared
>   (page 5)
> Fine-chopped parsley

Stir the mushrooms into the simmering casserole. Bring the ragout to serving temperature and garnish it with parsley.

Variations:

A pork ragout from Italy calls for olive oil to brown the pork (use 4 tablespoons). In step three, add 2 ripe medium tomatoes, peeled, seeded, and chopped. In step four, in place of the mushrooms add 3 cups chopped celery, boiled separately until just tender-crisp. This dish is made with either dry red or white wine.

A pork ragout from Spain omits the salt pork in step one and calls for browning the meat in olive oil (4 tablespoons); flaming the meat with brandy is optional. In step three, in place of red wine, use dry white wine (recommended: Riesling) and ¼ cup white wine vinegar; to the bouquet garni add the zest of 1 medium orange. In step four, the mushrooms are omitted. Serve the ragout with rice or boiled potatoes.

Another pleasant variation is the addition of 24 sausage balls made from ½ pound sausage meat cooked in a skillet until crisp and brown. Drain them on absorbent paper and add with the mushrooms in step four—or in place of the mushrooms, if desired.

Cassoulet du Midi-Pyrénées (FRANCE)

8 TO 10 SERVINGS
PREPARATION: ABOUT 40 MINUTES
COOKING: 3½ HOURS IN A 275° OVEN
REFRIGERATES; FREEZES

Not the classic cassoulet, but rather a homely country dish from the southwest.

> 1 **pound dried Great Northern or navy beans**
> 8 **cups cold water**

In a soup kettle, combine the beans and water. Over high heat, bring the water to a rolling boil, uncovered; allow the beans to cook for 10 minutes.

Away from the heat, allow them to stand, covered, for 1 hour. Return the water to the boil, reduce the heat, and simmer the beans, covered, for 1 hour.

6 thick slices bacon, diced
1½ pounds lean lamb, cut
    into 1½-inch cubes
1½ pounds lean pork, cut
    into 1½-inch cubes
2 carrots, scraped and
    sliced thin

2 large garlic cloves,
    peeled and chopped
    fine
3 large onions, peeled and
    sliced thin

In a flameproof casserole, cook the bacon until it is crisp and golden; with a slotted spoon, remove it to absorbent paper and reserve it. In the bacon fat, brown the lamb and pork, a few pieces at a time; remove them as they are done. Into the remaining fat, stir the carrot, garlic, and onion. Cook the mixture until the onion is translucent.

Prepared beans
Reserved bacon, lamb,
    and pork
1 pound highly seasoned
    sausage, such as chorizo,
    cut into ¼-inch rounds
Carrot-onion mixture
1 (6-ounce) can of tomato
    paste
1 cup chicken stock *or*
    canned chicken broth
1 teaspoon sugar

2 teaspoons salt
Bouquet garni (page 4),
    to which you add 5
    whole cloves and, if
    desired, the zest of 1
    medium orange
Dry white wine, as needed
    (recommended:
    Chablis)
½ cup fine-chopped
    parsley

Drain the beans and, in a large bowl, combine them with the bacon, lamb, pork, sausage, any liquid that may have accumulated from the meats, the carrot-onion mixture, and the tomato paste blended with the chicken stock. Sprinkle with sugar and salt. Gently stir the contents of the bowl to blend the ingredients. Put the bouquet garni in the bottom of the casserole. Over it spoon the bean-meat mixture. Add wine to cover. Bake the cassoulet, tightly covered, at 275° for 3½ hours, or until the meat and beans are very tender. If the completed dish seems too moist, spoon off a little of the liquid. Remove and discard the bouquet garni; garnish the cassoulet with parsley.

Choucroute Garnie Alsacienne (Sauerkraut with Pork and Sausage) (FRANCE)

6 SERVINGS

PREPARATION: ABOUT 25 MINUTES

COOKING: 2¼ HOURS IN A 300° OVEN

REFRIGERATES

This recipe for the celebrated Alsatian dish comes from a charming restaurant in Strasbourg, La Maison des Tanneurs, where, one early-spring day, I sat at a sun-flooded window banked with geraniums and enjoyed my *choucroute garnie*. To complete your meal, offer cheese (a chèvre goes well with this dish) and a compote of dried fruit (page 231).

½ pound thick-sliced
  bacon, diced

6 pork chops, trimmed of
  excess fat

1 pound sausage (chorizo
  or kielbasa), cut into
  1-inch rounds

2 pounds precooked
  sauerkraut, rinsed and
  drained

¼ cup brandy

In a flameproof casserole, cook the bacon until it is crisp and golden; with a slotted spoon, remove it to absorbent paper and reserve it. In the bacon fat, brown the pork chops and sausage, a few pieces at a time; remove them to absorbent paper and reserve them. In the remaining fat, cook the sauerkraut, stirring often, until it is just barely golden. Add the brandy and cook the mixture for 5 minutes.

2 large garlic cloves, peeled
  and chopped fine

1 large onion, peeled and
  stuck with 3 cloves

Bouquet garni (page 4),
  to which you add 6
  bruised juniper berries

Reserved bacon, pork
  chops, and sausage

3 cups dry white wine
  (recommended:
  Riesling *or* Sylvaner)

Push the sauerkraut aside so that you can put the garlic on the bottom and the onion in the center of the casserole. Add the bouquet garni. Arrange the sauerkraut in an even layer and over it lay the pork chops and sausage; over them, sprinkle the bacon. Add the wine and bake the casserole, covered, at 300° for 1 hour.

At this point you may stop and continue later.

> **6 medium potatoes, peeled**

Add the potatoes and continue baking the casserole for 1 hour more.

> **6 wurst sausages (frankfurters will do)**

Add the wurst and bake the choucroute 15 minutes longer, or until the sauerkraut and potatoes are very tender. Remove and discard the onion and bouquet garni. Serve the dish with Dijon mustard.

Variation:

From Poland: In step two, over the bottom of the casserole, in addition to the garlic, arrange 1 large carrot, scraped and sliced thin; over the layer of sauerkraut before adding the meat, arrange 2 tart apples, peeled, cored, and chopped.

Ham Steak in Wine

4 SERVINGS
PREPARATION: ABOUT 15 MINUTES
COOKING: 1½ HOURS IN A 350° OVEN
REFRIGERATES

1 (2-pound) cooked ham steak, about 1 inch thick	⅓ cup dark brown sugar, packed
Dijon mustard	1½ cups claret *or* ruby port
3 tart apples, peeled, cored, and chopped	Fine-chopped parsley

Put the ham in a shallow baking dish. Spread it very lightly with mustard. Over the ham, arrange the apples; sprinkle them with brown sugar and add the wine. Bake the ham, covered, at 350° for 1 hour; remove the cover and continue to bake it, basting it with the wine, for 30 minutes more. Transfer the ham to a heated serving dish, garnish it with a sprinkling of parsley, and offer the sauce, skimmed of any fat, separately.

Variation:

From Normandy, the French apple country: Omit the mustard; in 3 tablespoons butter, cook until translucent 2 large onions, peeled and chopped. Arrange the onion on top of the ham steak. In a small saucepan, warm ⅓ cup Calvados *or* applejack; ignite it and pour it over the ham. Allow the flame to die. Add the apples and brown sugar, as suggested. Add 1½ cups cider and complete the recipe as written.

Ham Mousse

6 TO 8 SERVINGS
PREPARATION AND COOKING: ABOUT 30 MINUTES
CHILLING TIME: 6 HOURS

A light and tasty way to use leftover ham, and a rather elegant main course for warm-weather meals.

Lightly oil and chill a 6-cup ring mold.

3½ cups diced cooked ham	1¼ cups chicken stock *or*
1 teaspoon Dijon mustard	1 (10½-ounce) can
1 envelope unflavored	of defatted chicken
gelatin	broth
	2 egg yolks, beaten

In the container of a food processor equipped with the steel blade, whirl the ham to a smooth paste. Transfer it to a mixing bowl and stir in the mustard. Soften the gelatin for 5 minutes in ¼ cup of the chicken stock. Heat the remaining broth in a saucepan and add the gelatin, stirring to dissolve it. Blend a little of the broth into the egg yolks; then add the yolks to the saucepan. Cook the mixture over gentle heat, stirring constantly, until it begins to thicken and coats a metal spoon. Allow it to cool, and then chill it until it just begins to set.

¼ cup Madeira	½ cup heavy cream,
½ cup fine-chopped parsley	whipped
or ¼ cup fine-chopped	3 egg whites, beaten until
gherkins	stiff but not dry
	Watercress

To the ham, add the contents of the saucepan, the Madeira, and the parsley, stirring to blend the mixture well. Fold in the whipped cream. Beat in one-fifth of the egg white; fold in the remainder. Using a rubber spatula, transfer the mixture to the prepared mold. Chill the mousse for at least 6 hours, or until it is thoroughly set. Unmold it onto a chilled serving platter and garnish it with watercress.

Veal

The delicacy of veal is a welcome alternative to the more robust flavor of beef. I believe you will find this selection of veal recipes light, refreshing, and tempting.

While I suggest using chicken stock in several of the dishes, veal stock is, of course, acceptable, if not, indeed, preferable; my recommendation of chicken stock derives from its greater availability (we simply eat more chicken than veal) and from the fact that, if you are unable to make your own stock, canned chicken broth is always at hand, whereas veal broth is not.

Some of the recipes call for pounding veal scallops with a meat hammer or the broad side of a heavy knife. When specifically directed, this step is integral to the recipe; when not suggested, the option is yours. Pounding always tenderizes the scallops somewhat, and thus may enhance the recipes.

The recipes for lamb shanks, pages 69–70, also apply to veal shanks. In place of red wine, use white wine, and follow the recipes as written.

While dry white wine is called for in these veal recipes, you may also use rosé, or a combination of French (dry) vermouth and white wine. The flavor of the vermouth is too distinctive to use on its own.

Roasted Leg of Veal

6 TO 8 SERVINGS
PREPARATION: ABOUT 20 MINUTES
COOKING: ABOUT 3 HOURS IN A 325° OVEN
REFRIGERATES; FREEZES

2 garlic cloves, peeled and
put through a press
1 teaspoon powdered thyme
¼ teaspoon fresh-ground
white pepper
1 (4½- to 5-pound) boned
leg of veal, rolled and
tied

½ pound salt pork, cut
into thin strips
2 cups dry white wine
(recommended:
Pinot Blanc)
1 bay leaf
1 medium onion, peeled
and sliced

In a small mixing bowl, blend the garlic, thyme, and pepper; rub the veal with this mixture. Arrange it on a rack in a roasting pan. Over the top, arrange the strips of salt pork. To the bottom of the pan, add the wine, bay leaf, and onion. Cover the veal (with heavy-duty aluminum foil, if your roasting pan is lidless) and roast at 325° for 40 minutes to the pound (a total of 2¾ to 3¼ hours). Baste it twice during the first half hour. Remove the cover for the final 45 minutes, basting the meat often with the pan juices. Remove the veal to a heated serving platter.

1 teaspoon cornstarch blended with a little cold water
12 small mushrooms, trimmed, sliced, and prepared (page 5)

Strain the pan juices; skim the fat from the liquid. In a saucepan, bring the liquid to a boil, add the cornstarch, and stir the sauce until it is somewhat thickened and smooth. Stir in the mushrooms and heat through. Offer the sauce separately.

Rouelle de Veau à l'Ancienne (Braised Fillet of Veal) (FRANCE)

6 SERVINGS
PREPARATION: ABOUT 25 MINUTES
COOKING: ABOUT 2 HOURS IN A 325° OVEN
REFRIGERATES; FREEZES

This dish from Lorraine makes an attractive main course for a dinner party.

4 tablespoons butter	1 garlic clove, peeled and
1 (3½-pound) fillet of veal	halved lengthwise
Salt	12 white onions, peeled
Fresh-ground pepper	(page 6)
1 thick slice bacon, diced	1½ cups dry white wine
1 smoked sausage, cut	(recommended:
into thin rounds	Sylvaner)

In a flameproof casserole, heat the butter and in it brown the veal. Season it to taste with salt and pepper. Add the bacon, sausage, garlic, and onions. Add the wine. Bring the liquid to the boil, reduce the heat, and simmer the veal, covered, for 10 minutes.

Transfer the casserole to a preheated 325° oven and cook it, covered, for 1½ hours, basting the veal often.

  ½ pound small mushrooms, trimmed, sliced thin, and prepared
       (page 5)
  ⅓ cup fine-chopped parsley

To the contents of the casserole, add the mushrooms and their liquid; continue to cook the veal for 30 minutes more. Transfer the fillet to a heated serving platter and garnish it with parsley.

Strain the pan juices. Discard the garlic. Around the veal, arrange the onions and mushrooms. Skim the fat from the liquid and offer it separately. If you wish, the sauce may be thickened with 1 teaspoon cornstarch blended with a little cold water.

Osso Bucco (Braised Veal Shanks) (ITALY)

4 SERVINGS
PREPARATION: ABOUT 35 MINUTES
COOKING: 1¼ HOURS IN A 325° OVEN
REFRIGERATES; FREEZES

This version, my own, of the famous dish is neither classic nor definitive, but one that I hope you will find satisfying.

4 thick veal shanks, cut into 2-inch pieces (ask your butcher to
    do this for you)
Seasoned flour (page 6)
4 tablespoons olive oil

Dredge the veal shanks in the seasoned flour; shake off any excess flour. In a flameproof casserole, heat the oil and in it brown the pieces of meat, a few at a time; remove them as they are done.

1 large carrot, scraped and sliced thin

1 celery rib, chopped

1 garlic clove, peeled and chopped fine

1 large onion, peeled and chopped fine

1 cup dry white wine (recommended: Soave or Chenin Blanc)

½ cup chicken stock or canned chicken broth

½ cup tomato sauce

½ teaspoon dried basil

¼ teaspoon crumbled rosemary

¼ teaspoon dried sage

In the fat remaining in the pan, cook the vegetables until the onion is translucent. Deglaze the casserole with the wine. Add the chicken stock, tomato sauce, and herbs. Return the veal to the casserole, together with any accumulated juices. Bake the veal at 325° for 1¼ hours, or until it is tender.

At this point you may stop and continue later. (Actually, the dish is now complete and may be served; my concluding step is optional.)

1 teaspoon anchovy paste
Grated rind of 1 medium lemon
¼ cup fine-chopped parsley

Bring the casserole to serving temperature. With a slotted spoon, transfer the veal to a heated serving platter. Into the sauce blend the anchovy paste and lemon rind. Pour the sauce over the veal and garnish the dish with parsley.

Côtes de Veau Morvandelle (Veal Chops in White Wine with Mushrooms) (FRANCE)

4 SERVINGS
PREPARATION: ABOUT 15 MINUTES
COOKING: 25 MINUTES, PARTIALLY IN A 400° OVEN

>   4 tablespoons butter
>   4 large veal chops
>   Salt
>   Fresh-ground pepper

In a skillet, heat the butter and in it cook the veal chops for 5 minutes on each side. Season them to taste with salt and pepper. Remove them to an ovenproof dish.

>   2 shallots, peeled and chopped fine, *or* 3 scallions (white part only), trimmed and chopped fine
>   12 mushrooms, trimmed and sliced thin
>   1 cup dry white wine (recommended: white Mâcon *or* Chablis)

In the fat remaining in the pan, cook the shallot until translucent. Add the mushrooms, stirring to coat them well. Add the wine and deglaze the skillet. Cook the vegetables, covered, for 5 minutes.

>   1 egg yolk
>   ¼ cup heavy cream
>   Salt
>   ½ cup grated Gruyère cheese

Blend the egg yolk and cream and, over gentle heat, add it to the contents of the skillet, stirring constantly until the sauce is somewhat thickened; do not allow it to boil. Season it to taste with salt. Spoon the sauce over the veal chops. Sprinkle the grated cheese over all. Bake the dish, uncovered, at 400° for 10 minutes, or until the cheese is melted and golden.

Blanquette de Veau (FRANCE)

6 SERVINGS
PREPARATION: ABOUT 30 MINUTES
COOKING: 1½ HOURS (ON TOP OF THE STOVE OR IN A 350° OVEN)
REFRIGERATES; FREEZES

This veal stew, enriched by the addition of a beurre manié, cream, and egg yolk, is pleasing to both eye and palate. Served with a hearty bread, it is a one-dish meal, especially if the variation (below) is used.

> 3 pounds stewing veal, cut into 1½-inch cubes
> 6 cups cold water

Put the veal in a large saucepan or soup kettle and add the water. Bring the liquid to the boil over high heat and cook the veal, uncovered, for 5 minutes. Drain the veal, refresh it in cold water, and return it to the kettle; *or*, if you plan to cook the blanquette in the oven, arrange it in an oven-proof casserole.

> 3 large celery ribs, with
>   their leaves, chopped
> Bouquet garni (page 4)
> A grating of nutmeg
> 1 teaspoon sugar
> 1½ teaspoons salt
>
> Fresh-ground white pepper
> 2 cups chicken stock *or*
>   canned chicken broth
> 2½ cups dry white wine
>   (recommended:
>   Chablis)

To the veal, add the celery, bouquet garni, and seasonings. Add the broth and wine (the liquid should just cover the ingredients; add more wine, if necessary). Bring the liquid to the boil, reduce the heat, and simmer the veal, covered, for 1 hour. *Or* bake the casserole, covered, at 350° for 1 hour.

At this point you may stop and continue later.

Return the veal to the simmer *or* to the designated oven heat.

Strained juice of 1 medium
    lemon
18 small white onions, peeled
    (page 6)
Beurre manié (page 4)
    of 3 tablespoons each
    softened butter and flour

½ pound mushrooms,
    trimmed, sliced, and
    prepared (page 5)
2 egg yolks beaten with
    ½ cup heavy cream
Salt
¼ cup fine-chopped
    parsley

Into the simmering veal stir the lemon juice and onions. Cook the veal 30 minutes longer, or until the onions are tender. Remove and discard the bouquet garni. Add the beurre manié, stirring gently until the sauce is thickened and smooth. At the time of serving, add the mushrooms, and when they are heated through, stir in the egg yolk–cream mixture. Do not allow the blanquette to boil. Adjust the salt to taste. Garnish the dish with parsley.

Variation:

HEARTY VEAL STEW: Follow step one as written. In step two, add 3 large carrots, scraped and cut into ½-inch rounds; 3 large yellow onions, peeled and cut into ¼-inch slices; and 3 medium white turnips, scraped and cut into large dice. Gently stir to mix. In step three, omit the white onions; make the beurre manié of 4 tablespoons each softened butter and flour; omit the eggs yolks, but retain the heavy cream. Complete the recipe as written.

Vitello alla Marengo (Veal Marengo) (ITALY)

6 SERVINGS
PREPARATION: ABOUT 30 MINUTES
COOKING: 1 HOUR
REFRIGERATES; FREEZES

This dish from Piedmont, a derivative, I should imagine, of Chicken Marengo (page 141), is easily prepared. Rice is a pleasant accompaniment to it.

½ cup olive oil

3 pounds lean veal, cut
   into 1½-inch cubes

1 small garlic clove, peeled
   and chopped fine

1 medium onion, peeled
   and chopped fine

1 teaspoon sugar

Salt

Fresh-ground pepper

1 cup chicken stock or
   canned chicken broth

1 cup dry white wine
   (recommended:
   Soave or Sauvignon
   Blanc)

6 ripe tomatoes, peeled,
   seeded, and chopped

1 small bay leaf

¼ teaspoon dried thyme

In a large skillet with a lid, heat the olive oil and in it brown the veal, a few pieces at a time; remove them as they are done. In the oil, cook the garlic and onion until translucent. Stir in the sugar and salt and pepper to taste. Add the chicken stock and wine; deglaze the skillet.

Return the veal to the skillet, together with any accumulated juices. Add the tomato, bay leaf, and thyme. Bring the mixture to the boil, reduce the heat, and simmer it, covered, for 45 minutes, or until the veal is tender.

4 tablespoons butter

12 small white onions, peeled (page 6)

12 small mushrooms, stems removed (use them in some other
   dish)

¼ cup fine-chopped parsley

In a second skillet, heat the butter and in it glaze the onions. Add them, together with the mushroom caps, to the veal; continue to cook the meat for 15 minutes more. Arrange the veal in a heated serving dish. Skim any excess fat from the sauce. Over high heat, cook it, stirring, for 5 minutes. Pour the sauce over the veal and garnish the dish with parsley.

Variation:

To cook the recipe in a 350° oven: Using a flameproof casserole as your cooking utensil, follow step one as written. Without glazing the white onions, add them to the casserole. Bake the veal, covered, at 350° for 45 minutes. Add the mushrooms and continue to bake the dish, covered, 15 minutes longer.

You may, if you like, substitute a 16-ounce can of Italian tomatoes, drained and chopped, for the fresh tomatoes.

Veal with Oranges (SPAIN)

6 SERVINGS
PREPARATION: ABOUT 30 MINUTES
COOKING: 1½ HOURS IN A 350° OVEN
REFRIGERATES

The orange and sherry flavors meld in a particularly appetizing way.

4 tablespoons butter	A grating of nutmeg
3 pounds lean veal, cut into 1½-inch cubes	1 teaspoon salt
2 tablespoons brown sugar	Fresh-ground pepper

In a flameproof casserole, heat the butter and in it brown the veal, a few pieces at a time; remove them as they are done. Return the veal to the casserole, together with any accumulated juices. Add the seasonings.

4 medium carrots, scraped and sliced thin
4 medium oranges, sliced paper-thin, seeded and cut into
    1-inch wedges (use oranges with thin rinds)
2 cups chicken stock *or* defatted canned chicken broth

To the casserole, add the carrots, oranges, and chicken stock. Bake the casserole, covered, at 350° for 1¼ hours.

At this point you may stop and continue later.

⅔ cup dry sherry
2 tablespoons cornstarch, blended until smooth in a little
    cold water
Fine-chopped parsley

Add the sherry and continue to bake the casserole, covered, for 15 minutes more. Add the cornstarch, stirring until the sauce is thickened. Garnish the dish with parsley.

Veal with Paprika (Veal Paprikash)

6 SERVINGS

PREPARATION: ABOUT 30 MINUTES

COOKING: 1 HOUR IN A 350° OVEN

REFRIGERATES; FREEZES

Originally a Hungarian dish, veal with paprika crept over the Austrian border and came to Vienna, whence this recipe, which I enjoyed at the home of Ljuba Welitsch, the Bulgarian prima donna who in the late 1940s made Richard Strauss's Salome the most glamorous figure to have appeared at the Metropolitan Opera since the creations of Geraldine Farrar and Maria Jeritza. (Given this background, I hesitate to designate a nationality for the recipe.)

2 tablespoons butter	Salt
2 tablespoons oil	Fresh-ground pepper
3 pounds lean veal, cut into 1½-inch cubes	

In a flameproof casserole, heat the butter and oil. Brown and season the veal, a few pieces at a time; remove them as they are done.

1 large garlic clove, peeled and chopped fine	2 tablespoons paprika (preferably sweet Hungarian)
3 medium onions, peeled and chopped	3 tablespoons flour
1 medium green pepper, seeded and chopped (optional)	

In the fat remaining in the pan, cook the vegetables until the onion is translucent. Stir in the paprika and then the flour. Over gentle heat, cook the mixture, stirring, for a few minutes.

1½ cups dry white wine (recommended: Chablis)
1 (8-ounce) can of tomato sauce

Gradually stir in the wine and then the tomato sauce. Over moderate heat, cook the mixture, stirring constantly, until it is thickened and smooth.

At this point you may stop and continue later.

> **Reserved veal**
> 2 **cups sour cream**
> ½ **pound mushrooms, trimmed, sliced, and prepared**
>   **(page 5) (optional)**
> **Fine-chopped parsley**

Return the veal to the casserole, together with any accumulated juices. Stir the mixture to blend the ingredients. Bake the veal, covered, at 350° for 1 hour, or until it is tender. Stir in the sour cream and mushrooms. Bring the dish to serving temperature, and garnish it with parsley. Veal paprikash goes well with noodles.

If you wish to offer the dish as a rather elegant main course, purchase veal cutlets and cut them into pieces of uniform size.

Veal Scallops with Apple (FRANCE)

6 SERVINGS
PREPARATION: ABOUT 20 MINUTES
COOKING: ABOUT 10 MINUTES
REFRIGERATES

> 12 (3-ounce) *or* 6 (6-ounce) **veal scallops, pounded thin**
> **Seasoned flour (page 6)**
> 8 **tablespoons butter**

Dredge the scallops in the seasoned flour; shake off any excess flour. In a large skillet, heat the butter and in it cook the scallops, about 3 minutes on each side (4 minutes on each side for the larger size), or until they are golden. Transfer them to a heated platter and keep them warm.

> 6 **shallots, peeled and**
>   **chopped fine,** *or* 6
>   **scallions (white part**
>   **only), trimmed and**
>   **chopped fine**
> 2 **tart apples, peeled, cored,**
>   **and cut into small dice**
>
> ⅓ **cup Calvados or**
>   **applejack**
> 1 **cup thickened cream**
>   **(page 6)** *or* **sour**
>   **cream**
> **Fine-chopped parsley**

In the butter remaining in the pan, cook the shallots until translucent. Add the apple and continue to cook the mixture, stirring gently, for 3 minutes, or until the apple softens. Warm the Calvados in a small saucepan, ignite it, and pour it over the apple; allow it to burn out. Over gentle heat, blend in the cream; do not allow the sauce to boil. Spoon the sauce over the veal scallops and garnish the dish with parsley.

Variation:

From the United States: Sprinkle 6 (6-ounce) veal scallops, pounded thin, with the strained juice of 1 small lemon; season them to taste with salt and fresh-ground white pepper. In a skillet, heat 4 tablespoons butter and in it brown the scallops. Remove them to a heated serving platter and keep them warm. In step two, in place of the Calvados, use ⅓ cup bourbon whiskey; do not ignite it, but, over high heat, cook it with the shallot-apple mixture for 2 or 3 minutes. Reduce the heat before adding the cream. Complete the recipe as written.

Veal Scallops with Mushrooms in Cream (Escalopes de Veau Vallée d'Auge) (FRANCE)

6 SERVINGS
PREPARATION: ABOUT 20 MINUTES
COOKING: 12 MINUTES
REFRIGERATES

Quickly prepared, this delicate dish is an excellent choice when you want to offer something special but do not want to linger for long in the kitchen.

8 tablespoons butter	⅓ cup Calvados *or*
6 (about 6-ounce) veal	applejack
scallops	Salt
	Fresh-ground white pepper

In a large skillet, heat the butter and in it, over moderate heat, cook the veal scallops for 4 minutes on each side, or until they are golden. Warm the Calvados in a small saucepan, ignite it, and pour it over the veal;

allow the flame to die. Season the scallops to taste with salt and pepper. Cover the skillet and, over gentle heat, cook them for 2 or 3 minutes. Remove them and keep them warm.

> ⅔ cup dry white wine (recommended: Muscadet *or*
>   Pinot Blanc)
> 1 pound mushrooms, trimmed, sliced, and prepared (page 5)
> 1 cup heavy cream
> Fine-chopped parsley

Over high heat, deglaze the skillet with the wine; allow the pan juices to reduce somewhat. Add the mushrooms and their liquid, together with the cream. Simmer the sauce, stirring, for 2 or 3 minutes. Return the scallops to the skillet and bring them to serving temperature; do not allow the sauce to boil. Arrange the scallops on a heated serving platter, spoon the sauce over them, and garnish the dish with parsley. This recipe goes well with saffron rice.

Veal Scallops with Orange

6 SERVINGS
PREPARATION: ABOUT 10 MINUTES
MARINATION TIME: 8 HOURS
COOKING: ABOUT 20 MINUTES

> 6 (about 6-ounce) veal scallops
> ½ cup orange-flavored liqueur

In a flat dish, arrange the scallops in a single layer. Warm the liqueur in a small saucepan, ignite it, and pour it over the veal; allow the flame to die. Marinate the scallops in the liqueur, covered and refrigerated, for 8 hours.

> 8 tablespoons butter
> Salt
> Fresh-ground white pepper

Remove the scallops from the marinade, allowing the liqueur to drain back into the dish; reserve the marinade. With absorbent paper, dry the scallops. In a skillet, heat the butter and in it, over moderate heat, cook the scallops for 4 minutes per side, or until they are golden. Season them to taste with salt and pepper.

Zest and strained juice of	Strained juice of 1 small
1 medium orange	lemon
Reserved marinade	2 tablespoons soft butter
	Fine-chopped parsley

Cut the orange zest into fine julienne. In a saucepan, combine it with 1 cup water; bring the liquid to the boil, reduce the heat, and simmer the zest, uncovered, for 5 minutes. Drain and reserve it. In a second saucepan, combine the orange juice, marinade, and lemon juice; over high heat, reduce the liquid by ¼ cup. Remove the scallops to a heated serving platter. Over high heat, deglaze the skillet with the reduced marinade. Add the orange zest and butter to the sauce, stirring. Spoon the sauce over the scallops and garnish the dish with parsley.

Veal Scallops with Parmesan Cheese (ITALY)

6 SERVINGS

PREPARATION: ABOUT 35 MINUTES

COOKING: 10 MINUTES IN A 400° OVEN

Scaloppine di vitello alla Bolognese is a classic dish from the Emilia-Romagna section of Italy, although I first enjoyed it at Dal Bolognese, a fine restaurant serving regional dishes, located on Rome's Piazza del Pòpolo.

12 (about 3-ounce) veal scallops, pounded thin
Seasoned flour (page 6)
6 tablespoons butter

Dredge the scallops in the seasoned flour; shake off any excess flour. In a skillet, heat the butter and in it, over moderate heat, cook the veal for 4 minutes per side, or until it is tender and lightly browned. Do not wash the skillet.

12 slices cooked ham
Fresh-grated Parmesan cheese, as needed

On each piece of veal, arrange a slice of ham to conform to the size of the scallop. Sprinkle each with the cheese. Roll up the scallops, cheese side in, and skewer them with toothpicks. Arrange them in a single layer in a lightly buttered ovenproof serving dish.

At this point you may stop and continue later.

1 cup dry white wine (recommended: Verdicchio *or* Chenin
   Blanc)
Fine-chopped parsley

To the skillet in which the veal was browned, add the wine and, over high
heat, deglaze the pan. Pour the wine over the scallops, and bake them,
uncovered, at 400° for 10 minutes, or until the cheese melts and the
scallops are thoroughly heated through. Garnish them with parsley and
serve them with buttered rice.

Veal Scallops with Wine and Lemon Sauce (Piccata di Vitello) (ITALY)

6 SERVINGS
PREPARATION: ABOUT 20 MINUTES
COOKING: 10 MINUTES
REFRIGERATES

The most celebrated Italian veal dish? Well, together with Vitello Tonnato (page 98), I daresay this is. And, like other simply sauced veal
scallop recipes, refreshing to both taste and appetite. Quickly done, too!

6 (about 6-ounce) veal   Soave *or* Chenin
   scallops   Blanc)
Seasoned flour (page 6)   Strained juice of 1 small
8 tablespoons butter   lemon
½ cup dry white wine   Fine-chopped parsley
   (recommended:

Dredge the veal scallops in the seasoned flour; shake off any excess flour.
In a large skillet with a lid, heat the butter and in it, over moderate heat,
cook the scallops for 4 minutes on each side, or until they are golden.
Combine the wine and lemon juice and add the mixture to the contents
of the skillet; continue to cook the scallops, covered, for 2 or 3 minutes.
Remove them to a heated serving platter. Spoon the sauce over them and
garnish the dish with parsley. Buttered rice is a pleasant accompaniment.

Variations:

In place of the white wine and lemon juice, use ½ cup Marsala and ¼
cup chicken stock *or* defatted canned chicken broth.

In place of the white wine and lemon juice, use ½ cup white port and ¼ cup chicken stock *or* defatted chicken broth.

VEAL SCALLOPS WITH MUSHROOMS AND OLIVES: Cook 3 strips of bacon, diced, until crisp and golden; remove and reserve the bacon. In the bacon fat, cook the flour-dredged scallops as directed (a little butter may be added as necessary). Add the white port and chicken stock, as in the preceding variation; cook the veal scallops, covered, for 2 or 3 minutes. Transfer them to a heated serving platter. Over them spread ½ pound mushrooms, trimmed, sliced, and prepared (page 5), 12 pitted ripe olives, halved lengthwise, and the reserved bacon. Spoon the sauce over all. Garnish the dish with fine-chopped parsley and lemon wedges.

Veal Rolls with Sausage Meat (Paupiettes de Veau à la Saucisse) (FRANCE)

6 SERVINGS
PREPARATION: ABOUT 25 MINUTES
COOKING: 45 MINUTES IN A 325° OVEN
REFRIGERATES

6 (about 6-ounce) veal scallops, pounded thin	Seasoned flour (page 6)
Fresh-grated nutmeg	6 tablespoons butter
Powdered thyme	1 cup dry white wine
1 cup pork-sausage meat, at room temperature	(recommended: white Burgundy)

Season the scallops to taste with nutmeg and thyme. Over them spread an even layer of sausage meat. Roll and tie the scallops. Dredge them in the seasoned flour; shake off any excess flour. In a flameproof casserole, heat the butter and in it, over moderate heat, cook the scallops, turning them so that they brown evenly, for 6 minutes. Remove them as they are done. Over high heat, deglaze the casserole with the wine.

At this point you may stop and continue later.

½ pound button
    mushrooms, trimmed
1 medium onion, peeled
    and chopped

½ medium green pepper,
    seeded and chopped
Bouquet garni (page 4)
Fine-chopped parsley

Return the paupiettes to the casserole. Over them arrange the prepared vegetables; tuck in the bouquet garni. Bake the paupiettes, tightly covered, at 325° for 40 minutes. (A sheet of heavy-duty aluminum foil, placed under the casserole lid and overlapping the sides of the utensil, is a good sealer.) Garnish the dish with parsley.

Veal with Tuna Fish Sauce (Vitello Tonnato) (ITALY)

6 SERVINGS
PREPARATION: ABOUT 45 MINUTES
COOKING: 1¾ HOURS
CHILLING TIME: 24 HOURS

This summer dish, found throughout Italy, is particularly enjoyed in Piedmont and Lombardy. The chilling time allows the flavors to meld. Properly covered and refrigerated, the veal keeps well for a week.

4 tablespoons olive oil
1 (2½-pound) boned veal roast, rolled and tied

In a flameproof casserole, heat the oil and in it, over moderate heat, lightly brown the veal. Remove the roast.

4 to 6 anchovy fillets,
    drained and chopped
    fine
2 tablespoons chopped
    capers
1 small carrot, scraped and
    chopped fine
2 medium celery ribs,
    with the leaves,
    chopped fine

2 large garlic cloves,
    peeled and chopped
    fine
1 large onion, peeled and
    chopped fine
1 teaspoon rubbed sage
½ teaspoon powdered
    thyme
1 teaspoon sugar
¼ teaspoon fresh-ground
    white pepper

In a mixing bowl, combine and blend the anchovy fillets, capers, vegetables, and seasonings. Spread the mixture in an even layer over the bottom of the casserole in which the veal was browned. Replace the veal
roast.

> 2 cups dry white wine (recommended: Soave *or* Chablis)
> 2 tablespoons white wine vinegar
> Chicken stock *or* defatted canned chicken broth, as needed

Combine the wine and vinegar and add the mixture to the casserole. Add
chicken stock just to cover. Bring the liquid to the boil, reduce the heat,
and simmer the veal, uncovered, for 1½ hours, turning it often. (The
liquid will reduce to about two-thirds of its original volume.)

> 1 (7-ounce) can oil-packed tuna, drained and mashed with a
>   fork until pasty (reserve the oil)

Stir the mashed tuna into the simmering liquid. Cook the veal 15 minutes
longer, or until it is fork-tender. Remove it from the heat and allow it to
cool, covered, turning it often so that it stays moist.

When the veal has reached room temperature, remove it from the casserole and slice it thin. Arrange it in a deep serving dish. Skim the fat from
the sauce.

> Reserved tuna oil
> Strained juice of 1 small lemon
> 4 tablespoons mayonnaise
> ½ cup fine- chopped parsley

Pour the contents of the casserole into the container of a blender. Whirl
it until the mixture is smooth. Add the reserved tuna oil, the lemon juice,
and the mayonnaise; more mayonnaise may be added if necessary to give
the sauce the consistency of cream. Pour the sauce over the sliced veal.
Chill the *vitello tonnato*, covered, for 24 hours. Garnish the dish with
parsley.

Variety Meats

Brains and sweetbreads, kidneys, liver, oxtail, tongue, tripe, and sausage—
these variety meats are all enhanced by being cooked with wine. From the
elegance of sweetbreads in white wine sauce to the robustness of oxtail

braised in red wine with vegetables, the many varying tastes and textures that derive from preparing variety meats will challenge your culinary imagination and add to your pleasure at mealtime.

BRAINS AND SWEETBREADS

The following recipes may be made with either brains or sweetbreads, although their textures differ. Both should be prepared and eaten absolutely fresh from butcher or freezer. One pound of brains or sweetbreads yields four servings.

Calf brains are preferred, but sheep brains are also very good. Veal sweetbreads are considered better, but lamb sweetbreads are totally acceptable. Sweetbreads, the thymus gland of the calf or lamb, which disappear before the animal is one year old, are very white. Both brains and sweetbreads are very tender and delicately flavored.

To prepare brains and sweetbreads: In a saucepan, soak them in cold acidulated water, refrigerated, for 3 hours. (Acidulated water: 4 cups of water with 2 tablespoons vinegar and 2 teaspoons salt.) Then, over medium heat, bring the acidulated water just barely to a simmer (do not allow it to boil); blanch the meat, uncovered, for 20 minutes. Drain and allow it to cool in cold water. Drain the brains or sweetbreads on absorbent paper. Discard any excess membrane, cartilage, or connective tissue. They are now fully cooked and need only to be sliced (brains) or separated with your fingers (sweetbreads) to complete the recipe of your choice.

Brains or Sweetbreads with Mushrooms

4 SERVINGS

PREPARATION: ABOUT 40 MINUTES (THE PREPARATION TIME DOES NOT
   INCLUDE READYING THE BRAINS OR SWEETBREADS)

COOKING: 10 MINUTES

Ris de veau régence is a classic French dish. I do not believe that "*cervelle de veau régence*" would be found on a restaurant menu, but I think you will enjoy brains prepared in this manner.

> 2 tablespoons butter
> 1 medium carrot, scraped and sliced *very* thin
> 1 medium celery rib, chopped fine
> 1 medium onion, peeled and chopped fine, *or* 4 scallions
>   (white part only), trimmed and chopped fine

In a skillet with a lid, heat the butter, tilting the pan to spread it evenly over the bottom. Add the vegetables and cook them, stirring, until the onion is translucent. Cover the skillet and, over gentle heat, continue to cook the vegetables for 5 minutes.

> ¼ cup ruby port
> ½ cup dry white wine (recommended: Chablis)
> ⅔ cup chicken stock *or* 1 (10½-ounce) can of defatted
>   chicken broth reduced to ⅔ cup

Add the port and, over high heat, reduce it somewhat. Add the white wine and continue to reduce the mixture for 3 or 4 minutes. Add the chicken stock. Cook the vegetables, covered, for 15 minutes.

At this point you may stop and continue later.

> 1 pound prepared brains *or* sweetbreads (page 100)
> Salt
> Fresh-ground white pepper

On top of the simmering vegetables, arrange the brains or sweetbreads. Season them to taste with salt and pepper. Cook them, covered, for 10 minutes, or until they are thoroughly heated through. Remove them to a heated serving dish and keep them warm.

> ½ cup heavy cream *or* thickened cream (page 6)
> ½ pound mushrooms, trimmed, sliced thin, and prepared
>   (page 5)
> Fine-chopped parsley

Over high heat, reduce the sauce by two-thirds. Add the cream and continue to reduce the mixture until it thickens sufficiently to coat a metal spoon. Stir in the mushrooms. Bring the sauce to serving temperature and spoon it over the brains or sweetbreads. Garnish the dish with parsley.

Variations:

In step one, after cooking the vegetables for 5 minutes, stir in 1 table-spoon flour and cook it briefly; add 1 cupful of Chablis *or* (if you feel posh) champagne, stirring until the mixture is thickened and smooth; reduce the heat and simmer the vegetables, covered, for 15 minutes. Omit step two. Follow step three as written. In step four, omit reducing the sauce. Complete the recipe as written.

Follow the preceding variation, using, in place of the Chablis or champagne, ½ cup dry sherry and ½ cup chicken stock *or* defatted canned chicken broth. Omit step two of the recipe; follow step three as written. In step four, omit reducing the sauce. Complete the recipe as written.

Follow step one of the recipe as written. Omit step two. In step three, before seasoning the brains or sweetbreads with salt and pepper, pour over them ¼ cup Calvados *or* applejack; complete step three as written. In step four, omit reducing the sauce and, in place of the heavy cream, use 1 cup light cream blended with 2 beaten egg yolks; over gentle heat, cook the sauce until it is thickened (do not allow it to boil). Complete the recipe as written.

Brains or Sweetbreads with Grapes

6 SERVINGS
PREPARATION: ABOUT 20 MINUTES (THE PREPARATION TIME DOES NOT
    INCLUDE READYING THE BRAINS OR SWEETBREADS)
COOKING: 20 MINUTES

> 1½ pounds prepared brains *or* sweetbreads (page 100)
> Seasoned flour (page 6)
> 2 tablespoons butter
> 2 tablespoons oil

Dust the brains or sweetbreads with the seasoned flour. Reserve the remaining flour. In a skillet, heat the butter and oil and sauté the brains or sweetbreads for 5 minutes on each side, or until they are faintly golden. Remove them to a heated serving dish and keep them warm.

2 teaspoons reserved seasoned
   flour
½ cup Chablis
½ cup Madeira
2 cups seedless grapes,

rinsed, drained, and
   halved lengthwise
2 tablespoons softened
   butter
Fine-chopped parsley

Into the fat remaining in the pan, stir the seasoned flour. Add the Chablis and Madeira; over high heat, deglaze the skillet, stirring the sauce until it is somewhat thickened. Add the grapes and heat them through. Stir in the butter and spoon the sauce over the meat. Garnish the dish with parsley.

Variation:

BRAINS OR SWEETBREADS WITH PEARS: In 2 tablespoons butter, sauté until tender 3 ripe pears, peeled, halved lengthwise, and cored; set aside and reserve them. Using the same skillet, follow step one of the recipe as written, adding ¼ cup pear brandy (recommended: poire Williams), warmed, ignited, and poured over the sautéed brains or sweetbreads. After removing them to a heated serving dish, deglaze the skillet over high heat with 1½ cups heavy cream, stirring until the sauce is somewhat thickened. Spoon the sauce over the meat and garnish the dish with the reserved pears and parsley.

KIDNEYS

Veal, lamb, and pork kidneys are interchangeable in these recipes.

Before being cooked, all kidneys require that the skin be removed, if the butcher has not already done so. The fat must also be cut out: Cut veal kidney into smallish pieces to expose the fat; lamb and pork kidney may be halved vertically to reveal it; then, with a sharp knife or pointed scissors, excise the fat. Soak the kidneys, refrigerated, in salted water to cover for at least 2 hours; drain and then dry them on absorbent paper before continuing with the recipe at hand.

Kidneys cook very rapidly; use gentle or medium heat and do not overcook them, for they quickly become dry and tough. It is customary to cook pork kidney longer than that of veal or lamb; increase the cooking time to about 30 minutes.

For 4 servings, use 1½ to 2 pounds of veal kidney, 16 to 20 lamb kidneys, and 12 to 16 pork kidneys.

Kidneys in Cream (FRANCE)

4 SERVINGS

PREPARATION: ABOUT 15 MINUTES (THE PREPARATION TIME DOES NOT
  INCLUDE READYING THE KIDNEYS)

COOKING: 10 MINUTES FOR VEAL OR LAMB KIDNEY, 30 MINUTES FOR PORK

REFRIGERATES

> 6 tablespoons butter
> Prepared kidneys for 4 persons (page 103)

In a skillet, heat the butter and in it, over medium heat, sauté the kidneys, turning them, for 2 minutes.

> 2 tablespoons Dijon mustard   ¼ cup white port
> Salt   ½ cup brandy
> Fresh-ground white
>   pepper

Stir in the mustard and season the kidneys to taste with salt and pepper. Continue to cook them over gentle heat, and when they just begin to brown, deglaze the skillet with the port. In a small saucepan, warm the brandy, ignite it, and pour it over the kidneys; allow the flame to die.

> 2 chicken livers, mashed and put through a strainer
> ½ cup heavy cream or thickened cream (page 6)
> Strained juice of ½ lemon
> Fine-chopped parsley

Stir in the chicken livers. Off heat, stir in the cream. Bring the sauce to serving temperature; do not allow it to boil. Stir in the lemon juice and garnish the kidneys with parsley. New boiled potatoes are a pleasant complement to this dish.

Braised Kidneys, Italian Style

4 SERVINGS

PREPARATION: ABOUT 15 MINUTES (THE PREPARATION TIME DOES NOT
  INCLUDE READYING THE KIDNEYS)

COOKING: 10 MINUTES FOR VEAL OR LAMB KIDNEY, 30 MINUTES FOR PORK

REFRIGERATES

In Italy, this recipe is made with pork kidneys.

> ¼ cup olive oil
> Prepared kidneys for 4 persons (page 103)
> 1 garlic clove, peeled and chopped fine
> 2 medium onions, peeled and chopped fine

In a skillet with a lid, heat the oil and in it sauté the kidneys, together with the garlic and onions, until the kidneys just begin to color.

> 1 cup dry red wine
>   (recommended:
>   Barbera or Zinfandel)
> 2 tablespoons tomato purée
>
> ¼ teaspoon crumbled
>   rosemary
> Salt
> Fresh-ground pepper
> Fine-chopped parsley

Blend the wine, tomato purée, and rosemary; pour the mixture over the kidneys and season them to taste with salt and pepper. Over gentle heat, simmer the kidneys, covered, for 10 minutes (or for 30, depending upon which variety you use). Garnish the dish with parsley.

Kidneys with Madeira

4 SERVINGS
PREPARATION: ABOUT 15 MINUTES (THE PREPARATION TIME DOES NOT
    INCLUDE READYING THE KIDNEYS)
COOKING: 25 MINUTES
REFRIGERATES

> 4 tablespoons butter
> Prepared Kidneys for 4 persons (page 103)
> Salt
> Fresh-ground white pepper

In a skillet, heat the butter and in it, over gentle heat, cook the kidneys for 2 to 3 minutes on each side, or until they just begin to color; season them to taste with salt and pepper. Transfer the kidneys and pan juices to a heated serving platter and keep them warm.

> 4 slices bacon, diced
> 2 medium onions, peeled
>   and chopped fine
>
> ½ cup Madeira
> ½ cup heavy cream
> Fine-chopped parsley

In the same skillet, cook the bacon until it is crisp and golden; remove it to absorbent paper and reserve it. To the bacon fat, add the onion and cook it until translucent. Add the Madeira and, over high heat, deglaze the skillet. Stir in the cream and simmer the sauce for 2 minutes; do not allow it to boil. Spoon the sauce over the kidneys and garnish the dish with parsley.

Variations:

In step one, before cooking the kidneys in the butter, dredge them in seasoned flour (page 6); shake off any excess flour. In step two, omit the bacon and onions; use 1 cup Madeira and, after deglazing the skillet, reduce the wine to ½ cup; in place of the heavy cream, use 6 tablespoons sour cream; do not allow the sauce to boil. Complete the recipe as written.

Follow step one as written. In step two, omit the bacon and onions, but sauté ½ pound mushrooms, trimmed and sliced, in the butter remaining in the pan; when they are limp, spoon them over the kidneys; in the same skillet, cook 4 scallions (white part only), trimmed and chopped, and when they are limp, transfer them to the serving dish; deglaze the skillet with 1 cup Madeira; add 1 teaspoon sugar and then reduce the wine to ½ cup; omit the heavy cream; spoon the sauce over the kidneys and garnish the dish with parsley. This variation is good served on toast.

Follow step one as written, adding 12 crushed juniper berries. Before removing the kidneys to the heated serving platter, flame them with ½ cup gin or Geneva. Omit step two as written, but deglaze the skillet with ¼ cup water and then reduce the mixture to a syrupy sauce; away from the heat, stir in 2 tablespoons softened butter; spoon the sauce over the kidneys and garnish the dish with parsley.

KIDNEYS WITH SHERRY (Spain): In 3 tablespoons olive oil, cook 1 small garlic clove, peeled and chopped, and 2 medium onions, peeled and chopped, until translucent; stir in 2 tablespoons flour and add 1 bay leaf and ½ cup beef stock *or* canned beef bouillon; cook the mixture, stirring constantly, until it is thickened and smooth; stir in ¼ cup of fine-chopped parsley. In a separate skillet, heat 2 tablespoons olive oil and in it cook the kidneys for 2 or 3 minutes on each side, or until they just begin to color; season the kidneys with salt and pepper to taste and transfer them to a heated serving platter. Deglaze the skillet with ½ cup dry sherry. Add the sherry to the onion mixture, stirring to blend the sauce; bring it to serving temperature and spoon it over the kidneys.

KIDNEYS WITH WHISKEY: In a skillet, cook until crisp and golden 4 slices of bacon, diced; remove the bacon to absorbent paper and reserve it. In the bacon fat, cook the kidneys for 2 or 3 minutes on each side, or until they just begin to color; season them to taste with salt and pepper; flame them with ½ cup dry whiskey (Canadian, Irish, or Scotch); with a slotted spoon remove the kidneys to a heated serving platter. Over high heat, deglaze the skillet with the whiskey remaining in the pan. Stir in ½ cup sour cream and 1 teaspoon Dijon mustard; do not allow the sauce to boil. Spoon the sauce over the kidneys and garnish the dish with parsley.

Kidney Sauce for Pasta

6 SERVINGS
PREPARATION: ABOUT 15 MINUTES (THE PREPARATION TIME DOES NOT
    INCLUDE READYING THE KIDNEYS)
COOKING: 30 MINUTES
REFRIGERATES

3 tablespoons olive oil	rosemary, and ½
2 veal kidneys, prepared for cooking (page 103), cut into 1-inch cubes and dried on absorbent paper	teaspoon sage
	¾ cup dry Marsala
	3 tablespoons tomato paste, blended until smooth with ¼ cup dry Marsala
½ pound mushrooms, trimmed and sliced thin	
	Salt
Bouquet garni of 1 bay leaf, 1 garlic clove, peeled and chopped fine, 1 teaspoon	Fresh-ground pepper
	¼ cup fine-chopped parsley

In a skillet, over high heat, bring the oil nearly to the point of smoking, add the kidney cubes, and cook them, stirring constantly, until they begin to brown. Reduce the heat and add the mushrooms, bouquet garni, and wine. Over gentle heat, simmer the mixture for 25 minutes, or until the sauce thickens somewhat. Stir in the tomato paste and continue to simmer the mixture for 5 minutes longer. Discard the bouquet garni and season the sauce to taste with salt and pepper. At the time of serving, stir in the parsley.

Kidney Stew (UNITED STATES)

6 SERVINGS

PREPARATION: ABOUT 20 MINUTES (THE PREPARATION TIME DOES NOT
   INCLUDE READYING THE KIDNEYS)

COOKING: 25 MINUTES (ON TOP OF THE STOVE OR IN A 300° OVEN)

REFRIGERATES

> 2 pounds veal kidneys, prepared for cooking (page 103), cut
>   into 1-inch cubes, and dried on absorbent paper
> Seasoned flour (page 6)
> 2 tablespoons butter
> 2 tablespoons oil

Dredge the kidneys in the seasoned flour. In a skillet, heat the butter and oil and, over high heat, quickly brown the kidneys; as the cubes are done, remove them to a flameproof casserole.

> 1 garlic clove, peeled and chopped fine
> 1 medium onion, peeled and chopped fine
> 2 teaspoons Dijon-style mustard
> 1½ cups dry red wine (recommended: Burgundy)
> ½ cup beef stock or canned beef bouillon
> 1 bay leaf

In the skillet, cook the garlic and onion until translucent. Stir in the mustard. Add the wine and, over high heat, deglaze the pan. Pour the mixture over the kidneys. Add the beef stock and bay leaf. Simmer the kidneys, covered (or bake them at 300°), for 25 minutes.

> 2 cups sour cream
> Salt
> Fresh-ground pepper
> ⅓ cup fine-chopped parsley

Blend the sour cream into the contents of the casserole. Season the stew to taste with salt and pepper. Bring it to serving temperature and stir in the parsley.

LIVER

Calf's liver, beef liver, and chicken livers are interchangeable in these recipes.

Liver cooks very quickly and dries and toughens when overcooked. Gentle heat and careful attention will assure your success with these dishes.

Liver in Wine Sauce (SPAIN)

4 SERVINGS
PREPARATION: ABOUT 15 MINUTES
MARINATION TIME: 3 HOURS
COOKING: 10 MINUTES

1 cup dry red wine (recommended: Rioja *or* Gamay Beaujolais)	½ teaspoon salt Fresh-ground pepper
2 tablespoons red wine vinegar	4 thin slices calf's or beef liver *or* 1 pound chicken livers (soaked for 1 hour in cold salted water, drained, and dried on absorbent paper)
1 bay leaf, crumbled	
1 small garlic clove, peeled and put through a press	

In a flat dish, combine the wine, vinegar, and seasonings. In this mixture, marinate the liver, refrigerated, for 3 hours.

2 tablespoons olive oil
3 thick slices bacon, diced

In a skillet, heat the olive oil and in it cook the bacon until crisp and golden; with a slotted spoon, remove it to asborbent paper and reserve it.

Reserved bacon
Fine-chopped parsley

Remove the liver from the marinade; dry it on absorbent paper and reserve the marinade. In the remaining bacon fat, over medium heat, cook the liver, 2 minutes on each side; do not overcook it. Remove it to a warmed

serving platter. Strain the marinade into the skillet. Over high heat, reduce it by one-half. Sprinkle the bacon over the liver; spoon the sauce
over all. Garnish the dish with parsley.

Variations:

In step one, make the marinade with either Madeira *or* Marsala; omit the
vinegar. In step two, omit the olive oil and bacon, but use 4 tablespoons
butter to cook until translucent 6 scallions (white part only), trimmed
and chopped fine. Complete the recipe as written.

LIVER WITH RAISINS: In step one, make the marinade with
Madeira (as in the preceding variation) and add to it ½ cup golden
raisins. In step two, omit the olive oil and bacon, but use 4 tablespoons
butter to cook until translucent 1 medium onion, peeled and chopped
fine. Into the onion stir 1 tablespoon flour. Remove the bay leaf from the
marinade. To the skillet, add the marinade, the raisins, and a bouquet
garni (page 4). Stir the mixture until it is thickened and smooth; simmer it, covered, for 20 minutes. Discard the bouquet garni. Add the
liver and, over gentle heat, cook it for 10 to 12 minutes, or until it is firm
but still tender. Garnish the dish with parsley.

OXTAIL

Braised Oxtail with Vegetables

6 SERVINGS
PREPARATION: ABOUT 30 MINUTES
COOKING: 2½ TO 3 HOURS IN A 300° OVEN, PLUS 30 MINUTES AT THE SIMMER
REFRIGERATES; FREEZES

3 to 4 pounds oxtail, disjointed	2 tablespoons butter
Seasoned flour (page 6)	2 tablespoons oil
	¼ cup brandy

Dredge the oxtail in the seasoned flour. In a flameproof casserole, heat
the butter and oil and in it brown the oxtail, a few pieces at a time; as they
are done, remove them to absorbent paper. Arrange the oxtail in a shallow

pan. In a small saucepan, warm the brandy, ignite it, and pour it over the oxtail; allow the flame to die.

2 garlic cloves, peeled and chopped

3 medium onions, peeled and chopped

2 cups dry red wine (recommended: Beaujolais)

2 cups beef stock *or* canned beef bouillon

1 (1-pound) can of tomatoes

2 bay leaves

1 teaspoon dried marjoram

½ teaspoon dried thyme

1 teaspoon sugar

Reserved oxtail

In the fat remaining in the casserole, cook the garlic and onion until translucent. Add the wine and, over high heat, deglaze the casserole. Add the beef stock, tomatoes, and seasonings. Replace the oxtail. Bake the casserole, covered, at 300° for 2½ to 3 hours, or until the meat separates easily from the bones.

At this point you may stop and continue later. (Recommended: Let cool and then refrigerate the oxtail overnight; the following day remove the solidified fat and proceed with the recipe.)

3 large carrots, scraped and sliced thin
3 large celery ribs, chopped
3 medium white turnips, scraped and diced

Over medium-high heat, bring the casserole to the simmer. Stir in the vegetables and continue to cook the dish, covered, for 30 minutes, or until the vegetables are tender.

Variations:

In place of the red wine, use Madeira.

In place of the red wine, use 1½ cups Marsala and 2½ cups beef stock.

TONGUE

Beef, veal, and lamb tongues are those generally used, although I find that a beef tongue of under 3 pounds has the best flavor. For this reason, the following recipe and its variations are written for beef tongue, but they may also be made with veal or lamb tongue, with adjustment of the cooking time, which will be less for veal and shorter still for lamb.

To prepare fresh tongue for cooking, scrub it well in warm water. In seasoned water to cover—use a bouquet garni (page 4)—simmer the tongue, uncovered, for 1½ hours. Refresh it in cold water, then slit it and peel off the skin, removing the roots, small bones, and gristle at the thick end.

You may also simmer the tongue for 2 to 3 hours, or until it is tender, refresh it in cold water, skin it, etc., and then offer it sliced and heated to serving temperature in a sauce of your choice (pages 289–304).

A 2-pound beef tongue yields 6 servings.

Braised Tongue

6 SERVINGS

PREPARATION: ABOUT 30 MINUTES (DOES NOT INCLUDE READYING THE
    TONGUE)
COOKING: 1 HOUR (ON TOP OF THE STOVE OR IN A 300° OVEN)
REFRIGERATES; FREEZES

¼ pound lean bacon
6 slices smoked ham (such
    as prosciutto)
3 medium carrots, scraped
    and sliced thin
3 medium onions, peeled
    and chopped fine
1 (about 2½-pound) beef
    tongue, prepared for
    cooking (page 112)

Bouquet garni (page 4)
1 cup dry white wine
    (recommended:
    Muscadet or Chenin
    Blanc)
⅓ cup brandy
1 cup beef stock or
    canned beef bouillon

Over the bottom of a flameproof casserole, arrange in layers the bacon, ham, carrots, and onions. Put the tongue on top. Add the bouquet garni and the liquids. Bring the mixture to the boil, reduce the heat, and simmer the tongue, covered, for 1 hour, or until it is fork-tender (or bake it, covered, at 300° for 1 hour).

Remove the tongue to a heated serving platter and garnish it with the bacon and ham. Strain the sauce into a saucepan, skim off any fat, and, over high heat, reduce it for 3 minutes. The sauce may be offered separately, as it is; or it may be thickened with 1½ teaspoons cornstarch blended until smooth with a little cold water.

Variations:

The tongue may be marinated for 6 hours in a mixture of 2 cups dry white wine, ¼ cup olive oil, 6 scallions (with all of the green that is crisp), trimmed and chopped, 1 large garlic clove, peeled and put through a press, 2 whole cloves, 1 bay leaf, ½ teaspoon thyme, ¾ teaspoon salt, and a grinding of fresh pepper. Simmer the tongue in the marinade as directed; strain and thicken the sauce with a beurre manié (page 4) made of 1½ tablespoons each softened butter and flour.

Mushrooms, up to 1 pound of them, if you wish, may be trimmed, prepared (page 5), and added for the final 30 minutes of cooking—a very palatable addition.

LANGUE DE BOEUF À LA BRETONNE (France): Omit the bacon and smoked ham; in the casserole, cook the carrot and onion in 4 tablespoons butter until the onion is translucent; add the prepared tongue and brown it lightly; remove and reserve it. To the casserole, add a split calf's foot, the bouquet garni, 2 cups Muscadet *or* Chenin Blanc, and ½ cup beef stock *or* canned beef bouillon. Simmer the calf's foot, covered, for 1 hour. Replace the tongue and continue cooking the meats for 1 hour longer, or until the tongue is fork-tender. Complete the recipe as written, dismembering and offering the calf's foot together with the tongue.

TRIPE

Tripe—eaten by the poor, it is said, because they can afford it, and by gourmets, because they can appreciate it! If it requires long and careful preparation, the results are entirely worth the effort.

Tripe, the inner lining of the stomach of steers, comes in three varieties:

honeycomb, pocket, and smooth. These recipes are written for fresh honeycomb tripe, the preferred variety, and the most delicately flavored.

Plain boiled potatoes complement tripe dishes.

Tripe in White Wine Sauce

6 SERVINGS

PREPARATION: ABOUT 25 MINUTES

COOKING: 2½ TO 3 HOURS

REFRIGERATES; FREEZES

3 or 4 pounds honeycomb tripe, cut into large bite-size pieces (it will shrink a bit while cooking)

3 large carrots, scraped and cut into ½-inch rounds

3 large celery ribs, with their leaves, chopped

2 medium garlic cloves, peeled and chopped

3 large onions, peeled and chopped

Bouquet garni (page 4)

1 teaspoon sugar

2 teaspoons salt

1 bottle dry white wine (recommended: Mâcon or other white Burgundy)

Chicken stock or canned chicken broth, as needed

In a soup kettle, combine all of the ingredients except the chicken stock. Then add chicken stock just to cover. Bring the liquid to the boil, reduce the heat, and simmer the tripe, covered, for 2½ to 3 hours, or until it can be easily pierced with the tines of a fork.

At this point you may stop and continue later. (Recommended: Let cool and then refrigerate the tripe overnight; the following day remove any solidified fat before proceeding with the recipe.)

Beurre manié (page 4) made of 6 tablespoons each softened butter and flour

Fine-chopped parsley

Discard the bouquet garni. Bring the tripe to a boil. Add the beurre manié, stirring until the sauce is thickened and smooth. Transfer the tripe to a heated serving dish and garnish it generously with parsley.

Variations:

TRIPE WITH BEANS (Italy): Prepare the tripe as directed. With a slotted spoon, remove it from the defatted cooking liquid and reserve it. Discard the bouquet garni. To the liquid, add 1 pound dried navy beans; bring the liquid to the boil and cook the beans, uncovered, for 10 minutes; remove the kettle from the heat and allow the beans to stand, covered, for 1 hour; return them to the heat and simmer them, covered, for 1 hour, or until they are just tender. Strain the liquid and reserve it. In a casserole, toss together the tripe, the beans, and the vegetables from the cooking liquid. Over high heat, reduce the liquid to 1½ cups; into it, blend a 6-ounce can of tomato paste. Pour the liquid over the contents of the casserole. Bake the casserole, covered, at 300° for 1½ hours, or until the beans are tender and the liquid is absorbed. The dish should be moist but not soupy.

TRIPE, SPANISH STYLE: Prepare the tripe as directed. With a slotted spoon, remove the tripe from the defatted cooking liquid and dry it on absorbent paper. Discard the bouquet garni. In a large skillet, heat ¼ cup olive oil and in it cook ¼ pound bacon, diced, until it is crisp and golden; remove and reserve it. In the bacon fat, brown the tripe, a few pieces at a time; as they are done, remove them to a casserole. Discard all but 4 tablespoons of the fat and into it stir 4 tablespoons flour; over gentle heat, cook the mixture for a few minutes. Strain the cooking liquid and measure out 2 cups of it; to the liquid, add 2 tablespoons tomato paste and 1 garlic clove, peeled and put through a press. Gradually add the mixture to the flour, stirring constantly until the sauce is thickened and smooth. Add ¼ cup brandy. Add salt to taste. Pour the sauce over the tripe, add the reserved bacon, and, over gentle heat, simmer the casserole, covered, for 30 minutes. (Save the remaining cooking liquid for use in soups or sauces; it makes a very rich stock.)

TRIPE IN MUSTARD SAUCE: Prepare the tripe as directed. With a slotted spoon, remove it from the defatted cooking liquid to a casserole. Discard the bouquet garni. Strain the cooking liquid and measure out 2 cups of it. In a saucepan, bring the liquid to the boil and stir in 1 tablespoon Dijon mustard; thicken the sauce with a beurre manié (page 4) made of 3 tablespoons each softened butter and flour. Pour the sauce over the tripe and, over gentle heat, bring it to serving temperature. Garnish the dish with parsley. (Save the remaining cooking liquid for use in soups or sauces.)

Tripes à la Mode de Caen (FRANCE)

6 TO 8 SERVINGS
PREPARATION: ABOUT 40 MINUTES
COOKING: 9 HOURS IN A 300° OVEN
REFRIGERATES; FREEZES

The most famous of all tripe dishes—and perhaps justly so. Serve it with
a hearty, crusty bread and a mixed green salad.

1 calf's foot, split (optional)	4 large garlic cloves,
Bouquet garni (page 4)	peeled and chopped
3 large carrots, scraped and	fine
sliced thick	3 large onions, peeled and
3 large celery ribs, with	sliced thick
the leaves, chopped	3 pounds honeycomb
coarse	tripe, cut into bite-size
	pieces

On the bottom of a large casserole, arrange the calf's foot and the bouquet
garni. Over them arrange the vegetables and tripe in alternating layers;
end with a layer of tripe.

2 teaspoons sugar	(recommended:
1½ teaspoons salt	white Mâcon or
⅓ cup Calvados or	Sauvignon Blanc)
applejack	Beef stock or canned beef
1 bottle dry white wine	bouillon, as needed

Over the tripe, sprinkle the sugar and salt. Add the wine and beef stock
just barely to cover. Bake the tripe, very tightly covered, at 300° for 9
hours.

The cooked tripe may be cooled and then refrigerated overnight to facilitate removing the solidified fat. To serve, allow the casserole to come to
room temperature before reheating it at 300° for about 1 hour.

One (6-ounce) can of tomato paste may be thoroughly blended with
some of the beef stock in step two; this is not traditional, but the addition
does tend to enrich the sauce.

SAUSAGES

Sausages cook well with wine, which tends to cut their richness. The following recipes will illustrate, I believe, how tasty and varied dishes made with sausages can be.

Sausages in White Wine

6 SERVINGS
PREPARATION: ABOUT 20 MINUTES
COOKING: 15 MINUTES
REFRIGERATES; FREEZES

    12 large pork sausages

With the tines of a fork, prick the sausages to prevent their bursting while cooking. In a skillet, brown the sausages; drain them on absorbent paper.

2 tablespoons butter	**¼ teaspoon powdered**
2 shallots, peeled and	**thyme**
chopped fine, *or* 3	**2½ cups dry white wine**
scallions (white part	**(recommended:**
only), trimmed and	**Chablis)**
chopped fine	**Fine-chopped parsley**
1½ tablespoons flour	

Discard the sausage fat and wipe the skillet clean with absorbent paper. In the skillet, heat the butter and in it cook the shallot until barely golden. Stir in the flour and, over gentle heat, cook the mixture for a few minutes. Stir in the thyme. Gradually add the wine, stirring constantly until the sauce is thickened and smooth. Simmer it, covered, for 15 minutes. Return the sausages to the sauce and heat them through. Remove them to a heated serving platter, spoon the sauce over them, and garnish the dish with parsley.

Variation:

Use 12 sweet Italian link sausages; increase the shallots to 4 (scallions to 6); reduce the flour to 1 tablespoon and the wine to 1½ cups; after heating the sausages through and removing them to the serving platter, add ¾ cup heavy cream to the skillet and, over gentle heat, simmer the mixture for 2 minutes before spooning it over the sausages. Garnish the dish with parsley.

Knackwurst with Ale (GERMANY)

6 SERVINGS
PREPARATION AND COOKING: ABOUT 20 MINUTES
REFRIGERATES

> 6 knackwursts
> 1 (12-ounce) can of ale

In a skillet with a lid, simmer the knackwursts, covered, in the ale for 15 minutes. Remove them to a heated serving platter and keep them warm.

> 2 tablespoons vinegar
> 1 teaspoon sugar
> A few grains of salt
> 6 peppercorns

To the ale in the skillet, add these four ingredients, and, over high heat, reduce the ale to ½ cup. Strain the sauce over the knackwursts and offer the dish with sauerkraut.

Red Cabbage with Sausage (POLAND)

4 SERVINGS
PREPARATION: ABOUT 30 MINUTES
COOKING: 45 MINUTES
REFRIGERATES

> 1 medium red cabbage, cored and shredded
> Boiling water

In a large bowl, arrange the cabbage and over it pour boiling water to cover. Allow it to stand for 5 minutes before draining it in a colander.

3 tablespoons butter
Strained juice of 2 large
   lemons
2 large tart apples, peeled,
   cored, and chopped
3 tablespoons sugar

1 teaspoon salt
Fresh-ground pepper
1 cup dry red wine
   (recommended: a
   hearty Burgundy)

In a flameproof casserole, heat the butter and in it toss the cabbage to coat the vegetable well. Sprinkle the cabbage with the lemon juice and then toss it again with the apples and seasonings. Add the wine and simmer the cabbage, covered, for 30 minutes.

At this point you may stop and continue later.

   1 pound kielbasa, cut into ¼-inch rounds

Over the cabbage, arrange the kielbasa. Continue to simmer the cabbage, covered, for 15 minutes longer, or until it is tender. Remove the cover and, over high heat, reduce the sauce somewhat.

Game

Wild duck, Cornish game hen, partridge, pheasant, pigeon or squab, rabbit, and venison—all lend themselves admirably and delectably to being cooked with wine.

Many of the recipes for domestic duck (pages 150–158) may be applied to wild duck if you allow for a somewhat drier meat and one that, because of the wild duck's life, is more muscular; in other words, cook wild duck longer than its domestic cousin.

Cornish game hen may be prepared in the same ways as chicken (pages 131–146); merely leave the game hens whole, and if you are adapting a recipe for chicken breasts, adjust the cooking time to 1 hour.

Similarly, venison may be cooked in the same manner as Boeuf Bourguignon (page 49) and Boeuf à la Mode (page 51).

Recipes for pheasant and rabbit are easily prepared and made attractive by the fact that butchers carry both varieties of game in season. Indeed, rabbit grown expressly as a food meat is available frozen, pan-ready and cut into serving pieces, at many supermarkets, so that you may enjoy this delicacy virtually throughout the year. If you use wild rabbit, ask your butcher to skin, draw, and dismember it. Soak the cut-up wild rabbit for 1½ hours in acidulated water, then drain it, dry it on absorbent paper, and proceed with the recipe at hand. (Acidulated water: 4 cups water, 2 tablespoons vinegar, and 2 teaspoons salt.)

Gin-Flamed Cornish Game Hen

4 SERVINGS
PREPARATION: ABOUT 30 MINUTES
COOKING: 50 MINUTES IN A 350° OVEN
REFRIGERATES; FREEZES

Stuffing of your choice	2 tablespoons butter
4 Cornish game hens,	2 tablespoons oil
¾ to 1 lb each	¼ cup gin *or* Geneva
2 cups stuffing of your choice	

Fill the cavities of the game hens with the stuffing of your choice. Skewer and truss them. In a flameproof casserole, heat the butter and oil and brown the hens, one at a time; remove the first one when it is done, and return it to the casserole when the second one is done. In a small saucepan, warm the gin, ignite it, and pour it over the hens; allow the flame to die.

1 teaspoon dried dill	4 tablespoons red currant
1 garlic clove, peeled and chopped fine	jelly
10 juniper berries, crushed	1 cup dry red wine (recommended:
Salt	Mâcon *or* Gamay
Fresh-ground pepper	Beaujolais)
1 teaspoon potato starch	Fine-chopped parsley
½ cup beef stock *or* canned beef broth	

Over the hens, sprinkle the dill, garlic, and juniper berries; season to taste with salt and pepper. Stir the potato starch into a little of the beef stock; when the mixture is smooth, add it, with the currant jelly, to the remaining stock, stirring to blend, and pour it over the hens. Add the red wine. Over high heat, bring the liquid to the boil. Transfer the casserole to a 350° oven and bake the hens, covered, for 50 minutes, or until they are fork-tender. Garnish them with parsley.

WILD DUCK BRAISED IN RED WINE: Use the recipe for Roast Duckling with Red Wine (page 157); follow step one as written; in step two, allow 2 (2-pound) wild ducks for the 4 servings and complete the step as written; follow step three as written; in step four, after thickening the sauce, add to it ½ pound small mushrooms, trimmed, halved, and prepared (page 5).

Partridge in Red Wine

4 SERVINGS
PREPARATION: ABOUT 20 MINUTES
COOKING: 1 HOUR IN A 350° OVEN
REFRIGERATES; FREEZES

This recipe may also be made with Cornish game hens.

4 (about 1-pound) partridge, halved lengthwise
Seasoned flour (page 6)
4 tablespoons butter
4 tablespoons oil

Dredge the partridge halves in the seasoned flour. In a flameproof casserole, heat the butter and oil and brown the partridge, a few pieces at a time; remove them as they are done.

1 medium onion, peeled and chopped	1 cup beef stock *or* canned beef bouillon
2½ cups dry red wine (recommended: Burgundy)	1 bay leaf Fine-chopped parsley

In the fat remaining in the casserole, cook the onion until it is barely golden. Add the wine and, over high heat, deglaze the casserole. Add the beef stock and bay leaf. Cook the sauce, stirring, until it thickens slightly.

Replace the partridge halves, spooning the sauce over them. Bake them, covered, at 350° for 1 hour, or until they are fork-tender. Transfer them to a heated serving platter, strain the sauce over them, and garnish them with parsley.

Pheasant in Chartreuse

4 SERVINGS
PREPARATION: ABOUT 20 MINUTES
COOKING: 1 HOUR IN A 350° OVEN
REFRIGERATES; FREEZES

4 tablespoons butter	Salt
4 tablespoons oil	Fresh-ground pepper
2 (about 2-pound) pheasants, quartered	

In a flameproof casserole, heat the butter and oil and brown the pheasant on both sides. Season it to taste with salt and pepper.

¼ cup green chartreuse
½ cup dry white wine (recommended: Chablis)
Additional chartreuse, as needed

Pour the ¼ cup chartreuse over the pheasant; add the wine and bake the pheasant, tightly covered, at 350° for 1 hour, or until it is tender. Add 2 or 3 tablespoons chartreuse after each 20 minutes of cooking. Remove the pheasant to a heated serving platter.

½ cup heavy cream
Fine-chopped parsley

Stir the cream into the pan juices and, over gentle heat, simmer the sauce for a few minutes; do not allow it to boil. Strain the sauce over the pheasant and garnish the dish with parsley.

This recipe may also be made with Cornish game hens or with chicken breasts; in the latter case, reduce the cooking time to 30 minutes, as suggested on page 131.

Pheasant with Sauerkraut (FRANCE)

4 SERVINGS
PREPARATION: ABOUT 30 MINUTES
COOKING: 1 HOUR IN A 350° OVEN
REFRIGERATES

Though not as famous as Choucroute Garnie (page 79), *faisan à la choucroute,* also from Alsace, makes a very tasty way to serve pheasant.

¼ pound salt pork, diced
2 (about 2-pound)
    pheasants, quartered
2 garlic cloves, peeled
    and chopped

2 large onions, peeled
    and chopped
1½ cups dry white wine
    (recommended:
    Riesling *or*
    Sylvaner)

In a large flameproof casserole, cook the salt pork until it is crisp and golden; with a slotted spoon, remove it to absorbent paper and reserve it. In the pork fat, brown the pheasant on both sides; remove the pieces as they are done. In the remaining fat, cook the garlic and onion until translucent. Add the wine and, over high heat, deglaze the casserole.

2 pounds precooked
    sauerkraut, rinsed and
    thoroughly drained
Pheasant giblets and necks
2 bay leaves
10 juniper berries, crushed

Reserved salt pork
2 large tart apples, peeled,
    cored, and sliced thin
½ teaspoon dried thyme
1 cup chicken stock *or*
    canned chicken broth

Over the bottom of the casserole, arrange a bed of sauerkraut. On top of it arrange the pheasant; tuck in their giblets and necks and the bay leaves, juniper berries, and salt pork. Over the pheasant arrange the apple slices and sprinkle them with thyme; add the chicken stock. Bake the pheasant at 350° for 1 hour, or until it is tender.

Variation:

In step one, omit the salt pork, but brown the pheasant in a combination of butter and oil; omit the garlic. In step two, omit the apples, but add 1

(1-pound) sausage, such as chorizo or kielbasa, cut into ¼-inch rounds. Complete the recipe as written.

Recipes for pheasant with sauerkraut may also be made with Cornish game hens.

Pheasant Braised with Sauterne

4 SERVINGS
PREPARATION: ABOUT 30 MINUTES
COOKING: 1 HOUR IN A 350° OVEN
REFRIGERATES; FREEZES

2 (about 2-pound) pheasants, quartered Seasoned flour (page 6), to which are added 1½ teaspoons sweet Hungarian paprika 3 tablespoons butter	3 tablespoons oil 6 scallions (with as much of the green as is crisp), trimmed and chopped 2 cups dry sauterne

Dredge the pheasant in the seasoned flour. In a flameproof casserole, heat the butter and oil and brown the pheasant; remove the pieces as they are done. In the fat remaining in the casserole, cook the scallion until it is wilted. Add the wine and, over high heat, deglaze the casserole. Replace the pheasant pieces and bake them, tightly covered, at 350° for 1 hour, or until they are tender.

½ pound mushrooms, trimmed, sliced, and prepared
(page 5)
Fine-chopped parsley

Add the mushrooms for the final 15 minutes of cooking. Garnish the dish with parsley.

This recipe may also be made with Cornish game hens.

Pigeons Braised in Marsala (Piccioni all' Cavour) (ITALY)

4 SERVINGS
PREPARATION: ABOUT 15 MINUTES
COOKING: 45 MINUTES
REFRIGERATES; FREEZES

Named for Camillo di Cavour, the famous nineteenth-century leader in the unification of Italy, this dish is especially popular in Piedmont. The recipe may also be made with squab or Cornish game hen.

6 tablespoons butter
4 pigeons, trussed
Salt
Fresh-ground pepper

4 scallions (with as much of the green as is crisp), trimmed and chopped
¾ cup Marsala

In a flameproof casserole, heat the butter and in it brown the pigeons on all sides; remove them as they are done. In the butter remaining in the casserole, cook the scallion until translucent. Add the wine and, over high heat, deglaze the casserole. Replace the pigeons and, over high heat, cook them, covered, for 5 minutes.

¾ cup chicken stock or canned chicken broth
¼ pound chicken livers
Fine-chopped parsley

Add the stock; reduce the heat and simmer the pigeons, covered, for 45 minutes, or until they are tender. Remove them to a heated serving platter. Over high heat, reduce the sauce somewhat; lower the heat to moderate and strain the chicken livers into the sauce. Spoon the sauce over the pigeons and garnish the dish with parsley.

Squab with Cherries

4 SERVINGS
PREPARATION: ABOUT 15 MINUTES
COOKING: 30 MINUTES IN A 350° OVEN
REFRIGERATES

4 tablespoons butter
2 tablespoons oil
4 squabs or young pigeons,
    trussed
¼ cup cherry-flavored
    liqueur

½ cup dry white wine
    (recommended:
    Burgundy)
Salt
Fresh-ground pepper

In a flameproof casserole, heat the butter and oil and brown the squabs on all sides; remove them as they are done. Return the squabs to the casserole. In a small saucepan, warm the liqueur, ignite it, and pour it over the squabs; allow the flame to die. Add the wine and season the squabs to taste with salt and pepper. Bake the squabs, covered, at 350° for 30 minutes, or until they are just tender.

At this point you may stop and continue later.

1 (16-ounce) can of pitted
    dark sweet cherries,
    drained (reserve the
    liquid)

1 teaspoon cornstarch
¼ cup cherry-flavored
    liqueur
Fine-chopped parsley

Add the cherries to the casserole and bring the squabs to serving temperature. Remove them to a heated serving platter and surround them with the cherries. Strain the pan juices into a saucepan and add ¼ cup of the reserved cherry liquid. Blend the cornstarch with the liqueur, and when the mixture is smooth, add it to the saucepan. Over high heat, cook the sauce, stirring constantly, until it is thickened and smooth. Pour the sauce over the squabs and garnish the platter with parsley.

Rabbit Braised in Spiced Wine Sauce (Hasenpfeffer) (GERMANY)

4 SERVINGS
PREPARATION: ABOUT 35 MINUTES
COOKING: 1 HOUR IN A 350° OVEN
REFRIGERATES; FREEZES

One of the most celebrated of dishes made with rabbit, hasenpfeffer is unsually comfortable fare for a brisk autumn evening.

½ pound lean bacon, diced
3 pounds rabbit, cut into
   serving pieces
Seasoned flour (page 6),
   to which is added an extra
   ¼ teaspoon pepper

1 small garlic clove, peeled
   and chopped fine
2 medium onions, peeled
   and chopped

In a flameproof casserole, cook the bacon until it is crisp and golden; with a slotted spoon, remove it to absorbent paper and reserve it. Dredge the rabbit in the seasoned flour. Brown the rabbit in the bacon fat, a few pieces at a time; remove them as they are done. In the same fat, cook the garlic and onion until translucent.

1 cup dry red wine
   (recommended:
   Zinfandel)
1 cup chicken stock *or*
   canned chicken broth

¼ cup brandy
3 teaspoons currant jelly
1 bay leaf
½ teaspoon crumbled
   rosemary
½ teaspoon dried thyme

Over high heat, deglaze the casserole with the red wine. Stir in the stock, brandy, jelly, and seasonings. Replace the rabbit and any juices that may have accumulated; over all, sprinkle the reserved bacon. Bake the rabbit, covered, at 350° for 1 hour, or until it is tender.

Rabbit Braised in Red Wine (Civet de Lapin) (FRANCE)

6 SERVINGS
PREPARATION: ABOUT 25 MINUTES
COOKING: 1½ HOURS IN A 350° OVEN
REFRIGERATES; FREEZES

4 thick slices bacon, diced
3 pounds rabbit, cut into
   serving pieces
Seasoned flour (page 6)
¼ cup brandy
1 garlic clove, peeled and
   chopped

2 medium onions, peeled
   and chopped
2 cups dry red wine
   (recommended:
   Mâcon *or* Gamay
   Beaujolais)

In a flameproof casserole, cook the bacon until it is crisp and golden; with a slotted spoon, remove it to absorbent paper and reserve it. Dredge the rabbit pieces in the seasoned flour. Reserve the flour. Brown the rabbit, a few pieces at a time, in the bacon fat; as they are done, remove them to a flat baking pan. In a small saucepan, warm the brandy, ignite it, and pour it over the rabbit; allow the flame to die. In the fat remaining in the casserole, cook the garlic and onion until translucent. Stir in 2 tablespoons of the reserved seasoned flour and, over gentle heat, cook the mixture for a few minutes. Add the wine and, over high heat, deglaze the casserole. Replace the rabbit and sprinkle it with the bacon.

Bouquet garni (page 4)
1 teaspoon sugar
1 teaspoon salt

Grated rind and strained
juice of 1 medium lemon
1 cup chicken stock *or*
canned chicken broth

Tuck in the bouquet garni; sprinkle on the sugar and salt. Add the lemon rind and juice and the stock. Bring the liquid to the boil on top of the stove, then transfer the casserole to the oven and bake it, covered, at 350° for 1 hour.

½ ounce bitter chocolate, grated
Fine-chopped parsley

Gently stir in the chocolate and continue to cook the rabbit for 30 minutes longer, or until it is fork-tender. Garnish the casserole with parsley. Serve the dish with buttered noodles or boiled new potatoes.

Variations:

Omit the onion in step one and add in step three, for the final 30 minutes of cooking, ½ pound mushrooms, trimmed, sliced, and prepared as on page 5, and 18 small white onions, peeled (page 6).

Use dry white or rosé wine in place of the red wine in step one; omit the chocolate in step four.

Follow the recipe as written, using 1½ cups dry sherry and 1½ cups chicken stock *or* canned chicken broth; omit the chocolate in step four.

RABBIT À LA MODE DE CAEN: In step one, flame the rabbit with Calvados *or* applejack; add 3 large carrots, scraped and cut into

½-inch rounds, and 3 medium white turnips, scraped and diced; use white wine in place of red. In step four, omit the chocolate.

RABBIT WITH PRUNES: In step one, in place of the red wine use dry white wine blended with 4 tablespoons tomato paste. In step two, add to the bouquet garni a 3-inch piece of cinnamon stick and 4 whole cloves. In step four, omit the chocolate; add 18 large tenderized pitted prunes for the final 20 minutes of cooking.

Venison Stew (UNITED STATES)

6 TO 8 SERVINGS
PREPARATION: ABOUT 35 MINUTES
COOKING: 1 HOUR IN A 325° OVEN
REFRIGERATES; FREEZES

Frontiersmen ate venison broiled or fried, and sometimes baked; in "great houses," however, it was served as a considerably more sophisticated dish, as this colonial recipe attests.

3 pounds haunch of venison,
    cut into 2-inch cubes
1 cup cider vinegar

1 large clove garlic, peeled
    and split lengthwise
8 thick slices bacon, diced
⅓ cup brandy

Dip each piece of venison in the vinegar and rub it with garlic. In a large flameproof casserole, cook the bacon until it is crisp and golden; with a slotted spoon, remove it to absorbent paper and reserve it. In the bacon fat, brown the venison, a few pieces at a time; remove them as they are done to a flat baking pan. In a small saucepan, warm the brandy, ignite it, and pour it over the venison; allow the flame to die. Return the venison and any accumulated juices to the casserole.

6 medium carrots, scraped
    and cut into ¼-inch
    rounds
3 large celery ribs, with the
    leaves, chopped
3 medium onions, peeled
    and chopped

3 medium white turnips,
    scraped and diced
Bouquet garni (page 4)
3 cups dry red wine
    (recommended:
    Burgundy)
1 cup beef stock *or*
    canned beef bouillon

To the casserole, add the vegetables, bouquet garni, wine, and beef stock. Bring the liquid to the boil; transfer the casserole to the oven and braise the venison, covered, at 325° for 1 hour, or until it is tender. With a slotted spoon, remove the meat and vegetables to a heated serving dish. Strain the liquid into a large saucepan.

> **Beurre manié (page 4) made of 6 tablespoons each softened butter and flour**
> **2 cups sour cream**
> **Reserved bacon**
> **Fine-chopped parsley**

Bring the strained liquid to the boil. Add the beurre manié and stir the sauce until it is thickened and smooth; simmer it for a few minutes and then, away from the heat, stir in the sour cream. Return the sauce to the heat and bring it to serving temperature; do not allow it to boil. Pour the sauce over the venison and vegetables and garnish the dish with the reserved bacon and the parsley. Serve the venison stew with boiled potatoes.

Poultry and Fowl

Chicken

Most of the following recipes call for "serving pieces of chicken," because I feel you should have the option to use that part of the bird's anatomy which you prefer. I admit to a prejudice for dark meat; I think it is more flavorful than the white and retains its moisture better. I have enjoyed these dishes made with thighs (second joints), and unless you are especially fond of white meat, I urge you to try a few recipes with the dark.

Another of my peculiarities is that I very often skin the serving pieces. Chicken skin is very fatty; discarding it at the outset makes for a finished dish that is less fat-laden. I do not waste the skin, however; it is wonderful for making chicken stock, lending both flavor and richness.

As for browning chicken, sometimes I do, sometimes I do not. First, browning chicken is a boring and messy business; second, I feel that frequently it does not add that much extra taste to the completed recipe. When browning skinned serving pieces, I do so gently to prevent the flesh from becoming stringy. Unless a recipe names a specific fat for browning, I suggest equal parts of butter and vegetable oil. Butter burns easily (which does, indeed, give extra—and unwanted—taste to the dish), and the oil acts as stabilizer, making it possible to brown the meat to one's liking without fear that the fat will suddenly burn.

In the recipes calling for chicken breasts, it is important not to overcook them. Chicken breasts become dry and stringy in a matter of minutes, if not seconds, when overcooked. For oven cooking, I recommend 30 minutes at 350°.

131

Now, having confessed some chicken-based idiosyncrasies and prejudices, I happily affirm that chicken takes to wine like a duck to water— so to speak. Wine enhances poultry, tenderizing it, bringing out its full flavor, and retaining its moisture. I believe you will enjoy making these recipes. I can vouch for my pleasure in having eaten them.

Chicken in Wine (Coq au Vin) (FRANCE)

6 SERVINGS

PREPARATION: ABOUT 30 TO 45 MINUTES, DEPENDING UPON WHICH VARIATION
   OF THE BASIC RECIPE YOU USE
COOKING: 1 HOUR (ON TOP OF THE STOVE OR IN A 350° OVEN)
REFRIGERATES; FREEZES (UNLESS OTHERWISE NOTED)

Coq au vin—what a variety of dishes this name embraces! Still, they are all versions of a single formula: chicken braised in a wine-based sauce.

According to Roger Lallemande, the great French gastronome and teacher of cooking, there is a legend that coq au vin was first created in the area now known as the Auvergne at the time of Caesar's invasion of Gaul. A Gallic leader sent as a "gift" to Caesar an old, feisty, and combative rooster—a symbol of the resistance the Roman warrior might expect. On the following day, Caesar invited the chieftain to a meal, at which the principal dish was the rooster, cooked slowly with herbs in local wine—a tacit but telling warning.

Customarily made with red wine, coq au vin may also be prepared with white or rosé. M. Lallemande has discovered sixty-one variations of the dish in France alone, where in virtually every region the local wine is used: in Alsace, Riesling (with marc to flame the chicken); in Anjou, vin d'Anjou (dry white) (with crème fraiche to enrich the sauce); in Auvergne, the chicken is marinated in local wine for twenty-four hours (and flamed with local eau-de-vie); in Berry, vin rouge de Sancerre (with beurre manié to thicken the sauce); in Bordelais, red Bordeaux (with bitter chocolate added to the sauce for enrichment and color); in Burgundy, any dry wine of the region, although Fleurie is considered especially good; in Brittany and Normandy, Meursault or Muscadet (with Calvados to flame the chicken); in Champagne, champagne (of course); in Flanders, beer; in the Nivernais, Pouilly-Fumé; in Provence, white Côtes de Provence (with marc to flame the chicken). And so on.

The dish may be made in the simplest possible manner: The chicken is dredged in seasoned flour and browned in a combination of butter and oil or in salt pork drippings; garlic and onion are cooked in the fat until translucent; the pan is deglazed with wine, a bouquet garni is added, and the chicken is simmered for 1 hour (or baked, tightly covered, in a 350° oven).

This simplicity, however, is merely a start. The browned chicken (and for *coq au vin* the chicken must be browned) may be flamed with brandy, Calvados, or applejack, marc, a flavored liqueur, or Pernod (in the last two cases, white wine is recommended). Three or four medium carrots and/or small white turnips, scraped and either sliced or diced, may be added for the total cooking time. Small white onions peeled (page 6), may be used in place of the chopped onion and added for the final 30 minutes of cooking. Tenderized pitted prunes may be added for the final 20 minutes of cooking. Last, and traditionally, mushrooms, trimmed, sliced, and prepared (page 5), may be added for the final 30 minutes of cooking.

If you do not dredge the chicken in seasoned flour, the sauce may be thickened with a flour-and-water paste, with beurre manié (page 4), or with egg yolks and cream. The sauce may be enriched by the addition of heavy cream, crème fraîche (thickened cream, page 6), or sour cream.

Cooking liquids other than red, white, and rosé wines are possible. For example, you may use 1½ cups dry vermouth plus chicken stock *or* canned chicken broth. An American version calls for ¾ cup bourbon whiskey, warmed, ignited, and poured over the browned chicken, 1 cup heavy cream, and chicken stock. And in Ireland, "cock of the north," a traditional dish, is made with ¾ cup Irish whiskey, warmed, ignited, and poured over the browned chicken, plus 1 cup dry red wine, chicken stock, and the strained juice of 2 medium lemons.

Having started with several (but by no means all) of the possibilities, let us move on to a basic recipe for *coq au vin*, so that you can play your own variations upon it.

> **2 tablespoons butter plus 2 tablespoons vegetable oil *or***
> **¼ pound salt pork, diced**
> **Serving pieces of chicken for 6 persons**
> **Seasoned flour (page 6)**
> **¼ to ⅓ cup brandy**

If you use salt pork, in a flameproof casserole, cook it until crisp and golden; with a slotted spoon remove it to absorbent paper and reserve it. Dredge the chicken pieces in the seasoned flour. Reserve the flour. In the combination of butter and oil (or in the salt pork fat) brown the chicken, a few pieces at a time; as they are done, remove them to a shallow baking pan. In a small saucepan, warm the brandy, ignite it, and pour it over the chicken; allow the flame to die.

> 2 garlic cloves, peeled and chopped fine
> 3 or 4 medium onions, peeled and chopped
> 1 or 2 tablespoons reserved seasoned flour (optional, for a
> thicker sauce)
> 3 cups dry red wine (recommended: Burgundy)

In the fat remaining in the casserole, cook the garlic and onion until translucent. Stir in the seasoned flour. Add the wine and, over high heat, deglaze the casserole.

At this point you may stop and continue later.

> Reserved chicken and any accumulated juices
> Bouquet garni (page 4)
> Reserved salt pork, if used
> Chicken stock *or* canned chicken broth, as needed

Return the chicken and its juices to the casserole. Tuck in the bouquet garni. Sprinkle on the salt pork. If necessary, add chicken stock just to cover. Simmer the chicken (or bake it, tightly covered, at 350°) for 30 minutes.

> ¼ pound (or more, if you wish) mushrooms, trimmed, sliced,
> and prepared (page 5)
> Fine-chopped parsley

Add the mushrooms and their juice and continue to cook the chicken, covered, for 30 minutes longer, or until it is tender. Discard the bouquet garni and garnish the dish generously with parsley.

You may complete the dish 24 hours in advance of serving, allow it to cool, refrigerate it overnight, and the following day remove any solidified fat. Allow the casserole to reach room temperature before reheating; do not overcook it. Garnish the dish with parsley at the time of serving.

BRAISED CHICKEN WITH ALMONDS (Spain): In step one, use 4 tablespoons olive oil to brown the floured chicken (add more oil as necessary); omit flaming the chicken. In step two, use 4 onions; deglaze the casserole with 2 cups dry white wine (recommended: white Burgundy). Follow step three as written. In step four, omit the mushrooms; in the container of a food processor or blender, combine ⅓ cup blanched almonds, 2 hard-cooked egg yolks, 3 large garlic cloves, peeled and chopped coarse, a generous pinch of saffron, and ¼ cup liquid from the casserole; whirl the mixture until it is smooth and then gently stir it into the casserole for the final 30 minutes of cooking. Complete the recipe as written and serve it with boiled rice.

BRAISED CHICKEN WITH APPLES (France) (does not freeze): In step one, omit the salt pork; flame the chicken with Calvados *or* applejack. In step two, omit the garlic, reduce the onions to 2, and add 4 large tart apples, peeled, cored, and sliced; deglaze the casserole with 2 cups dry white wine (recommended: Muscadet). In step three, omit the bouquet garni and, after replacing the chicken, add 1 cup apple juice blended with 1 cup thickened cream (page 6) *or* sour cream and seasoned with ½ teaspoon each cinnamon, clove, and nutmeg. In step four, omit the mushrooms. Complete the recipe as written.

BRAISED CHICKEN THIGHS WITH BACON: In step one, skin the chicken thighs, wrap each one in a thick slice of bacon, and skewer them so that the bacon is secure; dredge them in seasoned flour and brown them in butter and oil. In step two, add 3 medium carrots, scraped and sliced thin; to the wine, add 2 tablespoons tomato paste. Complete the recipe as written.

BRAISED CHICKEN WITH DRIED BEANS (France): Before starting the recipe, combine in a large saucepan 1 pound navy or pea beans and enough cold water to cover them by a full inch; bring the liquid to a boil and, over high heat, cook the beans, uncovered, for 10 minutes; remove the saucepan from the heat and allow the beans to stand, covered, for at least 1 hour.

In step one, cook 6 slices bacon, diced, until crisp and golden; proceed with the recipe as if you were using salt pork; do not dredge the chicken in seasoned flour. In step two, deglaze the casserole with 2 cups Riesling. In step three, drain the prepared beans and combine them with the chicken, 2 teaspoons salt, and 1 teaspoon sugar. In step four, omit the mushrooms; bake the casserole, very tightly covered, at 275° for 5 hours more, or until the beans are tender and the liquid is nearly absorbed; the dish should be moist but not soupy (if it seems too dry, add more chicken stock). Complete the recipe as written.

CHICKEN BRAISED IN BEER (Belgium): In step one, flame the chicken with Geneva. In step two, deglaze the casserole with 2 (12-ounce) cans of stale beer and 2 tablespoons cider vinegar. Complete the recipe as written.

BRAISED CHICKEN WITH CABBAGE (does not freeze): Follow step one as written. In step two, before wilting the garlic and onion, lightly glaze 3 medium potatoes, peeled and quartered; remove and reserve them; deglaze the casserole with 2 cups dry white wine (recommended: Chablis). In step three, combine 1 small cabbage, cored and shredded (about 4 cups), and 3 medium carrots, scraped and grated; arrange the mixture over the bottom of the casserole, add the chicken, and complete the step as written, adding the reserved potatoes. In step four, omit the mushrooms. Complete the recipe as written.

CHICKEN BRAISED IN CREAM: In step one, brown the chicken in butter and oil; use ½ cup brandy to deglaze the casserole (do not flame the chicken). Omit step two, but combine in the container of a food processor or blender an 8-ounce package of cream cheese, ¾ cup scalded milk, and 3 medium onions, peeled and chopped; whirl them until the mixture is smooth; transfer the mixture to the casserole and add 2 cups dry white wine (recommended: Mâcon or Pinot Blanc). Follow step three as written, omitting the chicken stock. In step four, in place of the parsley, garnish the dish with ½ cup grated Muenster cheese.

CHICKEN BRAISED IN TARRAGON CREAM: Follow the preceding variation, using, in place of the bouquet garni, ¼ cup chopped fresh tarragon leaves.

BRAISED CHICKEN WITH GARLIC (France): In step one, brown the floured chicken in butter and oil; flame the chicken with ¼ cup Calvados or applejack. In step two, omit the onions, but simmer, uncovered, 1 large head of garlic in water for 5 minutes; separate and peel the cloves, leaving them whole; deglaze the casserole with 2 cups vin rosé (recommended: Rosé d'Anjou or Grenache Rosé). In step three, distribute the garlic cloves throughout the casserole. In step four, omit the mushrooms. Complete the recipe as written.

BRAISED CHICKEN WITH GRAPES (Poulet Véronique) (France) (does not freeze): In step one, use butter and oil to brown the floured chicken. In step two, omit the garlic and onions; deglaze the casserole with 2 cups dry white wine (recommended: Muscadet or Sauvignon Blanc). Follow step three as written. In step four, omit the mushrooms but add for the final 15 minutes of cooking ½ cup toasted slivered almonds (page 4) and ½ pound (or more, to taste) seedless grapes, rinsed, drained on absorbent paper, and halved lengthwise. Complete the recipe as written.

BRAISED CHICKEN WITH LIME : In step one, use butter and oil to brown the floured chicken. In step two, use only 1 garlic clove and 1 onion; after cooking them until translucent, stir in ½ teaspoon chili powder, 1 tablespoon ground coriander, ½ teaspoon ground ginger, and ½ teaspoon turmeric; deglaze the casserole with 1½ cups dry white wine (recommended: Muscadet or Chablis); add ½ cup strained fresh lime juice. In step three, omit the bouquet garni. In step four, omit the mushrooms and add the grated rind of 2 limes for the final 15 minutes of cooking. Complete the recipe as written.

BRAISED CHICKEN WITH ONIONS (does not freeze): In step one, use butter and oil to brown the floured chicken. In step two, add butter and oil if necessary to glaze 24 small white onions, peeled (page 6); remove and reserve them; omit the garlic; deglaze the casserole with ¾ cup dry vermouth and 1¼ cups dry white wine (recommended: Chablis). In step three, omit the stock. In step four, omit the mushrooms, but add the reserved onions for the final 30 minutes of cooking. At the time of serving, stir in 1 cup heavy cream, scalded. Complete the recipe as written.

BRAISED CHICKEN WITH RED CABBAGE (Poland)(does not freeze) : Before starting the recipe, core and shred 1 medium red cabbage; cover it with boiling water; allow it to stand for 5 minutes and then drain it.

Follow steps one and two as written, using 2 cups dry red wine (recommended: Zinfandel) to deglaze the casserole. In step three, before replacing the chicken, add the cabbage to the casserole; bring the liquid to the boil, reduce the heat, and simmer the cabbage, covered, for 15 minutes; complete the step as written. In step four, omit the mushrooms. Complete the recipe as written.

CHICKEN BRAISED IN SHERRY WITH PRUNES (United States) (does not freeze): Before starting the recipe, soak for 1 hour 18 to 24 tenderized pitted prunes in dry sherry just to cover.

In step one, use butter and oil to brown the floured chicken. In step two, deglaze the casserole with 1¼ cups dry sherry. Follow step three as written. In step four, omit the mushrooms, but add the prunes together with their liquid for the final 20 minutes of cooking.

CHICKEN BRAISED IN SWEET WINE WITH PRUNES (Haiti) (does not freeze): Before starting the recipe, soak for 1 hour 18 to 24 tenderized pitted prunes in muscatel just to cover.

In step one, use butter and oil to brown the floured chicken. In step two, add to the garlic and onions 12 to 18 pitted green olives, sliced lengthwise, and ⅓ cup golden seedless raisins; deglaze the casserole with 1¼ cups muscatel. In step three, add a 3-inch piece of cinnamon stick to the bouquet garni; sprinkle the chicken with 3 tablespoons sugar. In step four, omit the mushrooms, but add the prunes with their liquid for the final 20 minutes of cooking.

BRAISED CHICKEN WITH VEGETABLES: Follow step one as written, using the salt pork. In step two, add to the garlic and onions 3 large carrots, scraped and cut into ½-inch rounds, 3 medium celery ribs, with the leaves, chopped, and 2 medium white turnips, scraped and diced; deglaze the casserole with 2 cups dry red or white wine. Complete the recipe as written.

CHICKEN BRAISED IN WHITE PORT (Portugal): In step one, use butter and oil to brown the floured chicken. In step two, increase the garlic to 3 cloves and reduce the onions to 2; deglaze the casserole with 2 cups white port; stir in 1½ teaspoons ground coriander. In step three, omit the bouquet garni. In step four, omit the mushrooms. Remove the fully cooked chicken pieces to a heated serving dish. Cook the sauce over high heat for a few minutes and then stir in 1 cup heavy cream; simmer the sauce briefly; do not allow it to boil. Spoon the sauce over the chicken. Complete the recipe as written.

Deep-Fried Chicken (Tatsuta-Age) (JAPAN)

4 SERVINGS
PREPARATION: ABOUT 15 MINUTES
MARINATION TIME: 2 HOURS (OR YOU MAY MARINATE THE CHICKEN, REFRIGERATED, OVERNIGHT)
COOKING: 7 MINUTES AT 375° IN A DEEP FRYER

A delicacy of chef Soji Kuwabara of the Fuji Restaurant, New York City.

½ cup sake (Japanese rice wine)
½ cup soy sauce (preferably Japanese)
1 teaspoon grated ginger root
2 whole chicken breasts, skinned, boned, and cut into
   bite-size pieces

In a mixing bowl, blend the sake, soy sauce, and ginger. Add the chicken to the marinade, coating it well. Allow the chicken to marinate, refrigerated, for at least 2 hours.

Cornstarch
Soybean oil
Lemon wedges

Drain the chicken; strain and reserve the marinade. Dredge the chicken in cornstarch; do not shake off any excess. In soybean oil preheated to 375°, deep-fry the chicken for 7 minutes, or until it is golden brown; do not overcook it. Drain it on absorbent paper and offer it garnished with lemon wedges. You may also make a sauce by straining the marinade and thickening it with 1 teaspoon cornstarch mixed until smooth with a little cold water.

Chicken with Eggplant (ITALY)

6 SERVINGS
PREPARATION: ABOUT 30 MINUTES
COOKING: 1 HOUR IN A 350° OVEN
REFRIGERATES

2 tablespoons butter   Salt
2 tablespoons oil   Fresh-ground pepper
Serving pieces of chicken
   for 6 persons

In a flameproof casserole, heat the butter and oil. Brown the chicken, a few pieces at a time, seasoning them to taste with salt and pepper.

¼ pound mushrooms,   ½ medium green pepper
   trimmed and sliced   seeded and chopped
1 medium eggplant,   12 small white onions,
   peeled and cut into   peeled (page 6)
   1-inch cubes   ½ teaspoon dried basil
2 large ripe tomatoes,   ½ teaspoon dried thyme
   peeled, seeded, and   ½ teaspoon salt
   chopped

Return the chicken to the casserole and over it arrange the vegetables in layers. Sprinkle them with the seasonings.

At this point you may stop and continue later.

   1½ cups dry white wine (recommended: Soave)
   Fine-chopped parsley

Add the wine to the casserole. Bake the chicken and vegetables, covered, at 350° for 1 hour, or until the chicken is tender. Garnish the dish with parsley.

Chilled Pickled Chicken (Escabeche de Gallina) (SPAIN)

6 SERVINGS
PREPARATION: ABOUT 40 MINUTES
COOKING: 40 MINUTES
CHILLING TIME: 6 HOURS
REFRIGERATES

This piquant dish serves as a welcome warm-weather main course for a light meal, or it may be offered as an hors d'oeuvre.

4 tablespoons olive oil
Serving pieces of chicken
   for 6 persons
1 cup dry white wine
   (recommended:
   Pinot Blanc)
1 cup malt vinegar
1 cup chicken stock *or*
   defatted canned
   chicken broth

3 carrots, scraped and
   sliced thin
1 leek (with a little of
   the green), rinsed and
   cut into ⅛-inch rounds
3 medium onions, peeled
   and sliced thin
Bouquet garni (page 4)
1 teaspoon sugar
2 teaspoons salt
Thin-sliced lemon

In a flameproof casserole, heat the oil and in it brown the chicken. Add the wine, vinegar, and stock. Add the vegetables and seasonings. Bring the liquid to the boil, reduce the heat, and simmer the chicken, covered, for 40 minutes, or until it is tender but does not fall apart. In a deep serving dish, arrange the chicken in a single layer. Discard the bouquet garni. Pour the liquid and vegetables over the chicken. Garnish the dish with lemon slices. Cover the dish, and when it has cooled to room temperature, chill it for at least 6 hours, or until it is thoroughly set. Offer the escabeche on chilled plates.

Chicken Marengo (FRANCE)

6 SERVINGS
PREPARATION: ABOUT 30 MINUTES
COOKING: 1 HOUR IN A 350° OVEN

A dish named, according to tradition, in honor of Napoleon's victory at Marengo. Napoleon never ate at set times; his chefs, therefore, were obliged to make several of the same dish, timing their completion so that they would be hot and properly done when the Emperor felt disposed to dine. He also ate with extreme rapidity. Because he was always served first and court etiquette prohibited anyone's eating after the Emperor had finished, many courtiers and guests left the table as hungry as they had come to it.

2 tablespoons butter   ¼ cup cognac
2 tablespoons oil   Salt
Serving pieces of chicken   Fresh-ground pepper
   for 6 persons

In a casserole or flameproof baking dish, heat the butter and oil and
brown the chicken. Warm the cognac, ignite it, and pour it over the
chicken. When the flame dies, season the chicken to taste with salt and
pepper. Remove and reserve the chicken.

1 medium onion, peeled and chopped
1 small garlic clove, peeled and chopped fine

In the fat remaining in the pan, cook the onion and garlic until translucent.

1¼ cups dry white wine   ¼ cup chopped parsley
   (recommended: ½ teaspoon dried tarragon
   Chablis)   ½ teaspoon dried thyme
¾ cup chicken stock *or*   1 teaspoon sugar
   defatted canned   Salt
   chicken broth   Fresh-ground pepper
1 bay leaf

To the contents of the casserole, add all these ingredients except the salt
and pepper. Over high heat, cook them, uncovered, for 10 minutes.
Adjust the seasoning to taste with salt and pepper.

3 large ripe tomatoes, peeled, seeded, and chopped
Reserved chicken pieces

Stir in the tomato and add the chicken, spooning the sauce over it.

At this point you may stop and continue later.

2 tablespoons butter
½ pound button mushrooms, trimmed, *or* regular mushrooms,
   trimmed and sliced

In a skillet, heat the butter and in it sauté the mushrooms, stirring them
often, until they are just barely limp. Bake the chicken, covered, at 350°
for 1 hour, or until it is tender. For the final 10 minutes of cooking, add
the mushrooms.

CHICKEN, HUNTER'S STYLE: known in France as *poulet chasseur*, in Italy as *pollo alla cacciatora*, this is remarkably like chicken Marengo, except that it is more stalwart. In step two, use 2 large onions, peeled and sliced thick, 2 large garlic cloves, and 1 medium celery rib, with some of the leaves, chopped. For the tarragon and thyme in step three, substitute ¾ teaspoon each dried oregano and rosemary, and when boiling the sauce, add 3 tablespoons wine vinegar. Finally, in step four, with the chopped tomato, add also an 8-ounce can tomato purée.

SAUTÉED CHICKEN BREASTS

Sautéing is, I find, the easiest and surest way of cooking chicken breasts, which can so easily be spoiled by overcooking. In these recipes, the butter in which the breasts are wholly or partially cooked becomes the base for a sauce of liqueur or wine and cream. Prepared in this way, chicken breasts are appetizing to eye and palate, ideal party fare. Let us start with *poulet Vallée d'Auge* from France and follow it with six variations.

Chicken Breasts in Apple-Flavored Cream (Poulet Vallée d'Auge) (FRANCE)

6 SERVINGS
PREPARATION: ABOUT 20 MINUTES
COOKING: 30 MINUTES
REFRIGERATES

6 tablespoons butter
3 large chicken breasts, boned, halved lengthwise, and trimmed of any cartilage or fat
2 shallots, peeled and chopped fine, *or* 3 scallions (white part only), trimmed and chopped fine
Salt
Fresh-ground white pepper

In a large skillet with a lid, heat the butter and in it, over medium heat, sauté the chicken breasts together with the shallot until the breasts are golden. Season them to taste with salt and pepper.

¼ cup Calvados *or* applejack
1 cup apple cider
½ pound small mushrooms, trimmed and prepared (page 5)

In a small saucepan, warm the Calvados, ignite it, and pour it over the chicken breasts; allow the flame to die. Add the cider and mushrooms. Over gentle heat, poach the chicken breasts, covered, for 30 minutes, or until they are fork-tender; do not overcook them. Remove them to a heated platter.

> 1 cup thickened cream (page 6) *or* sour cream
> Fine-chopped parsley

Over high heat, reduce the liquid for 3 minutes. Reduce the heat and blend in the cream; do not allow the sauce to boil. Spoon it over the chicken breasts, and garnish the dish with parsley.

CHICKEN BREASTS IN ARMAGNAC CREAM: In step one, sauté the chicken breasts until they are fully cooked (about 6 minutes on each side); after seasoning them, remove them to a heated serving platter. In step two, in place of flaming the breasts, deglaze the skillet with ¼ cup Armagnac *or* other brandy; omit the apple cider, but add the mushrooms. In step three, without reducing the liquid in the skillet, stir in 1½ cups thickened cream *or* sour cream; heat, but do not allow the sauce to boil. Complete the recipe as written.

CHICKEN BREASTS IN CHAMPAGNE: Follow step one as written. In step two, flame the chicken breasts with ¼ cup cognac; in place of the apple cider, use 1 cup champagne; complete the step as written. In step three, in place of the thickened cream or sour cream, use 1 cup heavy cream blended with 2 beaten egg yolks; over gentle heat, cook the sauce, stirring, until it thickens somewhat and coats a metal spoon; do not allow it to boil. Complete the recipe as written.

CHICKEN BREASTS WITH PERNOD: Follow step one as written. In step two, flame the chicken breasts with ⅓ cup Pernod; in place of the apple cider, use ½ cup chicken stock *or* canned chicken broth. Complete the recipe as written.

CHICKEN BREASTS WITH SCOTCH WHISKY: Follow step one as written. In step two, flame the chicken breasts with ½ cup Scotch; omit the apple cider but add ¾ cup chicken stock *or* canned chicken broth. Complete the recipe as written.

CHICKEN BREASTS IN SHERRY WITH CHEESE: In step one, sauté the chicken breasts until they are fully cooked (about 6 minutes on each side); after seasoning them, remove them to an ovenproof serving platter. In step two, omit the Calvados and cider, but stir into the chopped shallot 1 tablespoon flour; deglaze the skillet with ¾ cup dry sherry, stirring constantly until the mixture is thickened and smooth. Add the mushrooms. In step three, use ¾ cup of sour cream; spoon the sauce over the chicken breasts; sprinkle on ½ cup grated Parmesan cheese; bake the dish at 400° for 10 minutes, or until the cheese is melted and golden; omit the parsley.

CHICKEN BREASTS WITH VERMOUTH: Follow step one as written. In step two, omit the cider and flame the chicken breasts with ¼ cup brandy; add ½ cup dry vermouth and ½ cup chicken stock *or* canned chicken broth; tuck in a bay leaf; complete the step as written. In step three, omit the thickened cream or sour cream. Reduce the liquid, then add ½ cup heavy cream; heat but do not allow the sauce to boil. Complete the recipe as written.

Chicken Breasts with Cherries (Suprèmes de Volaille Montmorency) (FRANCE)

6 SERVINGS
PREPARATION: ABOUT 20 MINUTES
COOKING: 30 MINUTES IN A 350° OVEN
REFRIGERATES

6 tablespoons butter
3 large chicken breasts,
    boned, halved lengthwise,
    and trimmed of any
    cartilage or fat

Salt
Fresh-ground white pepper
¼ cup cherry-flavored
    liqueur (optional)

In a skillet, heat the butter and in it sauté the chicken breasts until they are just golden. Season them to taste with salt and pepper. Remove them to an ovenproof dish. Do not wash the skillet. In a small saucepan, warm the cherry liqueur, ignite it, and pour it over the chicken breasts; allow the flame to die. Bake the chicken, well covered, at 350° for 15 minutes.

2 (1-pound) cans of pitted dark sweet cherries,
    with their liquid
1 cup ruby port

While the chicken bakes, measure out 1 cup of the reserved cherry liquid, combine it with the port, and with this mixture deglaze the skillet; simmer the liquid for 10 minutes. Reserve an additional ½ cup cherry liquid and the cherries.

¼ teaspoon cinnamon	1 tablespoon cornstarch
2 tablespoons sugar (only if cherry liqueur has *not* been used)	Reserved cherry liquid
	Strained fresh lemon juice
	Reserved cherries

Blend the cinnamon, sugar, and cornstarch; add the mixture to the reserved cherry liquid, stirring until the liquid is smooth. To the contents of the skillet, add the cornstarch mixture, stirring constantly until the sauce is thickened and smooth. Stir in lemon juice to taste and then the reserved cherries.

Spoon the sauce over the chicken breasts and continue to bake them, covered, for 15 minutes longer.

CHICKEN BREASTS IN BITTER-ORANGE SAUCE: Follow step one as written, using orange-flavored liqueur to flame the chicken. In step two, into the butter remaining in the skillet, stir ½ teaspoon cinnamon, 1 teaspoon Dijon mustard, 1 cup strained fresh orange juice, 1 cup of dry white wine (recommended: Chablis), and ½ cup bitter-orange marmalade; when the mixture is well blended, add 2½ teaspoons cornstarch mixed until smooth with ¼ cup strained fresh orange juice; over moderate heat, cook the sauce, stirring constantly, until it is thickened and smooth. (The sauce may also be seasoned to taste with sugar.) Spoon the sauce over the chicken, garnish the dish with 6 paper-thin orange slices, and complete the recipe as written.

Roast Chicken, Italian Style

6 SERVINGS
PREPARATION: ABOUT 45 MINUTES
COOKING: 1 HOUR IN A 425°/350° OVEN

Giblets and neck from a roasting chicken
Dry white wine (recommended: Soave *or* Chardonnay)

In a small saucepan, combine the giblets, neck, and wine to cover; bring the liquid to the boil, reduce the heat, and simmer the giblets, covered, for 20 minutes, or until they are tender. Drain them, reserving the wine. Skin the neck and remove the meat from the bones; chop the meat and the giblets fine.

1 garlic clove, peeled and chopped fine	1 teaspoon fine-crumbled rosemary
1 medium onion, peeled and chopped fine	5 cups (about) bread stuffing of your choice
½ cup fresh-grated Parmesan cheese	Reserved giblets and wine
A generous grating of nutmeg	Additional wine, as needed

In a mixing bowl, using two forks, toss together the garlic, onion, Parmesan cheese, nutmeg, rosemary, stuffing, and giblets and wine. If necessary, add more wine to moisten the dressing; it should not be soggy.

1 (4- or 5-pound) roasting chicken	Salt
Olive oil	Fresh-ground pepper
	6 thin slices bacon

Stuff and skewer the chicken. Rub it with olive oil and season it to taste with salt and pepper. Arrange the chicken on a rack in a roasting pan with a cover. Over the chicken, lay the bacon. Put the roasting pan in the 425° oven and immediately reduce the heat to 350°.

1 cup wine

When the chicken is browned, add the wine. Continue to roast the chicken, covered, basting it often with the pan drippings. At the end of an hour, when the chicken is tender, use the pan drippings to make a thin sauce by skimming off the fat and adding ½ teaspoon cornstarch mixed until smooth with a little water.

Chicken with Rice and Seafood (Paella Valenciana) (SPAIN)

6 SERVINGS

PREPARATION: ABOUT 40 MINUTES

COOKING: 1 HOUR IN A 350° OVEN

REFRIGERATES

The unusual and seductive combination of flavors in this famous dish has made it almost our national favorite from Spain.

¼ pound salt pork, diced
Serving pieces of chicken
    for 6 persons

Olive oil, as needed
Salt
Fresh-ground pepper

In a large flameproof casserole, cook the salt pork until it is crisp and golden; with a slotted spoon, remove it to absorbent paper and reserve it. In the pork fat, brown the chicken pieces, a few at a time (add a little olive oil, as needed); season it to taste with salt and pepper. As the chicken is browned, remove it to absorbent paper.

2 garlic cloves, peeled and
    chopped fine
3 medium onions, peeled
    and chopped

1½ cups natural raw rice
A generous pinch of saffron
1 teaspoon turmeric

In the fat remaining in the pan, cook the garlic and onion until translucent. Stir in the rice and seasonings.

¾ pound raw shrimps,
    shelled and deveined
12 littleneck clams in their
    shells, well scrubbed
½ pound chorizo or other
    hard sausage, sliced
    thin

2 (20-ounce) cans of
    Italian tomatoes,
    drained (reserve the
    liquid)
Reserved chicken

Into the rice stir the shrimps, clams, chorizo, and tomatoes; over all, arrange the chicken.

At this point you may stop and continue later.

1 cup dry white wine
   (recommended:
   Sauvignon Blanc)
¼ cup brandy
1 (8-ounce) bottle of
   clam juice

Reserved tomato liquid
Chicken stock *or* canned
   chicken broth, as needed
1 teaspoon salt

Combine the liquids, in order, to equal 3 cups; stir in the salt.

Reserved salt pork
½ cup pitted green olives, halved lengthwise
1 (10-ounce) package of frozen tiny peas, fully thawed to
   room temperature
Fine-chopped parsley

Add the liquid mixture to the casserole. Sprinkle the salt pork over all. Bake the paella, covered, at 350° for 45 minutes. Over the top, sprinkle the olives and peas; continue to bake the dish, covered, for 15 minutes longer, or until the chicken is tender. When serving, garnish the casserole with parsley.

Chilled Chicken Mousse

6 SERVINGS
PREPARATION AND COOKING: ABOUT 25 MINUTES
CHILLING TIME: 6 HOURS

Lightly oil and chill a 5- or 6-cup ring mold.

1 pound boneless chicken breast, all fat removed
2 cups water
1 bay leaf
Salt

In a saucepan, combine the chicken, water, bay leaf, and salt to taste. Bring the liquid to a boil, reduce the heat, and simmer the chicken, covered, for 20 minutes. Allow it to cool, covered, in the broth; when it has cooled, dice it.

1½ envelopes unflavored gelatin, softened for 5 minutes in
   ¼ cup cold water

Dissolve the gelatin over simmering water; reserve it.

⅓ cup dry sherry

½ teaspoon paprika
   (preferably sweet
   Hungarian)

A few drops of Tabasco
   sauce

Reserved chicken and
   broth

Reserved gelatin

In the container of a food processor equipped with the steel blade, combine the sherry, paprika, Tabasco sauce, chicken and broth, and gelatin. Whirl them until the mixture is smooth. Transfer it to a mixing bowl and chill it until it just begins to set.

¼ cup fine-chopped gherkins

½ cup fine-chopped parsley

1 cup heavy cream, whipped

Briefly beat the chicken mixture to assure its smoothness. Stir in the gherkins and parsley. Fold in the whipped cream. Using a rubber spatua, transfer the mixture to the prepared mold. Chill the mousse for at least 6 hours, or until it is thoroughly set. Unmold it onto a chilled serving plate.

Duckling

The classic *caneton à l'orange* from France, together with its cousin, duckling in Bigarade sauce; duckling with grapes, with olives, and with peaches; duckling braised in red wine; duckling braised in *vin rosé*—these contrasting recipes will, I hope, make your cooking duck with wine a novel and enjoyable experience.

Oven-ready duckling is available at the supermarket, fresh or frozen. Usually the cavity contains a small package of the neck and giblets; use these and the wing tips to make stock for the sauce.

Before cooking a duck, whole or quartered, cut away and discard as much fat as possible. With the tines of a fork, prick the skin in several places.

Put a whole duck breast side up on the rack of a roasting pan; arrange quarters of duckling skin side down. Roast the duckling, uncovered, at 425° for 10 minutes; reduce the heat to 350° and continue to roast it 1 hour longer (rare), 1¼ hours longer (medium rare), or 1¾ hours longer (well done). Discard all fat from the roasting pan, reserving only as much as may be called for in an individual recipe. (Cooking directions in particular recipes may vary from this basic method.)

Caneton à l'Orange (Roast Duckling with Orange) (FRANCE)

4 SERVINGS
PREPARATION: ABOUT 1 HOUR
COOKING: ABOUT 1½ HOURS
REFRIGERATES; FREEZES

> Neck, giblets, and wing tips of the duckling
> 1 medium carrot, scraped and chopped
> 1 medium onion, peeled and quartered
> 1¼ cups water

In a saucepan, combine the neck, giblets, and wing tips, carrot, and onion; add the water; bring the liquid to the boil, reduce the heat, and simmer the mixture, covered, for 30 minutes. Strain and reserve the broth.

> 1 (5- to 6-pound) duckling   quartered, seeds removed
> Salt   1 cup dry white wine
> Fresh-ground pepper   (recommended:
> 2 oranges, unpeeled and   Muscadet or Riesling)

Rub the cavity of the duckling with salt and pepper to taste. Fill the cavity with the orange. Add the wine to the roasting pan and cook the duckling according to the suggested method (page 150).

> 2 oranges
> ⅓ cup sugar
> ½ cup dry white wine
> ½ cup orange-flavored liqueur

With a vegetable peeler, remove the zest from the oranges, and then cut it into julienne (page 5). Squeeze the oranges, strain the juice, and use it to baste the roasting duckling. In a saucepan, combine the zest, sugar, wine, and liqueur. Bring the mixture to the boil, reduce the heat, and simmer it, uncovered, for 10 minutes.

1 cup reserved giblet broth
½ cup wine
Strained juice of ½ lemon
1 tablespoon cornstarch
¼ cup brandy
Salt

1 orange, peeled, all white
   pith removed, divided
   into sections, the
   sections halved and
   seeded

Remove the duckling from the roasting pan and arrange it on a heated serving platter. Skim off all fat and, over high heat, deglaze the pan with the broth and wine. Strain this liquid into the contents of the saucepan and add the lemon juice. Blend the cornstarch with the brandy until the mixture is smooth, and stir it into the contents of the saucepan. Cook the sauce, stirring constantly, until it is thickened and smooth. Taste for salt. Add the orange sections. Spoon a little of the sauce over the duckling, and offer the remainder separately.

DUCKLING IN BIGARADE SAUCE: Follow the recipe as written, using, in place of sweet oranges, bitter or Seville oranges; if they are not available, an acceptable if unauthentic solution is to use, in place of the orange sections in the sauce, ½ cup bitter-orange marmalade.

Duckling Braised in Claret

4 SERVINGS
PREPARATION: ABOUT 25 MINUTES
MARINATION TIME: 6 HOURS
COOKING: 1½ HOURS IN A 350° OVEN
REFRIGERATES; FREEZES

2½ cups red Bordeaux
   or Cabernet Sauvignon
½ cup brandy
1 garlic clove, peeled and
   put through a press
2 medium onions, peeled
   and chopped

Bouquet garni (page 4)
1 teaspoon sugar
1 teaspoon salt
1 (5- to 6-pound)
   duckling, quartered

In a deep bowl, combine the wine, brandy, garlic, onion, bouquet garni, and seasonings. In the mixture, marinate the duckling at room temperature, turning the pieces occasionally, for 6 hours.

4 tablespoons oil

Remove the duckling from the marinade and dry it on absorbent paper. In a flameproof casserole, heat the oil and in it brown the duckling. Pour off all of the fat, replace the duckling, and add the marinade. Bake the casserole, covered, at 350° for 1½ hours, or until the duckling is tender.

At this point you may stop and continue later. (Recommended: Allow the casserole to cool to room temperature, refrigerate it overnight, and the following day remove the solidified fat.)

½ pound mushrooms, trimmed and prepared (page 5)
**4 tablespoons flour, blended until smooth with ½ cup cold
   water**
Chopped parsley

On top of the stove, bring the casserole to serving temperature. Remove the duckling to a heated platter. Discard the bouquet garni. Into the cooking liquid, stir the mushrooms and then the flour. Cook the sauce over high heat, stirring constantly, until it is thickened and smooth. Spoon some of the sauce over the duckling; offer the remainder separately. Garnish the dish with parsley.

Braised Duckling with Grapes

4 SERVINGS
PREPARATION: ABOUT 30 MINUTES
COOKING: ABOUT 1 HOUR
REFRIGERATES

2 tablespoons butter   **Nutmeg**
2 tablespoons oil   **Salt**
1 (5- to 6-pound)   **Fresh-ground pepper**
   duckling, quartered

In a flameproof casserole, heat the butter and oil; brown the duckling thoroughly and season it with a generous grating of nutmeg, salt, and pepper. Discard the fat.

    1½ cups muscatel
    4 tablespoons currant jelly

Blend the wine and jelly and pour the mixture over the duckling. Bring the casserole to the boil, reduce the heat, and simmer the duckling, covered, for 1 hour, or until it is tender.

At this point you may stop and continue later. (Recommended: Allow the casserole to cool to room temperature, refrigerate it overnight, and the following day remove the solidified fat.)

    1 tablespoon cornstarch, blended until smooth with ¼ cup
        cold water
    1 cup seedless grapes, rinsed, drained on absorbent paper, and
        halved lengthwise

Return the casserole to the boil. Remove the duckling to a heated serving platter. To the boiling wine, add the cornstarch, stirring constantly until the sauce is thickened and smooth. Add the grapes and continue to simmer the sauce for 5 minutes longer. Spoon the sauce over the duckling.

Duckling with Olives

4 SERVINGS
PREPARATION: ABOUT 30 MINUTES
COOKING: ABOUT 1½ HOURS IN A 450°/350° OVEN
REFRIGERATES

    Neck, giblets, and wing tips of the duckling
    1 medium carrot, scraped and chopped
    1 medium onion, peeled and quartered
    1¼ cups water

In a saucepan, combine the neck, giblets, and wing tips, carrot, and onion. Add the water. Bring the liquid to the boil, reduce the heat, and simmer the mixture, covered, for 30 minutes. Strain and reserve the broth.

    1 (16-ounce) can of pitted ripe olives or green olives, halved
       lengthwise

In a saucepan, cover the olives with cold water. Over high heat, bring the
water to the boil and cook the olives, uncovered, for 1 minute. Drain
them in a colander and refresh them in cold water. Reserve them.

    1 (5- to 6-pound) duckling
    Salt
    Fresh-ground pepper

Season the duckling to taste with salt and pepper. Arrange it on the rack
of a roasting pan. Bake the duckling, uncovered, at 450° for 20 minutes,
or until it is browned. Remove it from the pan and discard all but 2
tablespoons of the fat.

    2½ tablespoons flour
    1 cup reserved giblet broth
    1 cup dry white wine (recommended: Chablis)
    ¼ cup chopped parsley

Into the remaining fat, stir the flour. On top of the stove, cook the
mixture, stirring, until it is golden brown. Add the broth and wine and
continue to cook the sauce, stirring constantly, until it is thickened and
smooth. Add the parsley. Return the duckling to the roasting pan and
bake it, covered, at 350° for 1 hour, or until it is tender.

    Reserved olives

Add the olives to the sauce and heat them through.

Duckling with Peaches

4 SERVINGS
PREPARATION: ABOUT 30 MINUTES
COOKING: ABOUT 1½ HOURS, PARTIALLY IN A 325° OVEN
REFRIGERATES

    Neck, giblets, and wing tips of the duckling
    1 medium carrot, scraped and chopped
    1 medium onion, peeled and quartered
    1½ cups water

In a saucepan, combine the neck, giblets, and wing tips, carrot, and onion. Add the water. Bring the liquid to the boil, reduce the heat, and simmer the mixture, covered, for 30 minutes. Strain and reserve the broth.

> 1 (5- 6-pound) duckling, quartered
> Paprika
> Salt
> Fresh-ground pepper

Rub the duckling pieces with paprika, salt, and pepper to taste. Roast them according to the directions on page 150. Arrange the duckling in a baking dish, and discard all but 2 tablespoons of the fat.

> 6 scallions (white part
>   only), trimmed and
>   chopped
> 1 cup dry red wine
>   (recommended:
>   Mâcon or Gamay
>   Beaujolais)
>
> 1 cup reserved broth
> 1 tablespoon cornstarch,
>   blended until smooth
>   with ¼ cup cold water
> Worcestershire sauce

In a skillet, heat the remaining 2 tablespoons of duck fat and in it cook the scallions until translucent. Add the wine and broth. Add the cornstarch and, over high heat, cook the sauce, stirring constantly, until it is thickened and smooth. Stir in several drops of Worcestershire sauce.

> 4 firm ripe peaches, peeled, halved, and seeded, or
>   1 (29-ounce) can of peach halves, drained

Over the duckling, arrange the peach halves, round side up. Spoon the sauce over them. Bake the dish, covered, at 325° for 15 minutes, or until the peaches are thoroughly heated through.

Duckling Braised in Vin Rosé

4 SERVINGS
PREPARATION: ABOUT 30 MINUTES
COOKING: ABOUT 1½ HOURS IN A 400°/350° OVEN
REFRIGERATES; FREEZES

1 (5- to 6-pound) duckling, quartered	Ginger
	Paprika
1 small onion, peeled and grated	Salt

Roast the duckling at 400° for 20 minutes. Discard the fat and season the duckling with the onion, a generous sprinkling of ginger, paprika, and salt to taste. Arrange the duckling in a flameproof casserole.

1 cup rosé wine (recommended: Rosé d'Anjou or Grenache Rosé)	¼ cup granulated sugar
	2½ teaspoons cornstarch
	Grated rind of 1 small orange
¼ cup brown sugar, packed	

Over the duckling, pour half the wine. Bake the duckling, tightly covered, at 350° for 1 hour, or until it is tender.

While the duckling is cooking, make the sauce: In a saucepan, blend the sugars and cornstarch, add the remaining wine, and cook the sauce, stirring constantly, until it is thickened and smooth. Stir in the grated orange rind.

Remove the duckling to a heated serving platter. Into the contents of the saucepan, strain the pan juices. Over high heat, cook the sauce, stirring, for about 5 minutes, or until it is somewhat reduced and glazed. Spoon the sauce over the duckling.

Roast Duckling with Red Wine

4 SERVINGS
PREPARATION: ABOUT 25 MINUTES
MARINATION TIME: 24 HOURS
COOKING: ABOUT 1½ HOURS

Superficially akin to Duckling Braised in Claret (page 152), this dish is considerably more flavorful, and tastes very much like braised wild duck. The length of the marination time, which tenderizes the meat, allows you to use a larger duck, if you wish.

Neck, giblets, and wing tips of the duck
1 medium carrot, scraped and chopped
1 medium onion, peeled and quartered
1½ cups water

In a saucepan, combine the neck, giblets, and wing tips, carrot, and onion. Add the water. Bring the liquid to the boil, reduce the heat, and simmer the mixture, covered, for 30 minutes. Strain and reserve the broth.

1 (5- to 6-pound duckling or larger) (See page 157)	½ teaspoon crushed rosemary
3 anchovy fillets	½ teaspoon dried thyme
15 juniper berries, crushed	

Rub the cavity of the duckling with the anchovies, juniper berries, and herbs; leave them in the cavity. Put the duckling in a large bowl.

2 cups dry red wine (recommended: Burgundy or Zinfandel)	2 celery ribs, with the leaves, chopped
Reserved giblet broth	2 medium onions, peeled and chopped
1 large carrot, scraped and chopped	6 parsley sprigs

Combine the wine and broth; pour the mixture over the duckling and add the vegetables and parsley. Marinate the duckling, refrigerated, for 24 hours, turning it several times. Remove the duckling from the marinade and arrange it in a covered roasting pan. Add the marinade. Roast the duck, covered, according to the directions on page 150; remove the cover for the final 30 minutes of cooking.

4 tablespoons flour, blended until smooth with ½ cup
    cold water

Arrange the duck on a heated serving platter. Strain the marinade into a saucepan and skim off the fat. Over high heat, add the flour mixture, stirring constantly until the sauce is thickened and smooth. Offer it separately.

Fish and Seafood

Fish

In principle, fish cookery should be done as quickly as possible over high heat or in a very hot oven, in order to preserve the full flavor and texture of the fish. The Canadian Department of Fisheries has made an important contribution to this end. Simply called the Canadian Cooking Theory, it applies to lean- or fat-fleshed, salt- or fresh-water fish. It applies to fish that are stuffed and to fish that are plain. It holds true for baking, poaching, sautéeing, and steaming fish. It is easily followed, and it guarantees deliciously cooked, moist and flaky fish.

The Canadian Cooking Theory is simply this: Lay the fish—whole, filleted, or cut into steaks—on a flat surface; measure the depth of the fish at its deepest point; for each inch of depth, cook the fish 10 minutes. If you are using rolled fillets, measure their depth (diameter) *after* you have rolled them. If you are baking a stuffed fish, measure its depth *after* you have stuffed it.

The method also works for fish taken directly from the freezer (although I prefer to cook frozen fish after it is fully thawed to room temperature). If you cook still-frozen fish, double the cooking time to 20 minutes per inch of depth.

To bake fish: Preheat the oven to 450°; bake the fish on the top shelf.

To poach fish: Bring the poaching liquid (see page 160 for a suggested court bouillon) to the boil and place the fish in it; the liquid should not quite cover the fish. Time the cooking, covered, from when the liquid returns nearly to the boil (the water should shimmer at between 190° and 200°).

To sauté fish: Heat to very hot equal parts of butter and oil. Fry the fish on one side until golden; turn it and repeat the process; the total time will equal about 10 minutes per inch of depth of the fish. Drain the sautéed fish on aborbent paper.

To steam fish: Bring the water to a rolling boil; place the fish on a rack, making sure that the water does not touch it; cover the steaming utensil with a tight-fitting lid; time the cooking from the moment you put on the lid.

Armed with these four methods, you will be able to cook various fish in different ways, experimenting with the use of wines and with the sauces found on pages 289–304.

Court Bouillon for Poaching Fish

YIELD: ABOUT 6 CUPS
PREPARATION: ABOUT 45 MINUTES

Once the fish is cooked, the court bouillon becomes the basis for an accompanying sauce or for a soup.

2 medium carrots, scraped and sliced thin
1 garlic clove, peeled and chopped fine
3 medium onions, peeled and chopped
8 parsley sprigs
2 bay leaves, crumbled
2 whole cloves
½ teaspoon dried thyme
2 teaspoons salt
8 peppercorns
2 cups dry white wine (recommended: Mersault *or* Chenin Blanc)
4 cups water

In a large saucepan, combine the ingredients. Bring the liquid to the boil, reduce the heat, and simmer the mixture, covered, for 30 minutes. Strain and reserve the liquid.

FAT-FLESHED FISH DISHES

Baked Bluefish

6 SERVINGS
PREPARATION: ABOUT 20 MINUTES
COOKING: ABOUT 20 MINUTES IN A 450° OVEN

1 (5-pound) bluefish, drawn,
    the head and tail intact
Fresh dill
Parsley
1 medium lemon, sliced
    thin and seeded
Softened butter
8 scallions (with as much

of the green as is
crisp), trimmed and
chopped
Salt
Fresh-ground pepper
1 cup dry white wine
    (recommended:
    white Burgundy)

In the cavity of the fish, arrange a generous quantity of dill and parsley and the lemon slices. Line a baking pan with aluminum foil; coat the foil with softened butter. Sprinkle the scallion over the bottom of the pan. Lay the bluefish over the scallion, and season it to taste with salt and pepper.

At this point you may stop and continue later. (If you stop for longer than an hour, refrigerate the fish.)

½ cup heavy cream
1 egg yolk

Bake the fish at 450° according to the directions on page 159 (in this instance, about 20 minutes), or until it flakes easily when tested with a fork. Remove the fish to a serving platter. Remove the contents of the cavity to a saucepan. Add the cooking liquid and chopped scallion from the baking pan. Over high heat, reduce the liquid somewhat. Briefly beat together the cream and egg yolk. Add this, stirring, to the contents of the saucepan; do not allow the sauce to boil. When it is slightly thickened, strain the sauce into a gravy boat and offer it separately.

BAKED BASS: Have the fishmonger prepare a 3-pound striped bass, leaving the head and tail intact. Fill the cavity with the dill, parsley, and lemon slices (or, if you prefer, with your favorite stuffing) and skewer the cavity closed. Complete the recipe as written. Makes 4 servings.

Carp in White Wine (ITALY)

4 TO 6 SERVINGS
PREPARATION: ABOUT 30 MINUTES
COOKING: 30 MINUTES

> 4 tablespoons olive oil
> 1 medium onion, peeled
>   and chopped fine
> Beurre manié (page 4)
>   made of 4 tablespoons
>   each softened butter and
>   flour
> 1 cup dry white wine
>   (recommended:
>   Soave *or* Chablis)

> 1 cup water
> 1 tablespoon white wine
>   vinegar
> Salt
> Fresh-ground pepper
> ¼ cup fine-chopped
>   parsley

In a large skillet with a lid, heat the olive oil and in it cook the onion until translucent. Add the beurre manié and, over gentle heat, cook the mixture for a few minutes. Add the wine, water, and vinegar, stirring constanty until the sauce is thickened and smooth. Season it to taste with salt and pepper. Stir in the parsley.

At this point you may stop and continue later.

> 4 to 6 carp steaks (ask your fishmonger to prepare them)

To the simmering contents of the skillet, add the carp, spooning the sauce over it. Over moderate heat, braise the fish, covered, for 30 minutes, or until it flakes easily when tested with a fork. Serve the fish in the sauce.

Baked Shad and Roe (UNITED STATES)

6 SERVINGS
PREPARATION: ABOUT 20 MINUTES
COOKING: 25 MINUTES IN A 375° OVEN

If you wish to serve shad roe alone, the first step of the recipe, without the shad fillets, yields a delicious shad roe poached in wine (allow 1 roe per serving).

Softened butter	Salt
2 shad roe	Fresh-ground pepper
2 (about 1½ pounds total) boned shad fillets	1 cup dry white wine (recommended: Chablis)

Butter two baking pans. In one, arrange the roe. In the other, place the shad, skin side down. Season both to taste with salt and pepper. Dot the roe with butter and add to it the wine. Cover the roe tightly. Bake both the shad and the roe at 375°, the roe for 25 minutes and the shad for 20 minutes, or until it flakes easily when tested with a fork.

1 cup chicken stock or canned chicken broth	Beurre manié (page 4) made of 4 tablespoons each softened butter and flour
Liquid from the cooked roe	
1 teaspoon anchovy paste	1 cup heavy cream

In a saucepan, combine the stock and the roe cooking liquid. Stir in the anchovy paste. Add the beurre manié and, over moderately high heat, stir the mixture until it is thickened and smooth. Reduce the heat and stir in the cream; do not allow the sauce to boil. Strain the sauce into a gravy boat and offer it separately.

Fine-chopped parsley

Because cooked shad tends to break apart easily, I suggest that you transfer it directly from the baking plan to individual dinner plates. Divide the roe into 6 portions and put them on warmed plates with 6 portions of the shad. Garnish the fish with a sprinkling of parsley.

Norman Eel Stew (FRANCE)

4 SERVINGS
PREPARATION: ABOUT 35 MINUTES (DOES NOT INCLUDE READYING THE COURT
    BOUILLON)
COOKING: ABOUT 10 MINUTES
REFRIGERATES

Yes, the idea of coping with eel is unpleasant; but if your fishmonger
has eel, in all probability he will expect to skin, draw, and section it for
you. In that case, you are merely dealing with another fish.

    ¼ pound salt pork, diced
   12 small white onions, peeled (page 6)

In a large skillet with a lid, cook the salt pork until it is crisp and golden;
with a slotted spoon, remove it to absorbent paper and reserve it. In the
pork fat, glaze the onions (you may, if you wish, sprinkle them very lightly
with sugar to expedite this step); remove them to absorbent paper and
reserve them. Discard the remaining fat.

  2½ cups Court Bouillon   3 medium celery ribs,
      (page 160)   chopped fine
  1½ cups cider *or* apple juice   2 medium onions, peeled
   2 medium carrots, scraped   and chopped fine
     and cut into julienne

In the skillet, combine these five ingredients. Bring the liquid to the boil,
reduce the heat, and simmer the mixture, uncovered, for 15 minutes.

   2 pounds fresh eel, skinned, drawn, and cut into 2-inch
     segments

Return the contents of the skillet to the boil, add the eel, and when the
liquid returns just to the boil for the second time, reduce the heat and
simmer the eel, uncovered, for about 10 minutes, or until it flakes easily
when tested with a fork.

With a slotted spoon, remove the eel to a flat pan. Strain the contents
of the skillet into a saucepan and, over high heat, reduce it to 1½ cups.

    ¼ cup Calvados *or* applejack

In a small saucepan, warm the Calvados, ignite it, and pour it over the eel; allow the flame to die.

At this point you may stop and continue later.

> **Beurre manié (page 4) made of 3 tablespoons each softened butter and flour**
> **½ cup heavy cream**
> **Salt**
> **Fresh-ground pepper**

Return the reduced broth to the simmer. Add the beurre manié, stirring the mixture until it is thickened and smooth. Stir in the cream, and season the sauce to taste with salt and pepper.

> **Reserved eel**
> **Reserved onions**
> **Reserved salt pork**
> **Fine-chopped parsley**

Return the eel and onions to the simmering sauce only long enough to heat them through, about 3 minutes. When at serving temperature, transfer the stew to a heated bowl and garnish it with the salt pork and a sprinkling of parsley.

Eel in Green Sauce (Anguille au Vert) (BELGIUM)

6 SERVINGS
PREPARATION: ABOUT 30 MINUTES
COOKING: 25 MINUTES
REFRIGERATES; FREEZES

The eel may be served as a hot main dish or as a chilled first course. The sauce must be made with fresh, not dried, herbs.

3 tablespoons butter
2½ pounds eel, skinned,
    drawn, and cut into
    2-inch segments
1 medium celery rib, with
    the leaves, chopped fine
Zest of 1 medium lemon
4 large mint leaves,
    chopped
Chopped leaves of 1 bunch
    of parsley
3 large sage leaves,
    chopped

Chopped leaves of 2
    savory sprigs
2 shallots, peeled and
    chopped fine *or* 4
    scallions (with a little
    of the crisp green
    part), trimmed and
    chopped fine
Chopped leaves of 3
    tarragon sprigs
Chopped leaves of 1 bunch
    of watercress

In a skillet with a lid, heat the butter and in it cook the eel segments, turning them often, until they are lightly browned. Add the remaining ingredients and, over gentle heat, cook the mixture, covered, for 5 minutes; stir it frequently.

2 cups dry white wine
    (recommended:
    Muscadet *or* Chenin
    Blanc)
½ cup sour cream or
    thickened cream
    (page 6)

2 eggs
Strained juice of 2 medium
    lemons
1 teaspoon cornstarch
Salt
Fresh-ground pepper

To the contents of the skillet, add the wine. Bring the liquid to the boil, reduce the heat, and simmer the eel, covered, for 10 minutes, or until it flakes easily when tested with a fork.

While the eel is cooking, combine the sour cream, eggs, lemon juice, and cornstarch in a mixing bowl; with a fork, blend them well. Stir the mixture into the contents of the skillet; do not allow it to boil. When the sauce is thickened, season it to taste with salt and pepper.

LEAN-FLESHED FISH DISHES

Lean-fleshed fish lend themselves particularly well to being cooked with wine. The following recipes may be made with cod, flounder, haddock, halibut, lingcod, pike, scrod, or sole. Fillets of flounder and sole are attractive when presented rolled; to determine the cooking time, measure the diameter of the rolled fillet and proceed according to the directions on page 159–160.

Because the wine or liqueur used in these recipes most frequently wears two hats (as cooking liquid for the fish and, reduced somewhat, as the basis for the sauce), I urge you to have all ingredients measured and all utensils ready before you start the recipe at hand; this way, you will not have to keep the cooked fish waiting (and drying out) any longer than necessary.

Fish Fillets with Grapes (FRANCE)

4 SERVINGS
PREPARATION AND COOKING: ABOUT 30 MINUTES

An adaptation of the French culinary classic *filet de sole Véronique.*

Lean-fleshed fish fillets (page 166) for 4 persons
**1½ cups dry white wine (recommended: Meursault *or*
    Sauvignon Blanc)**

In a poacher or other utensil large enough to accommodate them in a single layer, arrange the fish fillets. In a saucepan, bring the wine to the boil, add it to the poacher, and cook the fish, covered, according to the directions on page 159. Remove the fish to a heated serving platter and keep it warm. Over high heat, reduce the wine to ¾ cup. Strain it into a saucepan.

2 teaspoons cornstarch
½ teaspoon salt
¾ cup light cream

Blend the cornstarch and salt; stir the mixture into ¼ cup of the cream. When it is smooth, add it and the remaining cream to the wine. Over moderately high heat, cook the sauce, stirring constantly, until it is thickened and smooth.

**1 cup seedless grapes, stemmed, rinsed, drained on absorbent
    paper, and halved lengthwise**
Fine-chopped parsley

To the sauce, add the grapes; bring the mixture to serving temperature, spoon it over the fish, and garnish the dish with parsley. Serve the fish with green peas.

FISH FILLETS WITH ORANGE: In step one, use ½ cup strained fresh orange juice and 1 cup white wine; complete the step as written. In step two, omit the cornstarch and thicken the liquid with a beurre manié (page 4) of 2 tablespoons each softened butter and flour; stir in ¼ cup orange-flavored liqueur; in place of the light cream, use ¼ cup heavy cream. In step three, omit the grapes, but add the grated rind of 1 small orange. Complete the recipe as written.

Baked Fish Fillets, Greek Style

4 SERVINGS
PREPARATION: ABOUT 15 MINUTES
COOKING: ABOUT 10 MINUTES IN A 450° OVEN

A simple but satisfying recipe I encountered on an Aegean Island when I was journeying among them on a fifty-five-foot ketch.

4 tablespoons olive oil	Salt
2 medium onions, peeled and sliced thin	Fresh-ground pepper
	½ cup dry white wine
2 garlic cloves, peeled and chopped fine	(recommended: Demestica *or* Chablis)
Lean-fleshed fish fillets (page 166) for 4 persons	Fine-chopped parsley

Coat a baking dish with 2 tablespoons of the oil. Over the bottom of the dish, arrange a layer of half the onion slices and half the chopped garlic. Over this, arrange the fillets in a single layer. Season them to taste with salt and pepper. Cover them with the remaining onion and garlic and drizzle with the remaining olive oil. Add the wine. Bake the fish, un- covered, at 450° according to the directions on page 159. Garnish it with parsley.

Fish Fillets Marguery

4 SERVINGS
PREPARATION: ABOUT 1 HOUR
COOKING: ABOUT 15 MINUTES IN A 450° OVEN

A somewhat simplified version of the French culinary classic *filet de sole Marguery*.

36 mussels, bearded and scrubbed under cold running water

In a large saucepan, combine the mussels and about ¼ cup water. Over high heat, steam the mussels, tightly covered, for 5 minutes, or until they open; discard any that do not open. Over a bowl, to catch their liquid, remove the mussels from their shells; reserve them. Strain the mussel liquid and reserve it.

Lean-fleshed fish fillets (page 166) for 4 persons
1½ cups dry white wine (recommended: Muscadet *or*
  Chenin Blanc)

In a poacher or other utensil large enough to accommodate them in a single layer, arrange the fillets. In a saucepan, bring the wine to the boil, add it to the poacher, and cook the fish, tightly covered, according to the directions on page 159. Remove the fillets to a heated platter and keep them warm. Strain the wine into a saucepan and add to it the reserved mussel liquid.

Beurre manié (page 4)   **1 cup light cream**
  made of 3 tablespoons   **Nutmeg**
  each softened butter and   **Salt**
  flour   **Fresh-ground white pepper**

To the contents of the saucepan, add the beurre manié and, over moderately high heat, cook the mixture, stirring constantly, until it is thickened and smooth. Stir in the cream. Season the sauce to taste with nutmeg, salt, and pepper; do not allow it to boil.

2 egg yolks, beaten
2 tablespoons dry sherry
Reserved mussels
Fine-chopped parsley

Whip the egg yolks and sherry into the sauce. Arrange the mussels around the fillets. Spoon the sauce over all, and garnish the platter with parsley. Serve the dish with boiled new potatoes.

Fish Fillets with Pears

4 SERVINGS
PREPARATION: ABOUT 35 MINUTES
COOKING: ABOUT 20 MINUTES

2 tablespoons butter	¼ teaspoon paprika
4 shallots, peeled and	(preferably sweet
chopped fine, *or* 6	Hungarian)
scallions (white part	½ teaspoon salt
only), trimmed and	½ teaspoon white pepper
chopped fine	¼ cup dry white wine
2 ripe pears, peeled, cored,	(recommended:
and chopped	Chablis)

In a saucepan, heat the butter and in it cook the shallot until translucent. Add the remaining ingredients and cook the sauce, covered, stirring occasionally, for about 20 minutes, or until the pears are very tender. Allow the mixture to cool somewhat. In the container of a food processor or blender, whirl the sauce until it is smooth. Return it to the saucepan.

Lean-fleshed fish fillets (page 166) for 4 persons
2 ripe pears, peeled, quartered, cored, each quarter cut into
   3 lengthwise pieces
1 cup dry white wine

In a poacher or other utensil large enough to accommodate them in a single layer, arrange the fillets. Over the fish, arrange the pear slices. In a saucepan, bring the wine to the boil, add it to the poacher, and cook the fish, tightly covered, according to the directions on page 159. Remove the fish and pears to a heated serving platter and keep them warm. Over high heat, reduce the liquid to ¼ cup; strain it into the sauce.

Strained juice of 1 small lemon
Fine-chopped parsley

Stir the lemon juice into the sauce. Spoon the sauce over the fish and pear slices, and garnish the platter with parsley.

Fish Fillets in White Wine Sauce (FRANCE)

4 SERVINGS
PREPARATION: ABOUT 30 MINUTES
COOKING: ABOUT 12 MINUTES IN A 450° OVEN

> Lean-fleshed fish fillets (page 166) for 4 persons
> 1½ cups dry white wine (recommended: Muscadet or
>   Riesling)

In a buttered baking dish, arrange the fillets in a single layer. In a saucepan, bring the wine to the boil, pour it over the fillets, and bake them at 450° according to the directions on page 159. Remove them to a heated platter and keep them warm. Over high heat, reduce the wine to ¾ cup, and strain it into a saucepan.

> Beurre manié (page 4)   1 tablespoon tomato paste
>   made of 2 tablespoons   ½ teaspoon anchovy paste
>   each softened butter and   ½ teaspoon dried tarragon
>   flour   Fresh-ground white pepper
> 1 cup heavy cream

To the reduced wine, add the beurre manié; over moderate heat, cook the mixture, stirring constantly, until it is thickened and smooth. Reduce the heat and add the cream, tomato and anchovy pastes, and tarragon. Cook the sauce for a few minutes, stirring constantly; do not allow it to boil. Season it to taste with pepper. Spoon the sauce over the fish.

Variations:

In step one, add to the white wine ¼ cup Pernod. In step two, omit the tomato and anchovy pastes. Complete the recipe as written.

In step one, use ¾ cup dry sherry and ¾ cup water in place of the wine. In step two, omit the anchovy paste and tarragon; add ¼ cup fine-chopped parsley. Complete the recipe as written.

In step one, use ¾ dry vermouth and an 8-ounce bottle of clam juice in place of the wine. In step two, omit the anchovy paste. Complete the recipe as written.

In step one, use 1½ cups dry red wine (recommended: Mâcon *or* Gamay Beaujolais) in place of the white. In step two, omit the tomato paste and tarragon; add ¼ cup fine-chopped parsley and the strained juice of 1 small lemon. Complete the recipe as written.

Fish Pudding (DENMARK)

6 SERVINGS AS A MAIN COURSE; 8 SERVINGS AS A FIRST COURSE
PREPARATION: ABOUT 30 MINUTES
COOKING: 1 HOUR IN A 325° OVEN

1 pound lean-fleshed fish fillets (page 166), chopped coarse	3 tablespoons potato starch
2 eggs	A grating of nutmeg
1 cup milk	1 teaspoon salt
1 small onion, peeled and chopped	Fresh-ground white pepper

In the container of a food processor equipped with the steel blade, reduce the fish to a smooth paste by dropping a few pieces at a time into the container with the motor running. Turn the motor on and off several times to assure the smoothness of the ground fish. With the motor running, add the remaining ingredients. Transfer the mixture to a bowl.

At this point you may stop and continue later.

1 cup heavy cream
½ cup dry white wine (recommended: French vermouth *or* sauterne)
¼ cup fine-chopped parsley

Blend the cream, wine, and parsley into the fish. Spoon the pudding mixture into a buttered 5-cup ring mold or other mold. Set the mold in a pan of hot water and bake the pudding at 325° for 1 hour, or until a knife inserted at the center comes out clean. Serve the pudding, if you like, with Sauternes Sauce (page 303).

Fish Stew (GERMANY)

6 SERVINGS
PREPARATION: ABOUT 25 MINUTES
COOKING: ABOUT 10 MINUTES

2 tablespoons butter
2 medium carrots, scraped and cut into 2-inch julienne
1 large onion, peeled and sliced thin, the rings separated

2 cups dry white wine (recommended: Rhine wine)
1 (8-ounce) bottle of clam juice
½ teaspoon dried basil
½ teaspoon crumbled rosemary

In a large saucepan, heat the butter and in it cook the carrot and onion, stirring, until the carrot is limp. Add the remaining ingredients, bring the liquid to the boil, reduce the heat, and simmer the mixture, uncovered, for 5 minutes.

2 pounds assorted lean-fleshed fish fillets (page 166), cut into bite-size pieces
¼ pound medium shrimps, shelled and deveined

¼ pound sea scallops, halved
Salt
Fresh-ground pepper
⅓ cup fine-chopped parsley

Over high heat, return the contents of the saucepan to the boil. Add the fish, shrimps, and scallops. Cook them, uncovered, for about 10 minutes, or until the fish flakes easily when tested with a fork. Season the stew to taste with salt and pepper. Stir in the parsley. Offer the dish with a good crusty bread and sweet butter.

Fish Stew (GUADALOUPE)

4 SERVINGS
PREPARATION: ABOUT 30 MINUTES
COOKING: ABOUT 10 MINUTES

3 tablespoons butter
2 tablespoons oil
1 garlic clove, peeled and
    chopped fine
1 medium onion, peeled
    and chopped fine

1½ pounds lean-fleshed
    fish fillet (page
    166), cut into
    bite-size pieces
¼ cup light rum

In a large skillet with a lid, heat the butter and oil and cook the garlic and onion until they are just golden. Add the fish and brown it lightly. In a small saucepan, warm the rum, ignite it, and pour it over the contents of the skillet; allow the flame to die.

2 ripe tomatoes, peeled,
    seeded, and chopped
12 mushrooms, trimmed
    and sliced thin
¼ cup dry white wine
    (recommended:
    Chablis)

1 teaspoon curry powder
    (preferably sweet
    Madras)
Strained juice of 1 small
    lemon

To the contents of the skillet, add the tomato, mushroom slices, and wine. Stir the curry powder into the lemon juice; when the mixture is smooth, add it to the skillet. Simmer the fish, covered, for 10 minutes, or until it flakes easily when tested with a fork. Serve the stew over rice.

Braised Salt Cod (FRANCE)

4 SERVINGS
SOAKING TIME: OVERNIGHT
PREPARATION: ABOUT 30 MINUTES
COOKING: 10 MINUTES IN A 350° OVEN

2 cups water
1 bay leaf, crumbled
½ teaspoon dried thyme
2 pounds salt cod, soaked overnight in cold water to cover,
    drained, and cut into bite-size pieces

In a skillet, bring the water to the boil; add the seasonings and then the salt cod; poach the fish, uncovered, for 10 minutes, or until it flakes easily

when tested with a fork. Allow it to cool in the liquid to lukewarm; remove the skin and bones; reserve the liquid. With the tines of a fork,
flake the fish. Arrange it in a buttered baking dish.

4 tablespoons butter	½ cup dry red wine
2 tablespoons olive oil	(recommended: a
2 garlic cloves, peeled and	full-bodied
chopped fine	Burgundy)
2 large onions, peeled and	1 cup reserved fish cooking
chopped fine	liquid
4 tablespoons flour	Bouquet garni (page 4)

In a saucepan, heat the butter and oil and cook the garlic and onion until
they are just golden. Stir in the flour and, over gentle heat, cook the mixture for a few minutes. Gradually add the wine, stirring until the mixture
is thickened and smooth. Add the reserved liquid and the bouquet garni.
Bring the sauce to the boil, reduce the heat, and simmer it, uncovered,
for 20 minutes. Discard the bouquet garni.

At this point you may stop and continue later.

    1 cup butter-toasted croutons

Spoon the simmering sauce over the contents of the baking dish. Bake
the dish at 350° for 10 minutes. Garnish it with the croutons.

Seafood

From a chilled clam mousse created in my kitchen in a moment of in-
ventiveness to a shrimp and scallop risotto created in Italy, quite possibly
for a hungry fisherman's family, seafood is complemented by being
combined with wine. Have I a favorite seafood dish? Difficult question;
but I happily admit that the mussel and oyster recipes rank high at my
table. And on purely personal grounds, I am partial to squid with garlic;
accompanied by two of my favorite foods—*hearty* crusty bread and mixed
salad—this recipe is peasant fare fit for a king.

    These recipes invite your invention; therein lies the pleasure of cook-
ing. Two words of warning worth repeating: *More* wine does not necessarily mean a *better* dish; and, when using wines and spirits, whenever

possible salt the dish *after* it is completed. Because wines and spirits bring out flavors, you will need less salt than you might expect.

Chilled Clam or Mussel Mousse

6 TO 8 SERVINGS
PREPARATION: ABOUT 35 MINUTES
CHILLING TIME: 6 HOURS

Lightly oil and chill a 6-cup ring mold or other mold.

2 envelopes unflavored gelatin, softened for 5 minutes in ½ cup dry white wine (recommended: Chablis)

2 (6½-ounce) cans of minced clams *or* mussels (you should chop the mussels coarse), with their liquid

1½ cups cream-style large-curd cottage cheese

Strained juice of 1 small lemon

A few drops of Tabasco sauce

1½ teaspoons Worcester-shire sauce

1 teaspoon salt

Dissolve the gelatin over simmering watcr. In the container of a food processor equipped with the steel blade or a blender, combine the gelatin with the remaining ingredients. Whirl the mixture until it is smooth. Transfer it to a mixing bowl and chill it until it just begins to set.

⅓ cup fine-chopped parsley
1 cup frozen small peas, fully thawed to room temperature
4 scallions (with as much green as is crisp), trimmed and chopped fine
1 cup heavy cream, whipped

Beat the gelatin mixture briefly to assure its smoothness. Fold in the parsley, peas, and scallion. Then fold in the whipped cream. Using a rubber spatula, transfer the mixture to the prepared mold. Chill the mousse for at least 6 hours, or until it is thoroughly set.

Salad greens of your choice

Arrange the salad greens on a chilled serving platter. On top of them, unmold the mousse.

Crab Meat Charentais (FRANCE)

6 SERVINGS AS A FIRST COURSE; 4 SERVINGS AS A MAIN COURSE
PREPARATION AND COOKING: ABOUT 25 MINUTES

4 tablespoons butter	1 pound lump crab meat,
½ small green pepper,	picked over
seeded and chopped	½ cup Chablis
fine	½ teaspoon dried tarragon
6 scallions (with as much	Salt
green as is crisp),	Fresh-ground white pepper
trimmed and chopped	
fine	

In a saucepan, heat the butter and in it cook the pepper and scallion until they are limp. Add the crab meat, wine, and tarragon. Heat the crab meat, stirring gently, for 5 minutes. Season it to taste with salt and pepper.

⅓ cup brandy
Fine-chopped parsley

In a small saucepan, warm the bandy, ignite it, and pour it over the crab meat; allow the flame to die. Serve the crab meat on toast; garnish with parsley.

Frogs' Legs (FRANCE)

4 SERVINGS
PREPARATION AND COOKING: ABOUT 25 MINUTES (DOES NOT INCLUDE
SOAKING THE FROGS' LEGS)

16 to 20 large frogs' legs
Seasoned flour (page 6)
4 tablespoons butter

In ice water to cover, soak the frogs' legs for 1 hour; dry them on absorbent paper. Lightly dredge them in the seasoned flour, shaking off any excess. In a skillet, heat the butter and in it, over moderate heat, sauté the frogs' legs on both sides, a few at a time, until they are golden. As they are done, transfer them to a warmed serving platter.

4 shallots, peeled and	1 cup white Burgundy
chopped fine, *or* 5	Salt
scallions (white part	Fresh-ground white pepper
only), trimmed and	Fine-chopped parsley
chopped fine	

In the butter remaining in the pan, cook the chopped shallot until it is golden. Add the wine and, over high heat, deglaze the skillet. Reduce the wine by half. Season the sauce to taste with salt and pepper. Spoon it over the frogs' legs, and garnish the dish with parsley.

Variations:

In step one, omit the seasoned flour and sauté the frogs' legs in butter only. In step two, after cooking the shallot, use 1 cup Riesling to deglaze the skillet; thicken the sauce with a beurre manié (page 4) made of 1½ tablespoons each softened butter and flour; into the sauce, stir ¼ cup heavy cream. Complete the recipe as written.

A variation from Tennessee: In step one, use 8 tablespoons butter. In step two, use scallions; omit the white wine, but use in its place ⅓ cup dry sherry and ⅔ cup beef stock *or* canned beef bouillon. Complete the recipe as written.

Grenouilles Sautées à la Provençale (*Frogs' Legs, Provence Style*) (France): Simmer a 16-ounce can of peeled Italian tomatoes, uncovered, for 25 minutes, or until thickened. Follow step one as written. In step two, in place of the shallots, use 3 medium garlic cloves, peeled and chopped fine; after deglazing the skillet with the wine, add the thickened tomato; over high heat, reduce the sauce somewhat, stirring constantly. Complete the recipe as written.

Lobster Thermidor

4 SERVINGS

PREPARATION: ABOUT 20 MINUTES (THE PREPARATION TIME DOES NOT
   INCLUDE READYING THE LOBSTER)

COOKING: 15 MINUTES IN A 350° OVEN

The recipe may be prepared with cooked Maine lobster, cooked rock
lobster tails, or canned lobster meat. For a tasty change, make the recipe
with sea scallops, halved and poached in dry white wine.

> 4 tablespoons butter
> 1 cup fine-chopped mushrooms
> Salt
> Fresh-ground white pepper

In a skillet, heat the butter and in it, over moderate heat, cook the
chopped mushroom, stirring, for 3 minutes. Season it to taste with salt
and pepper.

> 1 pound cooked lobster
>   meat, cut into small
>   bite-size pieces
> ½ cup soft bread crumbs
> ⅓ cup fine-chopped parsley
> ¼ cup brandy
> ¾ cup dry sherry
>
> 1 tablespoon Worcester-
>   shire sauce
> A few drops of Tabasco
>   sauce
> 1¾ cups heavy cream
> 4 egg yolks

Away from the heat, add to the contents of the skillet the lobster meat,
bread crumbs, parsley, brandy, sherry, Worcestershire sauce, and Tabasco sauce. In a small mixing bowl, briefly beat together the cream and
egg yolks. Add the mixture to the skillet, stirring to blend all of the
ingredients well.

> ½ cup grated Parmesan cheese
> Paprika (preferably sweet Hungarian)

Spoon the lobster mixture into individual ramekins. Over the top, sprinkle first the cheese and then a dusting of paprika. Bake the ramekins at
350° for 15 minutes.

LOBSTER NEWBURG: Follow step one as written. Omit all ingredients in step two except the lobster. Add to the skillet the Newburg Sauce on page 300; add the lobster and heat it through.

Steamed Mussels (*Moules à la Marinière*) (FRANCE)

4 SERVINGS
PREPARATION: ABOUT 1 HOUR (DOES NOT INCLUDE READYING THE MUSSELS)
COOKING: 15 MINUTES

One of the most famous dishes made with mussels is also one of the easiest to prepare and tastiest to eat. For a flavor variation, stir ¼ cup Pernod into the completed sauce.

5 dozen mussels

Under cold running water, scrub the mussels with a stiff brush; discard any with crushed shells and any that do not remain shut. Remove the beards, those fringes of sea vegetation adhering to the hinged side. Soak the mussels in cold water to cover for several hours: the addition of cornmeal to the water encourages their flushing out of sand and silt. Drain and rinse them in a colander under cold water. Reserve them.

> **5 shallots, peeled and chopped fine, *or* 8 scallions (with a little**
> **of the green part), trimmed and chopped fine, *or* 1 large**
> **onion, peeled and chopped fine**
> **¼ teaspoon powdered thyme**
> **½ teaspoon fresh-ground white pepper**
> **1¼ cups dry white wine (recommended: Muscadet *or* Chablis)**

In a soup kettle, combine these four ingredients. Over high heat, bring the liquid to the boil, reduce the heat, and simmer the mixture, covered, for 8 minutes.

Reserved mussels

Return the kettle to the boil, add the mussels, and, over high heat, steam them, tightly covered, for about 5 minutes, or until they open. With a slotted spoon, transfer them to a heated serving bowl; discard any that have not opened. Through a double layer of cheesecloth, strain the liquid into a saucepan.

Beurre manié (page 4) made of 2 tablespoons each softened
  butter and flour
Fine-chopped parsley

Bring the liquid to the boil, add the beurre manié, and stir the mixture
until it is thickened and smooth. Pour the sauce over the mussels and
garnish the dish generously with parsley.

Variations:

An old New England recipe for steamed mussels: In a soup kettle, cook
1 large onion, peeled and chopped fine, in 4 tablespoons butter; add
1½ cups dry white wine and 1 cup water; add ¼ cup fine-chopped parsley and ½ teaspoon dried thyme. Bring the liquid to the boil, add the
mussels, and, over high heat, steam them, covered, as directed above.
Transfer the mussels to a heated serving bowl and strain the liquid.
Bring the broth to serving temperature and offer it in cups, together
with individual dishes of melted butter, as an accompaniment to the
mussels.

An Italian version of steamed mussels: In a soup kettle, heat ¼ cup
olive oil and in it cook 3 garlic cloves, peeled and chopped, ½ medium
green pepper, seeded and chopped, and 5 scallions (with some of the
green part), trimmed and chopped. Add 1 cup dry white wine, 2 teaspoons dried basil, 1 teaspoon dried mint, 2 teaspoons dried oregano,
⅓ cup fine-chopped parsley, ½ teaspoon red pepper flakes, 1 teaspoon
sugar, and 1 teaspoon salt. Bring the liquid to the boil, reduce the heat,
and simmer the mixture, covered, for 8 minutes. Return the liquid to
the boil, add the mussels, and steam them as directed in the recipe above.
Transfer them to a heated serving bowl; strain the broth and offer it as
an accompaniment to the mussels.

Mussels in Cream (FRANCE)

6 SERVINGS
PREPARATION AND COOKING: ABOUT 50 MINUTES (DOES NOT INCLUDE
  READYING THE MUSSELS)
REFRIGERATES

This dish from the Charente-Maritime is usually served with the mussels on the half shell. Admitting the attractiveness of this tradition, I feel that removing the mussels entirely from their shells makes eating the dish considerably more carefree and therefore more enjoyable.

> 5 dozen mussels, prepared for cooking (page 180)
> 1 bottle dry white wine (recommended: Chablis)
> Bouquet garni (page 4)

In a soup kettle, combine the mussels, wine, and bouquet garni. Over high heat, bring the wine to the boil and cook the mussels, tightly covered, for about 5 minutes, or until they open; shake the kettle often to speed their opening.

Remove the kettle from the heat and drain the mussels through a colander, collecting the liquid in a bowl. Over the bowl (to collect more of the liquid), remove the mussels from their shells, discarding any that have not opened. Put them in a little of the mussel liquid to keep them moist. Discard the shells. Strain the mussel liquid through a very fine sieve or cheesecloth and reserve it. Reserve the bouquet garni.

> 4 tablespoons butter
> 2 medium onions, peeled and chopped
> 4 tablespoons flour
> A pinch of cayenne pepper
>
> ½ teaspoon curry powder (preferably sweet Madras)
> Fresh-ground white pepper

In a saucepan, heat the butter and in it cook the onion until translucent. Stir in the flour and, over gentle heat, cook the mixture for a few minutes. Stir in the seasonings.

> ½ cup milk, scalded
> Strained juice of ½ medium lemon
> Reserved mussel liquid
> Reserved bouquet garni

Into the contents of the saucepan, stir the milk. Combine the lemon juice and mussel liquid and add the mixture to the saucepan; add the bouquet garni. Bring the sauce to the boil, reduce the heat, and simmer it for 10 minutes. Discard the bouquet garni.

At this point you may stop and continue later.

    ¼ cup heavy cream
    Salt

Reheat the sauce and stir in the cream. Season it to taste with salt.

    Reserved mussels
    ½ cup fine-chopped parsley

In a heated serving bowl or terrine, arrange the mussels. Pour the sauce over them. Garnish the dish with parsley and offer it in heated soup plates.

Oysters in Sherry Cream

6 SERVINGS
PREPARATION: ABOUT 30 MINUTES
COOKING: 30 MINUTES IN A 300° OVEN

The ingredients may be readied ahead of time, assembled and cooked quickly—and the dish offered triumphantly for a gala late supper.

    6 tablespoons butter
    ¾ teaspoon anchovy paste
    3 cups unseasoned
        croutons

In a saucepan, heat the butter and blend in the anchovy paste. Add the croutons, cover the saucepan, and shake it vigorously to coat the croutons well. Remove the cover and, over medium heat, toast the croutons, stirring to brown them evenly.

    1 quart shucked oysters,   Strained juice of 1 medium
        drained   lemon
    4 scallions (with as much   ¾ cup heavy cream, scalded
        green as is crisp), trimmed   ⅓ cup dry sherry
        and chopped fine   ½ cup grated Gruyère
    ⅓ cup fine-chopped parsley   cheese

In a mixing bowl, blend the oysters, scallions, parsley, lemon juice, the cream and sherry. Grate the cheese and cover it.

At this point you may stop and continue later.

Put half the croutons in a buttered baking dish. Over them, arrange a layer of half the oysters. Sprinkle the oysters with half the scallions, parsley, and lemon juice. Repeat the layers. Over all, pour the cream mixture. Sprinkle the top with the grated cheese. Bake the oysters at 300° for 30 minutes. Serve them in patty shells or on toast.

POACHED OYSTERS: In step one, use 8 tablespoons butter; omit the rest of this step. In step two, to the heated butter add the oysters, scallions, parsley, and lemon juice; omit the heavy cream and cheese; in place of the sherry, use dry white wine. Shake the saucepan gently to cover the oysters with the sauce, when their edges curl, serve them on toast.

Coquilles St. Jacques (Scallops in Wine Sauce with Cheese) (FRANCE)

6 SERVINGS
PREPARATION: ABOUT 30 MINUTES
COOKING: 10 MINUTES IN A 400° OVEN

In France, *coquilles St. Jacques* means simply "scallops," and by extension the term has come to refer to this celebrated way of preparing the succulent mollusk.

1 bay leaf, crumbled	1½ pounds sea scallops,
1 parsley sprig	rinsed, drained, and
8 peppercorns	(depending upon
½ teaspoon dried thyme	their size) halved or
1 cup dry white wine	quartered, or bay
(recommended:	scallops, rinsed,
Muscadet *or* Chenin	drained, and left
Blanc	whole

In a saucepan, combine the first five ingredients. Bring the liquid to the boil, reduce the heat, and simmer the mixture, covered, for 5 minutes. Return the liquid to the boil, add the scallops, reduce the heat, and simmer them, covered, for 2 minutes. Allow the scallops to cool in the liquid. With a slotted spoon, remove the cooled scallops and reserve them. Strain the liquid through a fine sieve and reserve it.

6 tablespoons softened butter
3 tablespoons flour
Reserved broth
2 egg yolks

1 teaspoon strained lemon
  juice
A few grains of cayenne
  pepper
Salt

In a saucepan, heat 2 tablespoons of the butter and in it, over gentle heat, cook the flour for a few minutes, stirring. Add the broth, stirring constantly until the mixture is thickened and smooth. Away from the heat, with a whisk or electric beater, beat the mixture vigorously, adding the remaining butter one tablespoon at a time. Beat in the egg yolks and then the lemon juice and cayenne pepper. Adjust the seasoning to taste with salt. Continue beating the sauce until it cools.

Reserved scallops
Fresh-grated Parmesan cheese

Into 6 or 8 large scallop shells or ramekins, spoon a little of the sauce. Add the scallops in equal amounts. Cover them with the remaining sauce and sprinkle the top with the cheese. Bake the *coquilles St. Jacques* at 400° for 10 minutes, or until they are bubbly and golden.

Scallops in Madeira Sauce

6 SERVINGS
PREPARATION AND COOKING: ABOUT 30 MINUTES

I do not suggest a separate cooking time because the dish, once started, is nonstop, range to table. Before beginning the recipe, ready all the ingredients, including the rice, which may be kept warm in the top of a double boiler over simmering water.

1 cup Chablis
1½ pounds sea scallops, rinsed, drained, and (depending upon
      their size) halved or quartered, *or* bay scallops, rinsed,
      drained, and left whole

In a saucepan, bring the wine just to the boil, add the scallops, and when the wine returns to the simmer, lower the heat and cook the scallops for 3 minutes, or until they are just done; do not overcook them. With a slotted spoon, remove them to a serving bowl and keep them warm.

½ cup Madeira
½ cup heavy cream

To the wine in the saucepan, add the Madeira and cream. Over high heat, reduce the liquid to 1½ cups.

Beurre manié (page 4) made of 2 tablespoons each softened butter and flour	Salt Fresh-ground white pepper Fine-chopped parsley Cooked rice for 6 persons

Into the reduced liquid, stir the beurre manié. When the sauce is thickened and smooth, season it to taste with salt and pepper and spoon it over the scallops. Garnish the dish with a generous sprinkling of parsley and serve it over rice.

Variations:

Twelve medium mushrooms, trimmed and prepared (page 5), and 1 shallot, peeled and chopped fine, may be added to the completed sauce, if you like.

SHRIMP IN MADEIRA SAUCE: In step one, use 1½ pounds medium raw shrimps, shelled and deveined. Complete the step and the recipe as written.

SHRIMP AND CRAB MEAT IN MADEIRA SAUCE: In step one, treat the shrimps as suggested above. Then, in 4 tablespoons butter, sauté briefly 2 (6-ounce) cans of crab meat, picked over, with 4 scallions, trimmed and chopped fine. Complete the recipe as written.

Scallops in Newburg Sauce

6 SERVINGS

PREPARATION AND COOKING: ABOUT 30 MINUTES

Please see the note at the head of the recipe for Scallops in Madeira Sauce, page 185.

6 tablespoons butter

1½ pounds sea scallops, rinsed, drained, and (depending upon
their size) halved or quartered, *or* bay scallops, rinsed,
drained, and left whole

½ teaspoon nutmeg

1 teaspoon paprika (preferably sweet Hungarian)

In the top of a double boiler over boiling water, heat the butter and in it
cook the scallops for 2 minutes. Stir in the nutmeg and paprika and cook
the mixture 1 minute longer.

4 egg yolks

1½ cups heavy cream

⅓ cup dry sherry

Salt

Fresh-ground white pepper

¼ cup fine-chopped
parsley

In a mixing bowl, beat together the egg yolks and cream. Add the mixture to the contents of the double boiler, stirring the sauce constantly
until it is thickened and coats a metal spoon. Away from the heat, stir in
the sherry; adjust the seasoning to taste with salt and pepper. Stir in the
parsley. Offer the scallops over rice or on buttered toast.

SHRIMP IN NEWBURG SAUCE: In step one, use 1½ pounds
medium shrimps, shelled and deveined; complete the step and the recipe
as written.

Scallops in Orange Sauce

6 SERVINGS

PREPARATION AND COOKING: ABOUT 30 MINUTES

MARINATION TIME: 1 HOUR

Please see the note at the head of the recipe for Scallops in Madeira
Sauce, page 185.

1½ pounds sea scallops, rinsed, drained, and (depending upon
their size) halved or quartered, *or* bay scallops, rinsed,
drained, and left whole

⅔ cup orange-flavored liqueur

In a shallow dish, arrange the scallops and over them pour the orange-flavored liqueur. Marinate, stirring them occasionally, for 1 hour.

Zest of 1 medium orange, cut into julienne
1 tablespoon sugar

While the scallops are marinating, combine the orange zest and sugar in a small saucepan. Add water to cover, bring it to the boil, reduce the heat, and simmer the zest, uncovered, for 5 minutes. Drain and reserve the orange zest.

6 tablespoons butter
Salt
Fresh-ground white pepper

Drain the scallops, reserving the marinade. In a skillet, heat the butter and in it, over gentle heat, cook the scallops for 5 minutes. Season them to taste with salt and pepper.

Reserved marinade
1½ cups heavy cream
Reserved orange zest

In a small saucepan, warm the marinade, ignite it, and pour it over the scallops; allow the flame to die. With a slotted spoon, transfer the scallops to a warmed serving dish. To the liquid remaining in the skillet, add the cream and, over high heat, reduce the sauce, stirring, for 5 minutes. Spoon the sauce over the scallops and sprinkle them with the reserved orange zest. Serve the scallops over rice or on buttered toast.

Scallops in Wine and Cheese Sauce

6 SERVINGS
PREPARATION: ABOUT 20 MINUTES
COOKING: 10 MINUTES IN A 400° OVEN

¾ cup dry white wine
    (recommended:
      Muscadet *or*
      Sauvignon Blanc)
1 small onion, peeled and
    chopped fine

1 bay leaf, crumbled
A few grains of cayenne
    pepper
½ teaspoon salt

In a saucepan, combine these five ingredients. Bring the liquid to the boil, reduce the heat, and simmer the mixture, covered, for 5 minutes.

> 1½ pounds sea scallops, rinsed, drained, and (depending upon their size) halved or quartered, *or* bay scallops, rinsed, drained, and left whole

Return the wine to the boil, add the scallops, and cook them, uncovered, for 3 minutes. With a slotted spoon, remove them to a lightly buttered baking dish. Strain the liquid and return it to the saucepan.

> Beurre manié (page 4) made of 3 tablespoons each softened butter and flour
> ½ cup heavy cream
> 1 cup grated Muenster cheese

Bring the liquid to the boil; stir in the beurre manié. When the mixture is thickened and smooth, stir in the cream. Pour the sauce over the scallops, sprinkle the top with the grated cheese, and bake the scallops, uncovered, at 400° for 10 minutes, or until the cheese is melted.

Shrimp, Hunter's Style (Scampi Cacciatore) (ITALY)

6 SERVINGS
PREPARATION: ABOUT 40 MINUTES
COOKING: 20 MINUTES

> 4 tablespoons olive oil
> 2 garlic cloves, peeled and chopped fine
> 1 medium onion, peeled and chopped
> ½ medium green pepper, seeded and chopped

In a large skillet, heat the olive oil and in it, over moderate heat, cook the garlic, onion, and pepper for 5 minutes.

> 1 (8-ounce) can of tomato sauce
> 12 mushrooms, trimmed and sliced thin
> ¾ cup dry red wine (recommended: Barbera *or* Zinfandel)
>
> ¼ teaspoon ground allspice
> 1 bay leaf
> ¼ teaspoon dried oregano

To the contents of the skillet, add these six ingredients. Bring the mixture to the boil, reduce the heat, and simmer the sauce, uncovered, for 20 minutes, or until it is thickened. While the sauce is cooking, prepare the shrimps.

1½ pounds raw medium shrimps, shelled and deveined

In a saucepan, combine the shrimps and lightly salted cold water to cover. Over high heat, bring the liquid just to the boil. Drain the shrimps at once.

Salt
Fresh-ground pepper
Fine-chopped parsley

Season the sauce to taste with salt and pepper. Stir in the shrimps and heat them through. Garnish the dish generously with parsley and offer it over spaghetti or linguine.

Shrimp and Scallop Risotto (ITALY)

6 TO 8 SERVINGS
PREPARATION: ABOUT 30 MINUTES
COOKING: 20 MINUTES IN A 350° OVEN

¼ cup olive oil
3 celery ribs, chopped fine
1 medium garlic clove,
    peeled and chopped
    fine

1 medium onion, peeled
    and chopped fine
½ medium green pepper,
    seeded and chopped
    fine
1½ cups raw natural rice

In a flameproof casserole, heat the olive oil and in it cook the celery, garlic, onion, and pepper until the onion is translucent. Add the rice, stirring to coat each grain. Remove the casserole from the heat.

18 pitted ripe olives,
quartered lengthwise
⅓ cup fine-chopped
parsley
1 (4-ounce) jar pimientos,
drained and chopped
A generous pinch of
saffron, crumbled
1 teaspoon turmeric

1 pound sea scallops,
rinsed, drained, and
(depending upon
their size) halved or
quartered
1 pound raw medium
shrimps, shelled and
deveined

Into the rice mixture, stir these seven ingredients.

At this point you may stop and continue later.

1½ cups dry white wine (recommended: Verdicchio *or*
Riesling)
¼ cup brandy
1 (8-ounce) bottle of clam juice
Grated Parmesan cheese

In a saucepan, combine the liquid ingredients and bring them to the boil. Pour them over the contents of the casserole. Transfer the casserole to the oven and bake the risotto, covered, at 350° for 20 minutes, or until the rice is tender and the liquid is absorbed. Offer the cheese separately. Served with a mixed green salad vinaigrette, this dish provides a satisfying light meal.

Shrimp in White Wine with Feta Cheese (GREECE)

6 SERVINGS
PREPARATION: ABOUT 30 MINUTES
COOKING: 20 MINUTES IN A 400° OVEN

¼ cup olive oil
1 celery rib, chopped fine
1 garlic clove, peeled and
chopped fine

¼ cup chopped parsley
12 scallions (with as much
green as is crisp),
chopped

In a flameproof casserole heat the olive oil and in it cook the celery, garlic, parsley, and scallion until the scallion is limp.

- 1 (16-ounce) can peeled Italian tomatoes, drained
- 1 teaspoon dried thyme
- 1 (8-ounce) bottle of clam juice

To the contents of the casserole, add the tomatoes, thyme, and clam juice. Simmer the mixture, uncovered, for 25 minutes. Remove it from the heat.

- 2 tablespoons olive oil
- 1½ pounds raw medium shrimps, shelled, deveined, and
     sprinkled with the strained juice of 1 medium lemon

In a saucepan, heat the olive oil and in it cook the shrimps until they are barely pink; more olive oil may be added as necessary. Stir the shrimps into the sauce mixture.

At this point you may stop and continue later.

- ½ cup Chablis
- 1 pound feta cheese, crumbled

To the contents of the casserole, add the wine; over the top, sprinkle the cheese. Bake the dish, uncovered, at 400° for 20 minutes, or until it is heated through and the cheese is melted. Serve the dish with rice.

Squid with Garlic

6 SERVINGS
PREPARATION: ABOUT 35 MINUTES
COOKING: 1 HOUR IN A 300° OVEN

No, the sauce is not overpowering; it is smooth and delicately flavored. Hippocrates recommended garlic as a health-giving herb; the ancient Egyptians offered it to their gods; the early Chinese believed that eating it increased intelligence; the Romans thought it made men courageous; as late as World War I, the British used its juice as an antiseptic. We are fortunate just to be able to eat it!

3 pounds small squid, the
    ink sac and cuttlebone
    removed, cut into
    rings, thoroughly rinsed
    in cold water, and
    drained on absorbent
    paper (using a 3-pound
    package frozen squid,
    thawed in cold water
    and cut into rings,
    will save you consider-
    able time and effort)
2 cups dry white wine
    (recommended: white
    Burgundy)
1 bulb of garlic (about 20
    cloves), the cloves
    peeled and left whole
1 large bunch of parsley,
    the leaves chopped
    coarse, the stems tied
    in a bundle

In a flameproof casserole, combine the squid, wine, garlic, and parsley leaves and stems. Bring the liquid to the boil, cover the casserole, and transfer it to the preheated oven. Bake the squid for 1 hour.

Beurre manié (page 4) of 3 tablespoons each softened
    butter and flour
Salt
Fresh-ground pepper

Transfer the casserole to the top of the range, remove the cover, and, over high heat, reduce the liquid for 5 minutes. Discard the parsley stems. Add the beurre manié, and stir the mixture until it is thickened and smooth. Season the squid to taste with salt and pepper. Serve the dish with rice.

Squid in Red Wine Sauce (ITALY)

6 SERVINGS
PREPARATION: ABOUT 30 MINUTES
COOKING: 35 MINUTES

Squid as it is prepared in Genoa, simply and easily.

4 tablespoons olive oil
2 garlic cloves, peeled and halved lengthwise

In a skillet with a lid, heat the olive oil and in it cook the garlic until it is deep golden; with a slotted spoon, remove and discard it.

   3 pounds small squid, the ink sac and cuttlebone removed, cut
      into rings, thoroughly rinsed in cold water, and drained
      on absorbent paper (using a 3-pound package frozen squid,
      thawed in cold water and cut into rings, will save you
      considerable time and effort)
  ⅓ cup chopped parsley
  1 teaspoon salt
  Fresh-ground pepper

In the hot garlic-flavored oil, cook the squid and parsley for 5 minutes, stirring. Season the squid with the salt and a grinding of pepper.

  1 cup dry red wine (recommended: Barbera *or* Zinfandel)
  1 (24-ounce) can of peeled Italian tomatoes
  1 (10-ounce) package of frozen peas, fully thawed to room
      temperature

To the contents of the skillet, add the wine and tomatoes. With the back of a spoon, mash the tomatoes. Bring the mixture to the boil, reduce the heat, and simmer the squid, uncovered, for 20 minutes, or until it is tender and the sauce is somewhat thickened. Add the peas and continue to simmer the dish for 10 minutes, or until they are tender. Remove the skillet from the heat and allow the squid to stand, covered, for 5 minutes before serving. Offer the dish with rice.

Egg and Cheese Dishes

With the exception of *fondue neufchâteloise*—a one-dish meal, really— these egg and cheese recipes double in brass as either main dishes for light meals or as appetizers. The reason there are so few recipes in this category is that the delicate flavor of eggs can be easily overwhelmed by a hearty wine (you will notice that *oeufs à la nivernaise* and eggs in wine sauce are supported by very flavorful ingredients). Cheese served with wine at table (one of my favorite courses) is a gastronome's delight; but, once again, unless the flavor of the wine is very delicate, as in the fondue, the combination of wine *cooked* with cheese seems almost a redundancy of good tastes that are better enjoyed separately.

Cheese Fondue (Fondue Neufchâteloise)
(SWITZERLAND)

4 SERVINGS
PREPARATION: ABOUT 20 MINUTES
COOKING: 15 MINUTES

Possibly the most famous dish from Switzerland, *fondue neufchâteloise* makes delightful and informal supper fare as each person dunks crusty bread into the common pot of golden melted cheese.

    8 ounces Emmenthal cheese, grated
    8 ounces Gruyère cheese, grated
    3 tablespoons flour

In a mixing bowl, toss together the cheeses and flour. Set aside and reserve the mixture.

At this point you may stop and continue later.

1 large garlic clove, peeled
    and split lengthwise
2 cups dry white wine
    (Recommended:
    Neuchâtel *or*
    Sauvignon Blanc)
Reserved cheese

¼ cup kirschwasser
Fresh-grated nutmeg
Fresh-ground white pepper
2 small loaves crusty
    French bread, cut into
    bite-size cubes

With the garlic, vigorously rub the sides of a 2-quart chafing dish; discard the garlic. Add the wine and bring it nearly to the boil. Add the reserved cheese, stirring constantly until it is melted. Reduce the heat and stir in the kirschwasser. Season the mixture to taste with nutmeg and pepper. At the table, arrange the chafing dish in its cradle over a low flame. Offer the bread cubes separately. Serve the fondue with a mixed green salad and vinaigrette dressing.

Variations:

AMERICAN FONDUE: In step one, use 1 pound American cheese, grated. In step two, use California Chablis and ¼ cup bourbon. Complete the recipe as written.

CHEESE FONDUE WITH BEER: Follow step one as written. In step two, in place of the wine, use 2 cups stale beer; add 1 tablespoon tomato paste; in place of the kirschwasser, use ¼ cup vodka. Complete the recipe as written.

Welsh Rarebit

6 SERVINGS

PREPARATION AND COOKING: ABOUT 20 MINUTES (PREHEAT THE BROILER)

12 ounces Cheddar cheese, grated coarse
1 tablespoon butter
A pinch of cayenne pepper
¾ teaspoon dry mustard

In the top of a double boiler, toss together these four ingredients. Over boiling water, cook them, stirring constantly, until the cheese begins to melt.

½ cup warm beer
1 egg, beaten
1 teaspoon Worcestershire sauce

Add these three ingredients, stirring until the cheese is fully melted and the mixture is smooth.

6 slices buttered toast

On a lightly buttered baking sheet, arrange the toast slices. Over them, spoon the cheese mixture. Cook the rarebits under a hot broiler for 2 minutes, or until the cheese is bubbly.

Variation:

In step one, omit the dry mustard. In step two, add 2 teaspoons Dijon mustard; in place of the beer, use dry white wine.

Onion and Cheese Soufflé

4 SERVINGS
PREPARATION: ABOUT 30 MINUTES
COOKING: 30 MINUTES IN A 350° OVEN

Thoroughly butter a 2-quart soufflé dish.

1 cup stale beer
1 large onion, peeled and
    chopped fine
6 scallions (with some of
    the green), trimmed
    and chopped fine

½ teaspoon sugar
1 teaspoon salt
¼ teaspoon white pepper

In a saucepan, combine these six ingredients. Bring the liquid to the boil, remove the pan from the heat, and allow it to stand, covered, while you make the roux.

4 tablespoons butter
4 tablespoons flour
A grating of nutmeg

In a saucepan, heat the butter and in it, over gentle heat, cook the flour for a few minutes. Stir in the nutmeg. Gradually add the beer mixture to the roux, stirring constantly until the batter is thickened and smooth.

⅓ cup fresh-grated Swiss or Cheddar cheese
4 egg yolks

Into the mixture, beat the cheese and then the egg yolks.

At this point you may stop and continue later.

4 or 5 egg whites, beaten until stiff but not dry

Into the mixture, beat one-fifth of the egg white; fold in the remainder. Using a rubber spatula, transfer the batter to the prepared dish. Bake the soufflé at 350° for 30 minutes, or until it is well puffed and golden.

Oeufs à la Nivernaise (FRANCE)

4 SERVINGS
PREPARATION AND COOKING: ABOUT 35 MINUTES

If you use eight eggs, the recipe may be served as a main dish for luncheon or supper.

1 tablespoon butter
1 medium onion, peeled
   and chopped fine
2 cups dry red wine
   (recommended:
   Beaujolais)

2 cups court bouillon
   (page 160)
1 garlic clove, peeled and
   chopped
Bouquet garni (page 4)
Salt
Fresh-ground pepper

In a saucepan, heat the butter and in it cook the onion until translucent. Add all the remaining ingredients except the salt and pepper and simmer the mixture, uncovered, for 15 minutes. Season it to taste with salt and pepper.

At this point you may stop and continue later.

> 4 slices firm bread, crusts removed
> Softened butter

Spread the bread with the butter and, under a preheated broiler or in a skillet, toast it, buttered side toward the heat, until it is crisp and golden. Reserve the toast.

> 4 eggs
> Beurre Manié (page 4) made of 1 tablespoon each softened
>   butter and flour
> Fine-chopped parsley

Return the contents of the saucepan to the simmer and discard the bouquet garni. In the liquid, poach the eggs (one can manage four at a time with the aid of a slotted spoon). While they are poaching, arrange the toast on a warm serving plate. Arrange the cooked eggs on the toast. Strain the liquid. Pour half of it back into the saucepan. (Reserve the remainder for use in another dish or in soup making.) Over high heat, boil the liquid for 2 minutes. Thicken it with the beurre manié. Cook the sauce an additional 2 minutes. Spoon it over the eggs and garnish the dish with parsley.

Eggs Poached in Red Wine (Oeufs à la Matelote) (FRANCE)

3 SERVINGS

PREPARATION AND COOKING: ABOUT 25 MINUTES (DOES NOT INCLUDE
    PREPARING THE BEAN PURÉE)

This dish is traditionally served on a pureé of kidney beans. To make the purée, drain a 20-ounce can of white kidney beans and, in the container of a food processor equipped with the steel blade, reduce them to a smooth paste. Season the purée to taste with salt and pepper and heat it, covered, in the top of a double boiler over simmering water. Arrange the purée on a serving platter and keep it warm in a low oven while you prepare the eggs.

1 cup dry red wine
(recommended: a
hearty Burgundy)
1 cup beef stock *or* canned
beef bouillon
1 garlic clove, peeled and
halved

1 small onion, peeled and
quartered
A grating of nutmeg
Salt
Fresh-ground pepper

In a skillet with a lid, combine these seven ingredients. Bring the liquid to the boil, reduce the heat, and simmer the mixture, covered, for 10 minutes. With a slotted spoon, discard the garlic and onion.

6 eggs

In the simmering liquid, poach the eggs. With a slotted spoon, arrange them on top of the bean purée. Over high heat, reduce the liquid to 1 cup.

Beurre manié (page 4) made of 1 tablespoon softened butter
and 1½ tablespoons flour
Fine-chopped parsley

Into the reduced liquid, stir the beurre manié until the sauce is thickened and smooth. Spoon it over the eggs and garnish the dish with parsley.

Eggs in Wine Sauce

4 SERVINGS
PREPARATION: ABOUT 35 MINUTES
COOKING: 5 MINUTES

4 tablespoons butter
12 white onions, peeled
(page 6)
1 tablespoon flour
1 cup dry red wine

(recommended:
Bordeaux *or*
Cabernet Sauvignon)
½ cup water

In a skillet, heat 2 tablespoons of the butter and in it sauté the onions until they are golden. Remove and reserve them. To the skillet, add the remaining butter and the flour; over gentle heat, cook the mixture for a few minutes. Add the wine, stirring constantly until the mixture is thickened and smooth. Stir in the water.

1 shallot, peeled and chopped
    fine *or* 1 scallion, trimmed
    and chopped fine
½ garlic clove, peeled
    and chopped fine

1 bay leaf
1 clove
Salt
Fresh-ground pepper

To the sauce, add the shallot, garlic, bay leaf, and clove. Simmer the mixture, uncovered, for 30 minutes (a little water may be added if necessary). Discard the bay leaf and clove, and season the sauce to taste with salt and pepper.

At this point you may stop and continue later.

4 slices firm bread, the crusts removed
Softened butter

Spread the bread with butter and, under a preheated broiler or in a skillet, toast it, buttered side toward the heat, until it is crisp and golden. Reserve the toast.

4 eggs
Fine-chopped parsley

In boiling water, cook the eggs for 4 or 5 minutes; refresh them under cold water and peel them.

On each individual warmed plate, arrange a slice of toast; on it, arrange an egg; over the egg, spoon some of the hot sauce. Garnish each serving with parsley.

Vegetables and Side Dishes

Because the flavor of vegetables is often overwhelmed by wines and spirits, and because their color is not enhanced by being combined with red wine, there are considerably fewer vegetable recipes than those for meats and desserts, for example. Personally, I prefer vegetables simply prepared, slightly undercooked, dressed with sweet butter and perhaps a sprinkling of herbs.

If you enjoy the taste of anise, Pernod or another like-flavored liqueur may be used discreetly with leaf vegetables and summer squash; add a little as you add the butter. Curiously, mashed potatoes are very good given the same treatment. Green peas tossed with soft butter and a little crème de menthe are also very tasty.

Baked Bananas With Sherry (UNITED STATES)

6 SERVINGS
PREPARATION: ABOUT 15 MINUTES
COOKING: 30 MINUTES IN A 350° OVEN

This Creole side dish is a tasty accompaniment to roast meats.

⅓ cup dry sherry
⅓ cup dark brown sugar
4 tablespoons apricot jam

4 tablespoons butter,
  melted and cooled
Strained juice of 1 medium
  lemon

In a mixing bowl, combine and blend these five ingredients.

6 firm, ripe bananas, peeled and halved lengthwise

In a buttered baking dish, arrange the bananas, cut side down. Over them, spread the sherry mixture.

At this point you may stop and continue later.

Bake the bananas at 350° for 30 minutes, or until they are tender.

Sautéed Beets or Carrots

4 SERVINGS
PREPARATION: ABOUT 10 MINUTES
COOKING: ABOUT 50 MINUTES FOR BEETS, 20 MINUTES FOR CARROTS
REFRIGERATES

1 pound beets, unscraped *or* 1 pound carrots, scraped

In a saucepan, combine the beets or carrots and cold water to cover. Over high heat, bring the liquid to the boil, reduce the heat, and simmer the vegetable, covered, for 45 minutes (beets) or 15 minutes (carrots), or until it is fork-tender. Refresh it under cold water; peel (beets) and slice.

4 tablespoons butter
Grated rind of 1 medium orange
¼ cup orange-flavored liqueur
Salt

In a skillet, heat the butter and in it sauté the vegetable, stirring frequently to coat it well. Sprinkle on the orange rind. Add the liqueur, stirring gently as the alcohol evaporates. Season with salt, to taste, and serve the beets or carrots when they are heated through.

Variation:

In step two, omit the orange rind and, in place of the orange-flavored liqueur, use ¼ cup anise-flavored liqueur (pastis, Pernod).

Broccoli or Cauliflower, Roman Style (ITALY)

4 SERVINGS
PREPARATION: ABOUT 10 MINUTES
COOKING: 15 MINUTES
REFRIGERATES

1 medium bunch of broccoli
 or medium head of
 cauliflower
4 tablespoons olive oil
2 garlic cloves, peeled and
 halved lengthwise

Salt
Fresh-ground pepper
2 cups dry white wine
 (recommended:
 Soave or Chablis)

Trim the broccoli or cauliflower and cut it into flowerets. Rinse and drain them well. In a large skillet, heat the olive oil and in it brown the garlic. With a slotted spoon, remove and discard the garlic. To the flavored oil, add the vegetable and salt and pepper to taste. Over medium heat, cook it, stirring to coat it well. Add the wine, bring the liquid to the boil, reduce the heat, and simmer the vegetable, covered, for 10 minutes, or until it is tender.

Brussels Sprouts

6 SERVINGS
PREPARATION: ABOUT 15 MINUTES
COOKING: 15 MINUTES
REFRIGERATES

1½ pounds Brussels sprouts, trimmed, the wilted leaves
 removed
1 tablespoon salt

In a mixing bowl, combine the Brussels sprouts and cold water to cover; add the salt and allow the sprouts to soak for 15 minutes. Drain them.

In lightly salted boiling water to cover, cook the Brussels sprouts for 15 minutes, or until they are fork-tender; do not overcook them.

> 3 tablespoons softened butter
> Strained juice of ½ medium lemon
> ¼ cup anise-flavored liqueur (pastis, Pernod)

In a mixing bowl, combine the butter, lemon juice, and liqueur. Drain the cooked Brussels sprouts and add them, hot, to the contents of the bowl. Using a rubber spatula, gently stir them so that they are well coated.

Braised Cabbage

6 SERVINGS
PREPARATION: ABOUT 10 MINUTES
COOKING: 40 MINUTES IN A 350° OVEN

1 medium head of cabbage, the outer leaves removed	(recommended: Chablis)
1 cup chicken stock *or* defatted canned chicken broth	Softened butter Sugar Salt
1 cup dry white wine	Fresh-ground white pepper

Cut the cabbage into 6 equal portions; cut out and discard the core. In a shallow baking dish, arrange the cabbage with the cut surfaces exposed. Add the chicken stock and wine. On the exposed surfaces, spread a fairly generous amount of butter. Season the vegetable to taste with a sprinkling of sugar, salt, and pepper. Cover the dish tightly with foil.

At this point you may stop and continue later.

Bake the cabbage, covered, at 350° for 40 minutes, or until it is tender-crisp; baste it often with the pan juices.

Variations:

In step one, cut the cabbage into coarse shreds; in a skillet, heat 4 tablespoons butter, add the cabbage, and cook it until it is wilted; reduce the chicken stock to ½ cup; add 1 teaspoon dried tarragon. Instead of baking the cabbage, simmer it on top of the stove, covered, for 15 minutes, or until it is tender-crisp; remove the cover and, over high heat, reduce the sauce, stirring the cabbage as you do so.

In step one, reduce the chicken stock to ¾ cup and add ¼ cup Pernod. In step two, remove the cabbage to a heated serving dish after baking; thicken the pan juices with a beurre manié (page 4) made of 2 tablespoons each softened butter and flour; flavor the sauce with a grating of nutmeg and pour it over the vegetable.

In step one, cut the cabbage into coarse shreds; in a skillet, heat 2 tablespoons each butter and bacon fat; cook the cabbage in this mixture, tossing it lightly to coat it well, for 15 minutes, or until it is tender-crisp; season it with the sugar, salt, and pepper. Do not bake the cabbage, but add for the final 5 minutes of stovetop cooking 1 cup seedless grapes, stemmed, rinsed, drained on absorbent paper, and halved lengthwise.

Cabbage Braised in Champagne (GERMANY)

6 SERVINGS
PREPARATION: ABOUT 20 MINUTES
COOKING: 30 MINUTES

Although traditionally made with champagne, the dish may be prepared with any dry white wine.

4 tablespoons butter
2 medium onions, peeled and chopped fine
2 tart apples, peeled, cored, and sliced thin

In a skillet with a lid, heat the butter and in it cook the onion until translucent; add the apple slices and cook them for 5 minutes.

1 small (about ¾ pound) green cabbage, cored and cut into fine shreds	2 tablespoons sugar Strained juice of ½ large lemon
1 small (about ¾ pound) red cabbage, cored and cut into fine shreds	2 teaspoons grated lemon peel
½ cup champagne	Salt Fresh-ground white pepper

To the contents of the skillet, add the green and red cabbage, tossing the mixture to blend it; add the champagne, and sprinkle the lemon juice and seasonings over all. Bring the liquid to the boil, reduce the heat, and simmer the vegetable, covered, for 20 minutes, or until it is tender-crisp.

    1 cup champagne

Add the champagne to the cabbage. Cook the vegetable, uncovered, over high heat for 10 minutes more.

Broiled Eggplant Slices

6 SERVINGS
PREPARATION: ABOUT 15 MINUTES
COOKING: 6 MINUTES IN A PREHEATED BROILER

¼ cup dry red wine (recommended: Barbera or Zinfandel)	Salt
	Fresh-ground pepper
4 tablespoons olive oil	2 medium eggplants, sliced ½ inch thick
1 large garlic clove, peeled and put through a press	

Combine the wine, olive oil, and garlic. Blend the mixture and season it to taste with salt and pepper. With a pastry brush, generously coat one side of the eggplant slices. Arrange the eggplant, coated side up, on a large baking sheet. Broil the eggplant for 3 minutes. Turn it, coat the second side, and return the vegetable to the broiler for 3 minutes longer, or until it is tender.

Kidney Beans or Lentils

6 SERVINGS
PREPARATION: ABOUT 20 MINUTES
STANDING TIME: 1 HOUR
COOKING: 1¼ HOURS
REFRIGERATES; FREEZES

Dry flageolets may also be prepared in this way.

> 1 pound dried red kidney beans or lentils*
> Bouquet garni (page 4)
> Salt

In a large saucepan, combine the kidney beans and cold water to cover by at least 1 inch; add the bouquet garni and salt to taste. Over high heat, bring the liquid to the boil and cook the beans, uncovered, for 10 minutes. Remove the pan from the heat and allow the beans to stand, covered, for 1 hour. Over high heat, return the liquid to the boil, reduce the heat, and simmer the beans, covered, for 1 hour, or until they are tender but still hold their shape. Drain and refresh them under cold water; discard the bouquet garni. Please note that lentils are frequently packaged as precooked or tenderized; in that case, follow the cooking directions on the package.

> 3 slices bacon, diced
> 1 medium onion, peeled and chopped
> 1 tablespoon flour
> 1 cup dry red wine (recommended: a hearty Burgundy)
> Salt
> Fresh-ground pepper

In a skillet, cook the bacon until it is crisp and golden; with a slotted spoon, remove it to absorbent paper and reserve it. In the bacon fat, cook the onion until translucent. Stir in the flour and, over gentle heat, cook the mixture for a few minutes. Add the wine, stirring until the sauce is thickened and smooth. Season it to taste with salt and pepper.

> Reserved beans
> Reserved bacon

Into the sauce, gently stir the beans. Allow them to simmer until they are heated through. Garnish the beans with the bacon.

Mushroom Ragout

6 SERVINGS
PREPARATION: ABOUT 20 MINUTES
COOKING: 30 MINUTES
REFRIGERATES

A light-meal main dish for 4 persons.

> 4 tablespoons butter
> 1½ pounds mushrooms, trimmed and quartered
> 2 shallots, peeled and chopped fine, *or* 3 scallions (white part
>   only), trimmed and chopped fine

In a skillet, heat the butter and in it cook the mushrooms and shallots, tossing them often to coat them well, for 10 minutes.

> 3 tablespoons butter
> 3 tablespoons flour
> ¼ teaspoon powdered thyme
> ½ cup dry red wine
>   (recommended:
>   Médoc *or* other
>   claret)
>
> ¾ cup chicken stock *or*
>   canned chicken
>   broth
> Salt
> Fresh-ground pepper
> Fine-chopped parsley

In a saucepan, heat the butter and in it, over gentle heat, cook the flour for a few minutes. Stir in the thyme. Add the wine and chicken stock, stirring constantly until the mixture is thickened and smooth. Season it to taste with salt and pepper. Spoon the sauce over the mushrooms, bring them to serving temperature, and garnish them with parsley.

Variations:

MUSHROOMS WITH HAM (a pleasant supper dish): In step one, flavor the butter by cooking in it 1 large garlic clove, peeled and halved lengthwise (discard the garlic); break the stems from the mushrooms and chop them fine; cook the mushroom caps with the shallots, as directed. In step two, add to the butter, before the addition of the flour, the chopped mushroom stems and ½ pound lean boiled ham, chopped fine. Complete the recipe as written.

MUSHROOMS IN MUSTARD SAUCE: Follow step one as written. In step two, in place of red wine, use Chablis mixed with 4 teaspoons Dijon mustard. Complete the recipe as written. This variation makes an attractive first course, served on toast.

RUMANIAN MUSHROOM STEW: In step one, in place of the butter, use olive oil; after cooking the mushrooms, sprinkle them with the strained juice of 1 medium lemon. In step two, in place of the thyme, use 1 tablespoon fine-chopped chives and 1 teaspoon fennel seed, crushed in a mortar with a pestle; in place of the red wine use Chablis. Complete the recipe as written.

BRAISED MUSHROOMS WITH SAFFRON: Follow step one as written. In step two, omit the thyme, but use a generous pinch of saffron, crumbled; in place of the red wine, use Chablis; omit the chicken stock, but use an equal quantity of light cream. Complete the recipe as written.

Onions Monégasque

6 SERVINGS
PREPARATION: 20 MINUTES
COOKING: 30 MINUTES
REFRIGERATES

Onions, Monaco style, traditionally served chilled as a side dish with cold meats, are equally tasty as a first course. I serve them hot in cold weather, chilled in warm.

> 30 small white onions, peeled (page 6)
> 1½ cups dry white wine (recommended: Chablis)
> 1½ tablespoons white wine vinegar
>
> ½ small lemon, sliced very thin and seeded
> 1 teaspoon sugar
> ½ teaspoon salt
> Fresh-ground white pepper

In a saucepan, combine these seven ingredients. Bring the liquid to the boil, reduce the heat, and simmer the onions, covered, for 15 minutes, or until they are tender-crisp.

> 3 tablespoons tomato paste
> ⅔ cup golden seedless raisins

Into the contents of the saucepan, stir the tomato paste and raisins. Continue to simmer the mixture, covered, for 10 minutes.

With a slotted spoon, remove the onions to a serving dish. Over high heat, reduce the sauce, stirring constantly, until it is thick. Pour the sauce over the onions and allow them to cool before refrigerating, if they are to be served chilled.

Potato Salad (UNITED STATES)

6 TO 8 SERVINGS
PREPARATION AND COOKING: ABOUT 40 MINUTES

This recipe from New Orleans may be served warm or chilled.

½ cup dry white wine
(recommended:
Chenin Blanc)
½ cup Vinaigrette Sauce
(page 304)
2 tablespoons anise-flavored
liqueur (pastis,
Pernod) (optional)
2 medium celery ribs,
diced
1 large garlic clove, peeled
and put through a press

⅓ cup fine-chopped
parsley
1 small green pepper,
seeded and diced
5 shallots, peeled and
chopped fine, or 6
scallions (with as
much of the green as
is crisp), trimmed and
chopped fine
1 teaspoon dried tarragon
Salt, to taste

In a mixing bowl, combine and blend these ingredients. Allow the dressing to stand at room temperature for 6 hours.

2½ pounds red-skinned new potatoes

In boiling salted water to cover, cook the potatoes, uncovered, for about 12 minutes, or until they are just fork-tender. Drain and allow them to cool slightly. As soon as they can be handled, peel them and slice into ¼-inch rounds. Arrange the rounds in a large bowl.

If you wish to serve the salad hot, heat the prepared dressing, but do not allow it to boil. Pour it over the potatoes and toss the mixture gently.

If you wish to serve the salad chilled, pour the prepared dressing over the potatoes, toss the mixture gently, and chill it for at least 6 hours.

Braised Red Cabbage

6 SERVINGS
PREPARATION: ABOUT 20 MINUTES
COOKING: 1 HOUR
REFRIGERATES

4 tablespoons butter
1 large onion, peeled and
chopped fine
3 tablespoons dark brown
sugar

½ teaspoon allspice
½ teaspoon ground cloves
1 teaspoon salt
1 medium red cabbage,
cored and shredded

In a flameproof casserole, heat the butter and in it cook the onion until translucent. Add the sugar, stirring until it is dissolved; stir in the spices and salt. Add the cabbage. Toss the mixture to blend it well.

At this point you may stop and continue later.

Dry red wine (recommended: a hearty Burgundy)

Add wine just to cover. Bring the liquid to the boil, reduce the heat, and simmer the cabbage, covered, for 40 minutes. More wine may be added as needed.

½ cup golden raisins
2 medium apples, peeled, cored, and diced

Add the raisins and apples. Continue to simmer the cabbage for 20 minutes longer, or until it is tender-crisp.

¼ cup strained fresh orange juice
2 tablespoons cider vinegar
1½ teaspoons cornstarch

Combine the orange juice and vinegar; add the cornstarch, stirring until the mixture is smooth. Add it to the cabbage, stirring gently until the sauce is somewhat thickened and smooth.

Variations:

In step one, in place of the butter, use the fat from 6 slices of bacon, diced and cooked until crisp and golden. In step three, garnish the cabbage with the bacon bits.

In step one, increase the sugar to ½ cup. In step three, in place of the raisins, use 2 cups cranberries, rinsed and drained.

In step one, omit the sugar. In step two, in place of dry red wine, use ruby port.

Rice, Milan Style (Risotto alla Milanese) (ITALY)

6 SERVINGS
PREPARATION: ABOUT 15 MINUTES
COOKING: 15 MINUTES
REFRIGERATES

4 tablespoons butter
1 small onion, peeled
   and chopped fine
1½ cups raw natural rice
A generous pinch of saffron,
   crumbled
1 cup dry white wine
   (recommended:

Verdicchio *or*
   Chardonnay)
2 cups chicken stock *or*
   canned chicken broth
Salt
Fresh-ground white pepper
⅓ cup fresh-grated
   Parmesan cheese

In a saucepan, heat the butter and in it cook the onion until translucent. Add the rice, stirring to coat each grain. Stir in the saffron. Add the wine and chicken stock. Bring the liquid to the boil, reduce the heat, and simmer the rice, covered, for 15 minutes, or until it is tender and the liquid is absorbed. Season the rice to taste with salt and pepper. Stir in the Parmesan cheese.

Variations:

Cook ½ pound mushrooms, trimmed and sliced, in 2 tablespoons butter and ½ cup wine; when they are limp, strain them and add to their liquid wine to equal 1 cup; use this as the wine ingredient of the recipe. Before adding the Parmesan cheese to the cooked rice, fold in the mushrooms.

For a fresh vegetable taste, stir fine-chopped parsley into the cooked rice.

In place of dry wine, use dry vermouth; omit the Parmesan cheese, but stir into the cooked rice the grated rind of 1 medium lemon and ⅓ cup fine-chopped parsley.

Sautéed Spinach with Pears

6 SERVINGS
PREPARATION: ABOUT 30 MINUTES
COOKING: 5 MINUTES
REFRIGERATES

> 2 (10-ounce) packages fresh spinach, the woody stems removed, the leaves rinsed, wilted for 20 seconds in several quarts of lightly salted boiling water, drained, and chopped, *or* 2 (10-ounce) packages of frozen chopped spinach, fully thawed to room temperature

In a colander or heavy sieve, press the spinach until it is as dry as possible.

> 3 tablespoons butter
> 3 scallions (white part only), trimmed and chopped fine

In a large skillet, heat the butter and in it cook the scallion until translucent. Add the spinach and, over medium heat, cook it, stirring, until it is quite dry.

> 2 firm ripe pears, peeled, cored, and chopped fine
> A grating of nutmeg
> Salt
>
> Fresh-ground pepper
> ¼ cup pear-flavored liqueur (recommended: poire Williams)

Add the chopped pear and seasonings, tossing lightly to blend the ingredients. Stir in the liqueur; over high heat, cook the spinach, stirring, to evaporate the alcohol.

Baked Winter Squash

1 MEDIUM ACORN OR HUBBARD SQUASH YIELDS 2 SERVINGS
PREPARATION: ABOUT 10 MINUTES
COOKING: 1 HOUR IN A 350° OVEN

Halve the squash lengthwise, seed it, and score the flesh with a sharp knife. In the cavity of each half arrange:

- 1 tablespoon dark brown sugar
- 2 tablespoons butter
- 3 tablespoons dark rum *or* bourbon whiskey

Bake the squash at 350° for 1 hour, or until it is fork-tender.

Sweet Potato Casserole (UNITED STATES)

6 SERVINGS
PREPARATION: ABOUT 30 MINUTES (DOES NOT INCLUDE BOILING THE SWEET
   POTATOES)
COOKING: 30 MINUTES IN A 375° OVEN

A recipe from Tennessee, which may also be made with cooked winter squash.

6 medium sweet potatoes

In lightly salted boiling water to cover, cook the sweet potatoes in their skins for 25 minutes, or until they are very tender. Peel and mash them.

4 tablespoons softened butter	¼ cup dark brown sugar
3 eggs, beaten	½ teaspoon each
½ cup heavy cream	cinamon and nutmeg
⅓ cup bourbon whiskey *or* brandy *or* Madeira *or* sherry	*or* ginger and mace

Into the sweet potato, beat these ingredients.

½ cup golden raisins *or* pecan halves
Grated rind of 1 large orange (optional)

Stir in the raisins. Using a rubber spatula, transfer the mixture to a buttered baking dish. Sprinkle the top with orange rind.

At this point you may stop and continue later.

Bake the casserole at 375° for 30 minutes, or until it is lightly browned.

Sweet Potato and Banana Casserole

6 SERVINGS
PREPARATION: ABOUT 30 MINUTES
COOKING: 10 MINUTES IN A 450° OVEN
REFRIGERATES

5 medium sweet potatoes

In boiling water to cover, cook the potatoes in their skins for 20 minutes, or until they are very tender. Peel and chop them coarse.

2 ripe bananas, peeled and   **Fresh-grated nutmeg**
    chopped coarse   **Salt**
¼ cup dark rum   **Fresh-ground pepper**
2 egg yolks

In the container of a food processor equipped with the steel blade, combine the potatoes, bananas, rum, egg yolks, and nutmeg. Whirl the mixture until it is reduced to a smooth purée. Season the purée to taste with salt and pepper. Transfer it to a mixing bowl.

At this point you may stop and continue later.

2 egg whites, beaten until stiff but not dry

Into the potato mixture, fold the egg white. Using a rubber spatula, transfer it to a buttered casserole. Bake the potato at 450° for 10 minutes, or until it is heated through and lightly browned.

Tomato Aspic

6 TO 8 SERVINGS
PREPARATION AND COOKING: 1 HOUR
CHILLING TIME: 6 HOURS

Lightly oil and chill a 2-quart mold or serving bowl.

  4 tablespoons butter
  3 celery ribs, with their leaves, chopped coarse
  1 garlic clove, peeled and chopped
  2 medium onions, peeled and chopped

In a large saucepan or soup kettle, heat the butter and in it cook the celery, garlic, and onion, covered, for 10 minutes, or until they are tender.

  6 ripe medium tomatoes,   3 cloves
     chopped coarse   1 teaspoon dried tarragon
  3 cups white Burgundy   1 tablespoon sugar
  1 (6-ounce) can of tomato   1 tablespoon
     paste   Worcestershire sauce
  Grated rind and strained   1 teaspoon salt
     juice of 1 large lemon   ½ teaspoon fresh-ground
  1 bay leaf, crumbled   pepper

To the contents of the saucepan, add these ingredients. Simmer the mixture, covered, for 40 minutes.

  2 envelopes plus 1 teaspoon unflavored gelatin
  1 cup tomato juice

In a large mixing bowl, sprinkle the gelatin over the tomato juice and allow it to soften for 5 minutes. Into the gelatin, strain the hot tomato mixture, discarding the residue and stirring to dissolve the gelatin. Allow the aspic to cool.

  3 celery ribs, diced

Drop the celery into boiling salted water to cover for 15 seconds; refresh it in cold water and drain it. Stir it into the aspic. Pour the aspic into the prepared mold or bowl. Chill it for at least 6 hours, or until it is thoroughly set.

  Salad greens of your choice

Arrange the salad greens on a chilled serving platter. On top of them, unmold the aspic.

Vegetables Braised in Wine

6 SERVINGS
PREPARATION: ABOUT 10 MINUTES
COOKING: TIME WILL VARY DEPENDING UPON THE VEGETABLE

Celery, endive, fennel, leek, lettuce, and onion braise easily and tastily.

CELERY: Separate the stalks, cut off the leaves, rinse the vegetable thoroughly, and shake off any excess water. Cut it into uniform widths and lengths (½ inch × 4 inches is a size easy to handle and attractive to serve). Allow 6 to 8 pieces per serving. Cooking: 15 to 20 minutes.

ENDIVE: Trim the bottom end. If the endives are very large, halve them lengthwise; usually, however, you can select endives of about 1 inch in diameter and 5 inches long, a good size for an individual serving. Cooking: 20 minutes.

FENNEL: Cut off and discard the branches; trim the bottom end. Cut the bulbs in half. A small bulb will yield one serving; a large bulb, two. Cooking: 25 minutes.

LEEK: Cut off and discard the green part (reserve it for use in soup making); trim the bottom end. Separating the leaves, rinse the leeks thoroughly under fast-running cold water. Two medium leeks cut 6 or 7 inches long yield one serving. Cooking: 20 minutes.

LETTUCE: From a medium, firm head of leaf lettuce, remove the loose outer leaves; trim the bottom end. Rinse the lettuce under fast-running cold water, but do not pull it apart. Shake off any excess water. Tie the lettuce with string so that the leaves will lie in place. Afer you have braised the lettuce, remove the string, cut each head in half lengthwise, and arrange the halves on a heated serving plate. One medium head will yield two servings. Cooking: 10 minutes.

ONION: Use either 6 medium-large onions, peeled and cut into ¼-inch rounds, or 36 small white onions, peeled (page 6). Cooking in both instances: 15 minutes.

To Braise the Vegetables

> 4 tablespoons butter
> Salt
> Fresh-ground white pepper

In a large skillet with a lid, heat the butter, rotating the skillet to spread it evenly over the bottom of the pan. Add the vegetable of your choice, cut side down (if this instruction applies), and season it taste with salt and pepper.

Select a braising liquid, or create one of your own:

> 1 cup dry white wine (recommended: Chablis *or* sauterne) *or* ½ cup dry white wine plus ½ cup chicken stock (or defatted canned chicken broth) *or* ¾ cup dry vermouth plus ¼ cup chicken stock *or* ½ cup dry white wine plus ½ cup strained fresh orange juice *or* ¾ cup Madeira plus ¼ cup chicken stock *or* ¾ cup dry sherry plus ¼ cup strained fresh orange juice

Pour the braising liquid over the vegetable. Bring it rapidly to the boil and, over high heat, cook the vegetable, covered, for half the suggested cooking time. Remove the cover and reduce the liquid so that it is slightly thickened. If you like, sprinkle the vegetable with 2 teaspoons sugar to glaze it. While the sauce is reducing, baste the vegetable with a bulb baster. At this point, you may want to add another flavor by the addition of an alcohol.

Before removing the vegetable from the skillet, warm, ignite, and pour over it ¼ cup of one of the following: akvavit, Geneva, orange-flavored liqueur, or Pernod (this last is not advised with fennel, as both are anise-flavored).

Mixed Vegetable Casserole

8 TO 10 SERVINGS
PREPARATION: ABOUT 30 MINUTES
COOKING: 35 MINUTES
REFRIGERATES

3 large carrots, scraped
   and sliced thin
3 celery ribs, chopped
2 garlic cloves, peeled and
   chopped fine
1 medium bulb of fennel,
   chopped
1 large head of Boston
   lettuce, rinsed, shaken
   dry, and shredded
3 medium potatoes,
   peeled and quartered

2 large ripe tomatoes,
   peeled, seeded, and
   chopped
½ teaspoon thyme
1½ teaspoons salt
½ teaspoon fresh-ground
   pepper
1 cup chicken stock *or*
   defatted canned
   chicken broth
1 cup dry white wine
   (recommended:
   Chablis)

In a flameproof casserole, combine the ingredients and toss to blend them.

Bring the liquid to the boil, reduce the heat, and simmer the vegetables, covered, for 20 minutes, or until the potatoes are just tender.

1 (9-ounce) package of artichoke hearts, fully thawed to room
   temperature
1 (10-ounce) package of frozen peas, fully thawed to room
   temperature

Add the artichoke hearts and peas and continue to cook the vegetables 12 minutes longer.

2 tablespoons cornstarch, mixed with ¼ cup chicken broth

Add the cornstarch, stirring gently until the sauce thickens.

Curried Mixed Fruit Salad

6 SERVINGS
PREPARATION: ABOUT 25 MINUTES
COOKING: 5 MINUTES
REFRIGERATES

A rather exotic main course for light meals, especially welcome in warm weather.

> 1½ cups dry white wine (recommended: Sylvaner)
> 1 cup chicken stock *or* defatted canned chicken broth
> ½ cup pine nuts (pignoli) (optional)
> ½ cup golden raisins

In a saucepan, combine the wine and broth. Bring the mixture to the boil. Add the pine nuts and raisins and simmer them, uncovered, for 5 minutes.

> 1 to 1½ tablespoons curry powder (preferably sweet Madras)
> 2 tablespoons cornstarch
> ½ cup cold water

In a small bowl, blend the curry powder and cornstarch; add the water, stirring until the mixture is smooth. Add the curry to the contents of the saucepan; stir the sauce over the heat constantly until it is thickened and smooth.

> 3 ripe bananas, peeled and sliced
> 3 ripe peaches, peeled, seeded, and sliced
> 3 ripe pears, peeled, cored, and sliced
> 6 ripe purple plums, halved lengthwise and seeded
> Strained fresh lemon juice

Toss the fruits with lemon juice to prevent their discoloring, and reserve them.

At this point you may stop and continue later.

> **Sugar**
> **Salt**

To the sauce, add the fruits and simmer them, uncovered, for 5 minutes, or until they are heated through. Adjust the seasoning to taste with a little sugar and salt. Serve the curried fruit over rice; offer separately a selection of condiments: shredded coconut, diced cucumber, unsalted crushed peanuts, fine-chopped green or red sweet pepper, fine-chopped scallions.

Desserts

The variety of desserts that can be prepared with wines and spirits seems almost limitless. Just as meat dishes are enhanced by being cooked with wine, so do desserts gain from its addition. Fresh fruit that has been poached in wine takes on a very special flavor; that which has been flamed with liqueur, an exciting festiveness. Jellies, puddings, and creams are likewise given added glamour by the addition of spirits. And the same holds true for cakes and pies. Perhaps my favorite dessert, however, is a soufflé, either hot or chilled, that has been prepared with spirits; here, lightness, flavor, and elegance combine to bring the meal to a truly gala close.

Fruit Desserts

Baked Apple Slices (FRANCE)

6 SERVINGS
PREPARATION: ABOUT 30 MINUTES
MACERATION TIME: 8 HOURS
COOKING: 20 MINUTES IN A 475° OVEN
REFRIGERATES

This Norman recipe gives the homely apple considerable glamour.

> 8 large crisp apples, peeled, cored, quartered, each quarter cut
>   into 3 slices
> Strained juice of 1 large lemon

As you prepare the apples, toss them with the lemon juice (a large mixing bowl and rubber spatula facilitate this step), which will prevent the apples from discoloring.

¼ cup sugar
A few grains of salt
¾ cup Calvados *or* applejack

Into the apples, stir these three ingredients. Allow the apples to stand, refrigerated, for 8 hours; turn them occasionally.

Softened butter

Drain the apples, reserving the liquid. Generously butter an 8-inch aluminum pie pan. In the pan, arrange three overlapping layers of apple, dotting each layer with butter. Over the apples, pour the reserved liquid. Bake *the* apples at 475° for 20 minutes, or until the top is golden. Remove them to a flameproof serving plate.

¼ cup Calvados *or* applejack
Whipped cream or thickened cream (page 6)

At the time of serving, warm the Calvados in a small saucepan; ignite it and pour it over the apples, and present the dessert while it is still flaming. Offer the cream separately.

This dessert may be served hot from the oven, or you may warm it at the time of serving; it should not be chilled.

Variations:

APPLE SLICES WITH PORT WINE: Follow step one as written. Disregard the remainder of the recipe. In a saucepan, combine 3 cups ruby port, 1 cup sugar, a few grains of salt, a 3-inch piece of cinnamon stick, and 3 whole cloves; bring the mixture to the boil and, over high heat, cook it, uncovered, for 10 minutes. Add the apple slices and cook them, uncovered, for 3 minutes, or until they are just tender. Allow them to cool in the syrup; stir them gently every few minutes to assure that they color evenly. Transfer the apples to a serving bowl and chill them for at least 3 hours. Offer them with whipped cream.

SAUTÉED APPLE SLICES: Follow step one as written. Disregard the remainder of the recipe. Drain the apples and dry on absorbent paper. In 4 tablespoons butter, sauté them until they are golden. Sprinkle them with 3 tablespoons sugar and a few grains of salt. Flame the apple slices with ¼ cup Calvados *or* applejack, and offer them with whipped cream or thickened cream (page 6).

Bananas Baked with Rum

6 SERVINGS
PREPARATION: ABOUT 10 MINUTES
COOKING: 30 MINUTES IN A 350° OVEN

> **6 firm, ripe bananas, peeled and halved lengthwise**
> **4 tablespoons butter, melted**

In a buttered baking dish, arrange the bananas, cut side down. Brush them well with melted butter and pour over them any remaining butter.

> **¼ cup dark brown sugar**
> **¼ teaspoon cinnamon**

In a small mixing bowl, blend the sugar and cinnamon. Sprinkle the bananas with this mixture.

> **½ cup dark rum**
> **Whipped cream (optional)**

Bake the bananas at 350° for 30 minutes, or until they are tender. At the time of serving, warm the rum in a small saucepan, ignite it, and pour it over the bananas. Offer the dessert with whipped cream.

Bananas Baked in Rum Cream (NICARAGUA)

6 SERVINGS
PREPARATION: ABOUT 20 MINUTES
COOKING: 20 MINUTES IN A 375° OVEN
REFRIGERATES

> **8 tablespoons butter**
> **6 firm, ripe bananas, peeled and halved lengthwise**

In a skillet, heat the butter and in it sauté the banana halves, a few at a time, until they are golden. Remove them to absorbent paper as they are done.

1 (8-ounce) package of
    cream cheese, at room
    temperature
¼ cup dark rum
3 tablespoons
    fine-chopped candied
    ginger

3 tablespoons dark brown
    sugar
½ teaspoon cinnamon
A few grains of salt

In a mixing bowl, combine these six ingredients and, with a fork, beat them until the mixture is smooth.

In a buttered baking dish, arrange a layer of half the bananas. Over them, spread half the rum mixture. Repeat the layers.

At this point you may stop and continue later.

½ cup heavy cream

Pour the cream over the bananas. Bake the dessert at 375° for 20 minutes, or until the cream is absorbed and the top is golden.

Sautéed Bananas

6 SERVINGS
PREPARATION: ABOUT 10 MINUTES
COOKING: 12 MINUTES

6 tablespoons butter
⅓ cup dark brown sugar,
    packed
¼ teaspoon cinnamon
A few grains of salt

6 firm, ripe bananas,
    peeled and halved
    lengthwise
¾ cup dark rum

In a skillet, heat the butter and into it stir the brown sugar, cinnamon, and salt. In the mixture, sauté the bananas, until they are lightly browned (about 5 minutes on each side). In a small saucepan, warm the rum, ignite it, and pour it over the bananas; allow the flame to die.

Variations:

SAUTÉED BANANAS WITH ORANGE: In place of brown sugar, use granulated white sugar, and in place of the cinnamon, use the grated rind of 1 medium orange; add ¼ teaspoon sweet Madras curry; flame the sautéed bananas with ⅓ cup orange-flavored liqueur.

CARAMELIZED BANANAS: Use 8 tablespoons butter and ½ cup granulated white sugar; omit the cinnamon. Cook the bananas in the butter-sugar syrup and then flame them in ¼ cup each dark and light rum, blended.

Use granulated white sugar and nutmeg; flame the bananas with ¼ cup Pernod.

Use granulated white sugar and ¼ teaspoon ginger; flame the bananas with ¼ cup yellow chartreuse.

Cut the sautéed bananas into 1-inch pieces; flame them with ¼ cup each banana-flavored liqueur and dark rum. Offer the bananas as an accompaniment to vanilla ice cream.

Blueberries in Cassis

6 SERVINGS
PREPARATION: ABOUT 15 MINUTES
CHILLING TIME: 3 HOURS

The simplest summertime dessert, fresh, flavorful, and satisfying.

> 2 pints blueberries, stemmed, rinsed, and well drained in a
>   colander
> ⅓ cup cassis (black currant liqueur)
> Whipped cream (optional)

In a mixing bowl, using a rubber spatula, toss the blueberries with the cassis. Transfer them to a serving dish and chill them for 3 hours. Offer them with whipped cream.

Blueberries, strawberries, and sliced peaches are enhanced by being tossed with bitter-almond-flavored liqueur (recommended: amaretto). Chill the fruit before serving it.

Cherries Jubilee

6 SERVINGS
PREPARATION: ABOUT 15 MINUTES
COOKING: 10 MINUTES
REFRIGERATES

> 1 tablespoon cornstarch
> 2 tablespoons sugar
> 2 (1-pound) cans of pitted dark sweet cherries, thoroughly
>   drained (the liquid reserved)
> Ruby port

In a mixing bowl, combine and blend the cornstarch and sugar. In a saucepan, blend the cherry liquid and port to equal 2 cups. Into the liquid, stir the cornstarch mixture.

> Zest of 1 medium lemon, cut into julienne
> Zest of 1 medium orange, cut into julienne
> Reserved cherries
> Strained juice of ½ lemon

In a saucepan, combine the two zests, add water to cover, bring it to the boil, and simmer the zest for 5 minutes; drain it and add to the wine mixture. Cook the sauce, stirring constantly, until it is thickened and smooth. Stir in the cherries and lemon juice.

At this point you may stop and continue later.

> ½ cup brandy
> Vanilla Ice cream

Reheat the sauce. To serve, warm the brandy in a small saucepan, ignite it, and pour it over the cherries. While they are still flaming, spoon them over the ice cream.

Seedless Grapes with Almond Cream

6 SERVINGS
PREPARATION: ABOUT 15 MINUTES
CHILLING TIME: 3 HOURS

    1 cup sour cream
    ⅓ cup amaretto
    2 tablespoons sugar
    A few grains of salt

In a mixing bowl, combine and blend these four ingredients.

    1½ pounds seedless grapes, stemmed, rinsed, well drained in
        a colander, and halved lengthwise

Into the sour cream mixture, fold the grapes. Transfer the dessert to a
serving bowl and chill it for 3 hours.

Macédoine of Fruit

The following combinations of fruit are only a few of many possible ones.
It is difficult to go awry with mixtures of fruit, so I urge you to create
combinations of your own.

Refrigerate the macédoine of your choice for 3 hours.

Combine 1 cup each blueberries, raspberries, sliced fresh peaches, canta-
loupe balls, canned pineapple chunks, and canned pitted sweet cherries.
Toss the fruit with ¼ cup superfine granulated sugar and a few grains
of salt; add white crème de menthe to taste; stir the mixture to blend it
well. Makes 10 servings.

Combine 1 (1-pound) can of pitted sweet cherries, drained, with 1
(28-ounce) can of apricot halves, drained. Add ¼ cup orange-flavored
liqueur; stir the mixture to blend it well. Makes 6 servings.

Peel, core, and cut into cubes 1 ripe pineapple. Add 1 quart strawberries, hulled, rinsed, and drained. Toss the fruit with 3 tablespoons sugar and a few grains of salt; add ½ cup orange-flavored liqueur; stir the mixture to blend it well. Makes 6 servings.

Combine 2 cups stewed rhubarb, 1 pint strawberries, hulled, rinsed, drained, and halved, and 1 cup fresh pineapple cubes. Add the grated rind and strained juice of 1 medium orange, a sprinkling of ginger, and ¼ cup cherry-flavored liqueur; stir the mixture to blend it well. Makes 6 servings.

Combine 1 cup each strawberries, hulled, rinsed, drained, and halved; blueberries, stemmed, rinsed, and drained; honeydew balls; sliced banana; and watermelon balls. Add 3 tablespoons sugar, a few grains of salt, and ½ cup amaretto; stir the mixture to blend it well. Makes 8 servings.

Combine 3 cups sliced fresh peaches, 2 cups sliced fresh pears, and 1 pint blueberries, stemmed, rinsed, and drained. Add the strained juice of 1 large lemon, ⅓ cup sugar, a few grains of salt, and ½ cup brandy; stir the mixture to blend it well. Makes 6 servings.

Combine 1 cup each sliced banana, fresh pineapple cubes, and strawberries, hulled, rinsed, and drained. Add 3 tablespoons sugar and a few grains of salt. Combine and blend ½ cup brandy and ¾ teaspoonful ground ginger; pour the brandy over the fruit; stir the mixture to blend it well. Makes 6 servings.

Peel 2 small cantaloupes, seed them, and cut the flesh into bite-size pieces. Peel and slice 3 ripe peaches. Add 2 tablespoons sugar, a few grains of salt, and ½ cup Frangelico (hazelnut-flavored liqueur); stir the mixture to blend it well. Makes 6 servings.

Fruit-flavored liqueurs complement macédoines of fruit; brandy and nut-flavored liqueurs are also reliable. Crème de menthe and dry red and white wines should be used with discretion because of the strong individual flavor of the former and the "sourness" of the latter, unless a compensatory amount of sugar is used.

Any of the above fruit combinations, without the addition of a liqueur, go well with . . .

Sherry Custard

6 TO 8 SERVINGS
PREPARATION AND COOKING: ABOUT 15 MINUTES
CHILLING TIME: 3 HOURS

> 6 egg yolks
> ¾ cup sugar
> A few grains of salt
> 1 cup cream sherry

In the top of a double boiler, beat the egg yolks until they are lemon-colored. Gradually add the sugar, beating constantly. Stir in the salt and sherry. Over simmering water, cook the mixture, stirring, until it thickens and coats a metal spoon. Remove it from the heat, allow it to cool, and chill it, covered, for 3 hours.

At this point you may stop and continue later.

> 1 cup heavy cream, whipped

At the time of serving, fold in the whipped cream. Into the sherry custard, fold the chilled and drained fruit combination of your choice.

Dried Fruit Compote

8 SERVINGS
PREPARATION: ABOUT 25 MINUTES
STANDING TIME: 6 HOURS
COOKING: 25 MINUTES
CHILLING TIME: 3 HOURS

> ¾ cup sugar
> A few grains of salt
> 1½ cups dry red *or* white
>   wine (recommended:
>   Burgundy)
> Zest and strained juice of
>   1 medium lemon

> Zest and strained juice of
>   1 medium orange
> 4 allspice berries, bruised
> 1 (3-inch) piece of
>   cinnamon stick
> 4 cloves

In a saucepan, combine the sugar, salt, wine, zests, and juices. Tie the allspice berries, cinnamon stick, and cloves loosely in cheesecloth; add them to contents of the saucepan. Bring the liquid to the boil, over high heat, cook the mixture, uncovered, for 10 minutes.

> ½ pound each dried apricot halves, dried peach halves, dried
>   pear halves, and pitted prunes
> 1 cup golden raisins
> Boiling water

In a large saucepan, combine the fruits. Add the hot syrup, zests, and spices. Add boiling water, if necessary, just to cover. Allow the mixture to stand, covered, for 6 hours.

Bring the liquid to the boil, reduce the heat, and simmer the fruit, uncovered, for 25 minutes, or until it is just tender. With a slotted spoon, remove it to a serving bowl. Discard the zests and spices. Over high heat, reduce the liquid until it is slightly syrupy. Allow it to cool, pour it over the fruit, and chill the compote for 3 hours.

Orange in White Wine

6 SERVINGS
PREPARATION: ABOUT 30 MINUTES
COOKING: 15 MINUTES
REFRIGERATES

> 6 large navel oranges
> Zest of 2 large lemons, cut into julienne

With a vegetable peeler, remove the zest from the oranges, reserving the fruit. Cut the zest into julienne and combine it with the lemon zest. In rapidly boiling water, cook the zest, uncovered, for 5 minutes. Drain and reserve it.

> 1¼ cups sugar   Sauvignon
> A few grains of salt   Blanc)
> 1 cup dry white wine   Reserved zest
>   (recommended: ¼ cup orange-flavored
>   Muscadet or   liqueur

In a saucepan, combine the sugar, salt, wine, and zest. Over high heat, bring the liquid to the boil. After the sugar is dissolved, continue to boil the syrup until it is faintly caramel-colored. Remove the saucepan from the heat and stir in the liqueur.

Reserved oranges

Remove all pith from the oranges. Cut a slice from the bottom so that they will stand. Arrange them on a serving platter. Over and around the oranges, spoon the syrup.

Baked Peaches

6 SERVINGS
PREPARATION: ABOUT 20 MINUTES
COOKING: 20 MINUTES IN A 350° OVEN
CHILLING TIME: 3 HOURS

This simple and satisfying dessert, known throughout Europe for centuries, appears in English cookbooks of the Tudor era.

1 cup sugar
A few grains of salt
1 cup dry red wine *or* white
    wine (recommended:
    Burgundy) *or* ruby
    port

¼ cup fruit-flavored
    liqueur (optional)
Zest and strained juice of
    1 medium lemon
½ teaspoon mace

In a saucepan, combine these seven ingredients. Over high heat, bring them to the boil, stirring to dissolve the sugar. Cook the mixture, uncovered, for 10 minutes.

6 large firm ripe peaches
Boiling water

Immerse the peaches in boiling water for 1 minute. Peel them and cut a thin slice from the bottom so that they will stand Arrange them in a baking dish and over them pour the wine mixture. Bake the peaches, covered, for 20 minutes, or until they are tender.

Allow the peaches to cool in the baking dish. Transfer them to a serving bowl and strain the syrup over them. Chill them for 3 hours.

Peaches Flamed with Scotch Whisky

6 SERVINGS
PREPARATION: ABOUT 15 MINUTES
COOKING: 15 MINUTES
REFRIGERATES

The recipe may be made with either fresh or canned peaches. In place of Scotch whisky, you may use bourbon, brandy, kirschwasser, amaretto, or any *dry* cordial. Peaches prepared this way are a fine accompaniment to vanilla ice cream.

> 2 tablespoons butter
> ½ cup dark brown sugar
>   (packed)
> A few grains of salt
>
> Strained juice of 1 medium
>   lemon
> ½ teaspoon vanilla
>   extract

In a skillet, heat the butter and to it add the brown sugar and salt. Cook the mixture, stirring, until it becomes syrupy. Away from the heat, stir in the lemon juice and vanilla.

> 12 peach halves
> ⅓ cup Scotch whisky

If using fresh peaches, immerse them in boiling water for 1 minute to facilitate peeling them. To the contents of the skillet, add the peach halves, one at a time, and spoon the syrup over them; transfer them, cut side down, to a flameproof serving dish.* In a small saucepan, warm the Scotch, ignite it, and pour it over the peaches; allow the flame to die.

*If the skillet is large enough, the peach halves may be left in the syrup until after they have been flamed, and then transferred to a serving dish.

Peaches in Strawberry Sauce

6 SERVINGS
PREPARATION: ABOUT 20 MINUTES
CHILLING TIME: 3 HOURS

1 quart strawberries, hulled,
    rinsed, and drained on
    absorbent paper
1 cup superfine granulated
    sugar

A few grains of salt
½ cup kirschwasser *or*
    orange-flavored
    liqueur
½ cup heavy cream

In the container of a food processor equipped with the steel blade, combine these five ingredients; whirl the mixture until it is smooth and the sugar is dissolved. (In the absence of a food processor, force the strawberries through a sieve and, in a mixing bowl, blend the pulp with the other ingredients.)

6 large ripe peaches
Boiling water

Immerse the peaches in the boiling water for 1 minute. Peel, halve, and pit them. Arrange them in a serving bowl and spoon the strawberry mixture over them. Chill the dessert for 3 hours.

Flaming Pears

6 SERVINGS
PREPARATION AND COOKING: ABOUT 25 MINUTES
REFRIGERATES

2 tablespoons butter
½ cup dark brown sugar
    (packed)
½ cup strained fresh orange
    juice

Strained juice of 1 medium
    lemon
½ teaspoon cinnamon
1 teaspoon vanilla extract
A few grains of salt

In a chafing dish or saucepan, combine these seven ingredients. Over gentle heat, cook them, stirring, only until the butter is melted.

6 ripe Bartlett pears, peeled, halved lengthwise, and cored, *or*
    12 canned pear halves, well drained

Arrange the pears in the chafing dish, spooning the sauce over them.

At this point you may stop and continue later.

Grated rind of 1 medium lemon
Grated rind of 1 medium orange

Over gentle heat, cook the fruit until it is thoroughly heated. Remove it to a flameproof serving dish. Over high heat, reduce the syrup somewhat; pour it over the pears and sprinkle them with the grated rinds.

½ cup brandy

In a small saucepan, warm the brandy, ignite it, and pour it over the pears. Present the dessert while it is still flaming.

Poached Pears (ENGLAND)

6 SERVINGS
PREPARATION: ABOUT 15 MINUTES
COOKING: 5 HOURS IN A 250° OVEN

The basic instructions for "Peris in Sirrop" are taken from a twelfth-century "cookbook," *The Forme of Cury* (which meant "cooking"), a collection of recipes set down by the chefs of Richard II.

1 (3-inch) piece of
    cinnamon stick
8 cloves
3 walnut-sized pieces of
    ginger root, bruised
Zest of 1 medium orange
A few threads of saffron

⅔ cup sugar
A few grains of salt
2 cups dry red wine
    (recommended:
    claret)
1 cup water

In an ovenproof and flameproof dish, combine these nine ingredients. Bring the mixture to the boil, stirring to dissolve the sugar.

6 firm-fleshed pears (Bosc *or* Comice), peeled, unstemmed,
    with a small slice cut from their bottoms so that they stand
    upright

To the contents of the baking dish, add the pears, and bake them at 250° for 5 hours, basting them thoroughly once an hour. They should be tender but still retain their shape. Allow the pears to cool in the liquid, basting them frequently. Transfer them to a serving bowl and strain the liquid over them (or you may reduce the liquid to a syrup and then strain it over the fruit). Chill the pears before serving them.

The recipe may also be made with white or rosé wine, with Madeira or ruby port, or with cognac (in this case, 2 cups water, 1 cup cognac, and 1 teaspoon vanilla extract).

When serving the pears, add, if you wish, ¼ cup amaretto, warmed and ignited. The dessert may be garnished with a 3-ounce package of slivered almonds, toasted (page 4). To make it even more festive, offer separately a bowl of thickened cream (page 6) or whipped cream.

Flaming Pineapple

6 SERVINGS
PREPARATION: ABOUT 25 MINUTES
CHILLING TIME: 3 HOURS

> 1 large ripe pineapple, peeled and cored
> ½ cup sugar
> ¼ cup kirschwasser

Cut the pineapple into 12 or 18 lengthwise pieces, arrange them on a flameproof serving platter, and sprinkle them with the sugar and kirschwasser. Cover the fruit and chill for 3 hours.

> ⅓ cup brandy or orange-flavored liqueur

At the time of serving, warm the brandy in a small saucepan, ignite and pour it over the pineapple. Present the dessert while it is still flaming.

Pineapple in Rum

6 SERVINGS
PREPARATION: ABOUT 20 MINUTES
MACERATION TIME: OVERNIGHT

> 1 large ripe pineapple, peeled, cored, and cut into bite-size chunks
> 3 tablespoons sugar
> A few grains of salt
> ½ cup light rum

In a mixing bowl, toss together the pineapple, sugar, and salt. In a small saucepan, warm the rum, ignite it, and allow the flame to die. Pour the rum over the pineapple; toss the fruit once again. Transfer it to a serving bowl and allow it to macerate, covered, overnight in the refrigerator.

Baked Plums (POLAND)

6 SERVINGS
PREPARATION: ABOUT 15 MINUTES
COOKING: 50 MINUTES IN A 350°/400° OVEN
REFRIGERATES (WITHOUT THE MERINGUE)

> 1½ cups dry red wine (recommended: Burgundy)
> 1½ cups sugar
> A few grains of salt
> Zest of 1 medium lemon

In a saucepan, combine these four ingredients. Over high heat, bring the liquid to the boil. After the sugar is dissolved, continue to boil the syrup for 5 minutes.

> 3 pounds purple plums, rinsed, drained on absorbent paper,
>   and pricked in several places with a pin (to keep their
>   skins from bursting)

Arrange the plums in a lightly buttered baking dish. Over them, pour the syrup. Bake the plums, uncovered, at 350° for 45 minutes, or until they are tender. Discard the lemon zest.

At this point you may stop and continue later.

> 3 eggs whites
> ½ cup sugar
> ½ teaspoon almond extract

In a mixing bowl, beat the egg whites until frothy; gradually add the sugar and then the almond extract, beating until the whites are stiff but not dry. Over the plums, spread the meringue. Bake the dish at 400° for 5 minutes, or until the meringue is golden.

The compote may be served hot or at room temperature.

Variation:

Omit step one. In step two, halve the plums lengthwise and remove the pits; using 2½ cups sugar, layer the plums alternately with the sugar; add 1 cup dark rum; bake the plums as suggested. Omit step three. Serve the plums in their syrup.

Prunes Baked in Wine

6 SERVINGS
PREPARATION: ABOUT 15 MINUTES
MACERATION TIME: OVERNIGHT
COOKING: 45 MINUTES IN A 325° OVEN
CHILLING TIME: 3 HOURS

> 36 large pitted prunes
> 2 cups dry red wine (recommended: Burgundy) *or* Madeira
>   *or* Marsala *or* ruby port

In a mixing bowl, arrange the prunes. Add the wine and allow them to macerate overnight.

Drain the prunes in a colander, reserving the wine. Remove the prunes to a baking dish; transfer the wine to a saucepan.

> 1 cup sugar (if you use dry red wine) *or* ½ cup sugar (if you use a sweet wine)
> A few grains of salt
> 1 (3-inch) piece of cinnamon stick
>
> Zest and strained juice of 1 medium lemon *or* 1 medium orange
> 1 teaspoon vanilla extract
> Additional wine, as needed

To the wine in the saucepan, add the first five ingredients. Over high heat, bring the liquid to the boil. When the sugar is dissolved, continue to cook the syrup, uncovered, for 10 minutes. Pour the syrup over the prunes. If necessary, use additional wine to cover the prunes.

> Sour cream, thickened cream (page 6), or whipped cream
>   (all optional)

Bake the prunes, uncovered, at 325° for 45 minutes, or until they are tender. Allow them to cool in the syrup. Transfer them and the syrup to a serving bowl and chill the dessert for 3 hours. Offer it with the cream of your choice.

Strawberries in Benedictine Cream

6 SERVINGS
PREPARATION: ABOUT 25 MINUTES
COOKING: 10 MINUTES
CHILLING TIME: 3 HOURS

> 1 quart strawberries, hulled, rinsed, and drained on absorbent
> paper

Halve the strawberries lengthwise. Chill them in the refrigerator while you prepare the cream.

> 4 egg yolks   2 cups milk
> ¼ cup sugar   ¼ cup benedictine
> A few grains of salt

In the top of a double boiler, beat the egg yolks lightly. Add the remaining four ingredients and, over simmering water, cook the mixture, stirring constantly, until it thickens and coats a metal spoon. Remove the custard from the heat and allow it to cool, stirring to keep it from crusting. When it is lukewarm, pour it over the strawberries. Chill the dessert for 3 hours.

Gelatin Desserts

Basic Wine Gelatin

4 SERVINGS
PREPARATION: ABOUT 15 MINUTES (THE PREPARATION TIME WILL VARY
   WITH THE INGREDIENTS USED)
CHILLING TIME: 6 HOURS

Wine gelatins make fresh, cooling desserts, ideal for spring and summer. They may be made with dry red or white wine, champagne, port, sherry, Madeira, or Marsala. To the wine may be added fruit-flavored liqueurs to equal the 2 cups required (see below). Fresh fruits are refreshing complements to the gelatin, either as part of the jelled mold or as an accompaniment to fill the unmolded gelatin ring. These recipes may be prepared well in advance of serving and offered with assurance that they will please. The basic recipe is easily doubled.

Lightly oil and chill a 5-cup ring mold or other mold, or chill a serving bowl or individual dessert glasses.

> 1 envelope unflavored gelatin, softened for 5 minutes in ¼ cup
>   cold water *or* fruit juice

Over simmering water, dissolve the gelatin and reserve it.

> 2 cups wine, as called for   Special seasoning, as
>   in the variation (below)   called for
> Sugar, as called for   A few grains of salt
>   Reserved gelatin

In a mixing bowl, combine the wine, sugar, special seasoning, salt, and gelatin. Stir the mixture until the sugar is dissolved. Chill it until it just begins to set.

> 1 to 1½ cups prepared fruit, as called for
> 2 or 3 egg whites beaten until stiff but not dry, with 2 to 3
>   tablespoons sugar (optional)

With a rotary beater, briefly whip the chilled gelatin. Fold in the fruit and egg whites. Using a rubber spatula, transfer the mixture to the prepared mold or dish. Chill it for at least 6 hours, or until it is thoroughly set.

> Dessert sauce of your choice (pages 304–310) (optional)

Unmold the dessert onto a chilled serving plate; or you may serve it directly from its dish. Offer separately the sauce of your choice.

Note: Although a single quantity of the recipe will not fill a 5-cup ring mold, this utensil is suggested so that you can fill the center with fruit. If the recipe is doubled, as it should be for 6 servings, the gelatin will fill the mold.

CHAMPAGNE GELATIN WITH FRUIT: Follow step one as written. In step two, use champagne as the wine; complete the step as written. In step three, use 1 cup seedless grapes, stemmed, rinsed, dried on absorbent paper, and halved lengthwise, or 1 (16-ounce) can of mandarin orange sections, thoroughly drained. Complete the basic recipe as written.

GRAPES IN WINE GELATIN: Follow step one as written. In step two, use dry red or white wine, ½ cup sugar, and 2 or 3 drops of almond extract; complete the step as written. In step three, with red wine use red grapes, stemmed, rinsed, drained on absorbent paper, halved lengthwise, and seeded; with white wine use green seedless grapes, prepared the same way. Complete the basic recipe as written.

PORT WINE GELATIN: Follow step one as written. In step two, use 1 cup ruby port and to it add the strained juices of 1 medium-size lemon and 1 medium-size orange, plus additional port to equal the 2 cups; use ⅓ cup sugar. Omit the fruit. Complete the basic recipe as written. Recommended: Fill the unmolded ring with Blueberries in Cassis (page 227) or with sliced fresh peaches tossed with ¼ cup orange-flavored liqueur.

SHERRY GELATIN: Follow step one as written. In step two, use 1 cup dry sherry and 1 cup strained fresh orange juice; use ⅔ cup sugar; add 2 tablespoons strained fresh lemon juice. Complete the basic recipe as written.

SAUTERNES GELATIN WITH MIXED FRUIT: Follow step one as written. In step two, use Sauternes; add 2 tablespoons strained fresh lemon juice; complete the step as written. In step three, add 1½ cups cut mixed fresh fruit. Complete the basic recipe as written.

Puddings and Cremes

Apricot Pudding (Kissel) (RUSSIA)

6 SERVINGS
PREPARATION AND COOKING: ABOUT 40 MINUTES
CHILLING TIME: 3 HOURS

1 (11-ounce) package of tenderized dried apricot halves
Honey
A few grains of salt

In water just to cover, simmer the apricot halves, covered, for 20 minutes, or until they are very tender. Allow them to cool somewhat. In the container of a food processor or blender, reduce the apricots and their liquid to a smooth purée. Return the purée to the saucepan and add honey to taste and salt.

2 tablespoons potato starch
¼ cup brandy
Whipped cream (optional)

Blend the potato starch and brandy until the mixture is smooth. Stir it into the apricot purée and simmer the kissel, stirring constantly, until it is thickened and smooth. Spoon the dessert into a serving bowl or individual glasses. Refrigerate it for at least 3 hours. Offer it with whipped cream.

Athol Brose (SCOTLAND)

6 TO 8 SERVINGS
PREPARATION: ABOUT 10 MINUTES
CHILLING TIME: 1 HOUR

Really a traditional drink, but so thick that it can be eaten like Zabaglione (page 256), athol brose was traditionally quaffed at Hogmanay (New Year's Eve). Compare it with Posset (page 333).

2 cups Scotch whisky
2 cups heavy cream
1 cup honey (preferably heather or buckwheat)
A few grains of salt

In a mixing bowl, combine the ingredients and, with a rotary beater, whip the mixture until it is frothy and thick. Chill it for 1 hour before serving it in dessert glasses.

Banana Pudding (PORTUGAL)

6 SERVINGS
PREPARATION: ABOUT 25 MINUTES
COOKING: 50 MINUTES IN A 325° OVEN

8 ripe bananas, peeled	⅔ cup sugar
½ cup white port	A few grains of salt
3 tablespoons butter, melted	4 egg yolks, beaten

In a little water (just enough to keep the fruit from scorching), simmer the bananas, covered, until they are very soft. Purée the bananas in the container of a food processor or blender (or force them through a sieve). In a mixing bowl, combine and blend the banana purée with the remaining ingredients.

Whipped cream (optional)

Using a rubber spatula, transfer the mixture to a buttered 2-quart soufflé dish. Bake the pudding at 325° for 50 minutes, or until the top is golden. Offer the dessert hot, accompanied by whipped cream.

Brandy Pudding (UNITED STATES)

6 TO 8 SERVINGS
PREPARATION AND COOKING: ABOUT 30 MINUTES
CHILLING TIME: 6 HOURS

This traditional dessert from South Carolina is very good and very rich— a calorie counter's nemesis.

Chill a serving bowl.

    4 egg yolks
    1 cup sugar
    A few grains of salt
    1 cup brandy

In the top of a double boiler, using a rotary beater, beat the eggs until they are thick and lemon-colored. Gradually add the sugar and salt, beating constantly. Stir in the brandy. Over simmering water, cook the custard until it thickens and coats a metal spoon. Allow it to cool, covered, to room temperature.

> 12 ladyfingers, split
> 2 cups heavy cream, whipped
> 4 egg whites, beaten until stiff but not dry

Arrange the ladyfingers over the bottom and around the edge of the chilled bowl. Into the custard, fold the whipped cream and then the egg white. Using a rubber spatula, transfer the pudding to the prepared dish. Chill it, covered, for at least 6 hours.

Eggnog Pudding (UNITED STATES)

6 SERVINGS
PREPARATION AND COOKING: ABOUT 30 MINUTES
MACERATION TIME: OVERNIGHT
CHILLING TIME: 6 HOURS

From Kentucky—where else?—the bourbon capital of the world, comes this handsome dessert, really a chilled soufflé.

Lightly oil and chill a 5-cup ring mold or other mold.

> ½ cup chopped mixed candied fruit
> 3 tablespoons golden raisins
> ⅓ cup brandy

In a small bowl, combine the fruit, raisins, and brandy. Allow the fruit to macerate, covered, overnight in the refrigerator. In a saucepan, bring the mixture just to the boil, then remove it from the heat and reserve it.

> 1½ envelopes unflavored gelatin, softened for 5 minutes in
>   ⅓ cup cold water
> 1½ cups bourbon whiskey

Over simmering water, dissolve the gelatin. Add the bourbon.

> 6 egg yolks   ¼ cup dark rum
> ⅓ cup sugar   Reserved bourbon mixture
> A few grains of salt

In the top of a double boiler, beat the egg yolks until they are light. Add the sugar and salt, beating constantly. Stir in the rum and the bourbon mixture. Over simmering water, cook the custard until it thickens and coats a metal spoon. Cover the custard and allow it to cool, and then chill it until it just begins to set.

> 1 cup heavy cream, whipped
> Reserved fruit and its liquid
> 1 tablespoon vanilla extract

With a rotary beater, briefly beat the custard to assure its smoothness. Fold in the whipped cream. Into the reserved fruit, stir the vanilla; fold the mixture into the pudding. With a rubber spatula, transfer the pudding to the prepared mold. Chill it for at least 6 hours, or until it is thoroughly set. Unmold it onto a chilled serving platter.

Indian Pudding (UNITED STATES)

6 SERVINGS
PREPARATION: ABOUT 30 MINUTES
COOKING: 1 HOUR IN A 350° OVEN

> 4 cups milk
> 6 tablespoons corn meal

In the top of a double boiler, over direct heat, scald the milk. Add the corn meal, stirring, and cook the mixture over boiling water for 20 minutes.

> 2 tablespoons butter   ¼ teaspoon ginger
> ¾ cup molasses   ¾ teaspoon salt
> 1 teaspoon cinnamon

Into the contents of the double boiler, stir these five ingredients.

> 2 eggs, beaten

Away from the heat, stir in the eggs.

> ¾ cup cold milk
> ¼ cup bourbon whiskey, dark rum, or Southern Comfort
> Whipped cream or heavy cream

Combine and blend the milk and liquor. Spoon the corn meal mixture into a buttered baking dish. Add the cold milk. Bake the pudding, uncovered, at 350° for 1 hour, or until it is set (the consistency will be soft). Serve it at once, with the cream offered separately.

Lemon Cream (NETHERLANDS)

4 SERVINGS
PREPARATION AND COOKING: ABOUT 20 MINUTES
CHILLING TIME: 6 HOURS

Chill a serving bowl.

> 4 egg yolks
> ½ cup sugar
> A few grains of salt
> Grated rind of 1 large lemon
> Strained juice of 2 large
>   lemons
> ½ cup dry white wine
>   (recommended:
>   Chablis)
>
> ½ envelope (1½
>   teaspoons)
>   unflavored gelatin,
>   softened for 5
>   minutes in ¼ cup
>   cold water

In the top of a double boiler, beat the egg yolks with the sugar and salt until they are thick. Add the lemon, lemon juice, and wine and, over simmering water, cook the mixture, stirring constantly, until it is thickened and coats a metal spoon. Add the gelatin, stirring until it is dissolved. Allow the custard to cool, covered, and then chill it until it just begins to set.

4 egg whites, beaten until stiff but not dry

With a rotary beater, briefly beat the custard to assure its smoothness. Beat in one-fifth of the egg white; fold in the remainder. With a rubber spatula, transfer the cream to the prepared bowl and chill it for at least 6 hours, or until it is thoroughly set.

Lemon Syllabub (UNITED STATES)

8 TO 10 SERVINGS
PREPARATION: ABOUT 15 MINUTES
CHILLING TIME: 3 HOURS

A recipe from colonial Maryland.

All ingredients and the dessert glasses should be thoroughly chilled.

> 1 cup cream sherry
> 1 cup Madeira
> Zest of 1 medium lemon

In a mixing bowl, combine the wines and lemon zest; allow the mixture to stand, refrigerated, for 3 hours. Discard the lemon zest.

> 4 cups heavy cream, whipped   1 cup superfine granulated
>   until it just begins to   sugar
>   hold its shape   A few grains of salt
> Chilled sherry-Madeira   A grating of nutmeg
> ⅓ cup strained fresh
>   lemon juice

Into the whipped cream, gradually beat, in order, the reserved wine, the lemon juice, and the sugar and salt. Pour the syllabub into the chilled glasses and garnish it with a grating of nutmeg. Serve it at once.

Nesselrode Pudding (UNITED STATES)

6 SERVINGS
MACERATION TIME: 1 HOUR
PREPARATION AND COOKING: ABOUT 30 MINUTES (PLUS 1 HOUR FOR
    CHILLING)
CHILLING TIME: 6 HOURS

Lightly oil and chill a 5-cup ring mold or other mold.

> ½ cup currants
> ⅓ cup golden raisins
> ½ cup dark rum

In a small mixing bowl, combine the currants and raisins. Add the rum and allow them to macerate for 1 hour.

4 egg yolks
¾ cup sugar
A few grains of salt
2 cups heavy cream

1 (8¾-ounce) can of
   unsweetened chestnut
   purée
1 teaspoon vanilla extract
Reserved fruit and rum

In the top of a double boiler, beat the egg yolks until light. Add the sugar and salt and continue to beat the mixture until it is thick and lemon-colored. Add the cream and, over simmering water, cook the mixture, stirring constantly, until it is thickened and coats a metal spoon. Away from the heat, beat in the chestnut purée and the vanilla. Stir in the re-served fruit and rum. Chill the mixture for 1 hour.

1 cup heavy cream
2 tablespoons sugar
Glazed Chestnuts (Marrons glacés)

Whip the cream, adding the sugar as it thickens. Fold it into the chilled Nesselrode mixture. Using a rubber spatula, transfer the pudding to the prepared mold and chill it for at least 6 hours. Unmold the dessert onto a chilled serving plate and garnish it with marrons glacés.

Orange Cream

6 TO 8 SERVINGS
PREPARATION: ABOUT 30 MINUTES
CHILLING TIME: 6 HOURS

Chill a serving bowl.

1½ envelopes (4½
    teaspoons) unflavored
    gelatin, softened for
    5 minutes in ½ cup
    cold water
1 (6-ounce) can of frozen
    orange juice concentrate,
    thawed

1 cup water
⅔ cup sugar
A few grains of salt
½ cup orange-flavored
    liqueur

Over simmering water, dissolve the gelatin. In a mixing bowl, combine the orange juice concentrate, water, and dissolved gelatin; add the sugar and salt, stirring until the sugar is dissolved. Stir in the liqueur. Chill the mixture until it just begins to set.

2 cups heavy cream, whipped

With a rotary beater, briefly beat the chilled mixture to assure its smoothness. Fold in the whipped cream. With a rubber spatula, transfer the orange cream to the chilled serving bowl. Refrigerate it for at least 6 hours, or until it is thoroughly set.

LEMON CREAM: In step two, omit the orange juice, in its place using ¼ cup strained fresh lemon juice; increase the sugar to 1¼ cups; in place of the liqueur, use 1 cup Sauternes; add the grated rind of 1 medium lemon. Complete the recipe as written. (Another recipe for lemon cream appears on page 242).

Plum Pudding (ENGLAND)

6 SERVINGS PER PUDDING MOLD
PREPARATION: ABOUT 45 MINUTES
MACERATION TIME: OVERNIGHT
COOKING: 3 HOURS
REFRIGERATES; FREEZES

Like many traditional recipes, this one for the classic English plum pudding requires some effort; therefore, I suggest using one of the puddings and freezing the second, so that you may offer it, effortlessly, at a later date.

½ cup currants
½ cup golden raisins
½ cup brandy

In a small bowl, combine the currants, raisins, and brandy. Allow them to macerate overnight.

½ cup sugar	½ teaspoon ground ginger
3 cups flour	½ teaspoon grated
1 teaspoon baking powder	nutmeg
1 teaspoon cinnamon	1½ teaspoons salt
½ teaspoon ground cloves	

In a large mixing bowl, sift together these dry ingredients.

Reserved macerated fruit
  and its liquid
¼ cup chopped nuts
¼ cup chopped candied
  citron

¼ cup chopped candied
  orange peel
1 large tart apple, peeled
  and grated

Into the contents of the mixing bowl, stir these five ingredients.

1 cup suet, chopped fine
1½ cups milk
½ cup dark molasses

To the contents of the bowl, add these three ingredients. Beat the mixture vigorously to blend it well. Spoon the batter into two 1½-quart pudding molds. Cover the molds well, securing the covers with string. Arrange them on a rack in a large kettle. To the kettle, add boiling water to reach halfway up the molds. Reduce the heat so that the water simmers gently, cover the kettle tightly, and steam the puddings for 3 hours.

½ cup brandy
Hard Sauce (page 308)

Unmold the puddings onto a flameproof serving platter. In a small saucepan, warm the brandy, ignite it, and pour it over the puddings. Present the dessert while aflame. (If you reserve one pudding for later use, flame each pudding with ¼ cup brandy.) Offer the hard sauce separately.

Pots de Crème à l'Orange (FRANCE)

6 SERVINGS
PREPARATION AND COOKING: ABOUT 15 MINUTES
CHILLING TIME: 6 HOURS

Not the traditional French recipe, but the taste, texture, and satisfaction are undoubtedly Gallic.

1 (6-ounce) package of semisweet chocolate bits
2 eggs
¼ cup orange-flavored liqueur

In the container of a blender, combine these three ingredients.

2 tablespoons sugar
A few grains of salt
½ cup milk
Grated rind of 1 small orange

In a saucepan, combine these four ingredients. Over high heat, bring the milk to the boil, stirring. Immediately pour the milk in a steady stream into the blender container, simultaneously turning the blender on at low speed. Blend the dessert for about 15 seconds, or until the chocolate is melted and the mixture is smooth. Pour the dessert into individual cups or dishes and refrigerate it for at least 6 hours.

Variation:

In place of the orange-flavored liqueur, use a mocha-flavored cordial or light rum.

Pumpkin Cream

6 SERVINGS
PREPARATION: ABOUT 10 MINUTES
COOKING: 50 MINUTES IN A 325° OVEN
CHILLING TIME: 6 HOURS

1 cup canned pumpkin
  purée
3 eggs plus 1 egg yolk
⅓ cup sugar
A few grains of salt
1⅔ cups heavy cream

¼ cup dark rum
2 teaspoons grated orange
  rind
¼ teaspoon allspice
½ teaspoon cinnamon

In the container of a food processor, combine all the ingredients and whirl them for 15 seconds, or until the mixture is smooth (or combine them in a mixing bowl and blend them with a rotary beater.) Pour the mixture into a lightly buttered ring mold. Set the mold in a pan of hot water and bake the custard at 325° for 50 minutes, or until it is set. Allow it to cool to room temperature and then chill it for 6 hours before unmolding it onto a chilled serving platter. Offer Crème Anglaise (page 306).

Rum Bavarian Cream

6 TO 8 SERVINGS
PREPARATION AND COOKING: ABOUT 25 MINUTES
CHILLING TIME: 6 HOURS

Chill a 6-cup ring mold or serving bowl.

> 1 envelope unflavored gelatin
> ½ cup sugar
> A few grains of salt

In the top of a double boiler, combine and blend the gelatin, sugar, and salt.

> 1½ cups milk
> 4 egg yolks
> ½ cup dark rum

To the contents of the double boiler, add the milk and egg yolks. Using a rotary beater, blend the mixture well. Stir in the rum and, over simmering water, cook the custard, stirring constantly, until it thickens and coats a metal spoon. Remove it from the heat, allow it to cool, covered, and then chill it until it just begins to set.

> 1 cup heavy cream, whipped
> 4 egg whites, beaten until stiff but not dry

With a rotary beater, briefly beat the custard to assure its smoothness. Fold in the whipped cream. Beat in one-fifth of the egg white; fold in the remainder. Using a rubber spatula, transfer the cream to the mold (rinsed with cold water) or serving bowl. Chill the dessert for at least 6 hours, or until it is thoroughly set. Unmold it onto a chilled serving platter or serve it from the bowl.

CHARLOTTE RUSSE: Line a spring-form pan with split ladyfingers (about 20); sprinkle them with ¼ to ⅓ cup light rum, cream sherry, Marsala, *or* orange-flavored liqueur (rum is traditional, but the others are equally tasty). Double the recipe for Rum Bavarian Cream. Follow step two as written. In step three, use ½ cup of the liquor with which you sprinkled the ladyfingers. In step four, omit the egg whites. Spoon the cream into the spring-form pan. To serve the charlotte, unmold it onto a chilled serving platter and offer it cut into wedges, as you would serve a cake. Makes 10 to 12 servings.

Sherry Cream

6 TO 8 SERVINGS
PREPARATION AND COOKING: ABOUT 30 MINUTES
CHILLING TIME: 6 HOURS

Chill a serving bowl.

8 egg yolks	Grated rind of 1 small
1 cup sugar	lemon
A few grains of salt	1 cup milk
1 cup dry sherry	½ cup slivered almonds,
½ cup water	toasted (page 4)
¼ cup kirschwasser	and crushed with a
	rolling pin

In the top of a double boiler, beat the egg yolks until they are thick and lemon-colored. Gradually beat in the sugar and salt. Beat in the sherry, water, lemon rind and kirschwasser. Stir in the milk. Over simmering water, cook the mixture, stirring constantly, until it thickens and coats a metal spoon. Allow it to cool somewhat, then fold in the almonds. With a rubber spatula, transfer the cream to the chilled bowl. Chill the dessert for 6 hours.

Sherry Parfait

6 SERVINGS
PREPARATION: ABOUT 15 MINUTES
CHILLING TIME: 6 HOURS

Chill 6 parfait or champagne glasses.

1 envelope unflavored	⅔ cup confectioners'
gelatin, softened for	sugar
5 minutes in ¼ cup	A few grains of salt
cold water	¾ cup medium dry sherry
¼ cup boiling water	

In a mixing bowl, dissolve the gelatin in the boiling water. Add the sugar and salt, stirring until the sugar is dissolved. Stir in the sherry. Chill the mixture until it just begins to set.

1 cup heavy cream, whipped

With a rotary beater, briefly beat the chilled mixture to assure its smoothness. Fold in the whipped cream. Spoon the mixture into the prepared glasses and chill it for at least 6 hours, or until it is thoroughly set.

Sweet Potato Pudding (CARIBBEAN ISLANDS)

4 TO 6 SERVINGS
PREPARATION: ABOUT 25 MINUTES
COOKING: 2½ HOURS IN A 300° OVEN

6 medium sweet potatoes, peeled
¾ cup corn syrup

Grate the sweet potatoes into a mixing bowl containing the corn syrup; stir the mixture with each addition to prevent the potatoes from discoloring.

2 eggs
4 tablespoons butter,
** melted**
¾ cup milk

⅓ cup dark rum
Grated rind of 1 large
** orange**

Into the potato pulp, beat these ingredients.

½ cup flour
¾ teaspoon salt

Sift together the flour and salt; beat the mixture into the contents of the mixing bowl.

Spoon the pudding batter into a well-buttered 1½-quart soufflé dish. Bake it, uncovered, at 300° for 2 hours, stirring every 30 minutes. Bake it for 30 minutes longer without stirring. Offer the pudding with a sauce of your choice (pages 304–310).

Variation:

Follow step one as written. In step two, omit the orange rind. In step three, sift with the flour and salt ¾ teaspoon allspice, ¾ teaspoon cinnamon, and ½ teaspoon mace. Complete the recipe as written.

Zabaglione (ITALY)

4 TO 6 SERVINGS
PREPARATION AND COOKING: ABOUT 15 MINUTES
CHILLING TIME: 2 HOURS

In France, the dessert is called *sabayon*; legend tells us that it journeyed across the Alps from Italy with Catherine de Medici when that formidable lady went to France to marry Henry II.

Chill 4 to 6 dessert glasses.

> **6 egg yolks**
> **6 tablespoons superfine granulated sugar**
> **A few grains of salt**
> **6 tablespoons Marsala**

In the top of a double boiler, combine these four ingredients and, with a rotary beater, whip them until the mixture is light. Over simmering water, cook it, stirring, until it thickens and coats a metal spoon. Allow it to cool.

> **½ cup heavy cream, whipped**

Fold in the whipped cream. Spoon the dessert into the prepared glasses and chill it for at least 2 hours.

Variations:

In place of Marsala, you may use champagne, Sauternes, sherry, bourbon whiskey, white Burgundy, or amaretto; in the last case, reduce the sugar to 1 tablespoon.

Zabaglione is a delicious accompaniment to fresh fruit (berries or sliced peaches). Make the dessert with 5 tablespoons sauterne and 1 tablespoon brandy or orange-flavored liqueur.

Ice Cream

Basic Ice Cream

YIELD: ABOUT 5 CUPS
PREPARATION AND COOKING: ABOUT 30 MINUTES

The freezing time will depend upon the method used; see below.

> 1¼ cups light cream
> ⅓ cup liqueur or liquor
> ⅓ cup sugar
> A few grains of salt

In the top of a double boiler, combine the cream and alcoholic ingredient; over direct heat, scald the cream. Add the sugar and salt, stirring until the sugar is dissolved. Remove the mixture from the heat.

> 4 egg yolks, lightly beaten
> Special ingredients, as called for in variations below

To the egg yolks, add a little of the hot cream, stirring. In a steady stream, pour the egg mixture into the remaining cream, stirring constantly. Over simmering water, cook the custard, stirring, until it thickens and coats a metal spoon. Remove it from the heat and stir in the special ingredients.* Allow the custard to cool, and then chill it.

*If you will be freezing the mixture in freezer trays, hold off on adding solid ingredients until then, as directed below.

> Special flavoring, as called for (vanilla extract, almond
>   extract, etc.)
> 2 cups chilled heavy cream, two days old

Into the chilled custard, stir the flavoring and heavy cream. Freeze the ice cream in one of the following ways.

In an ice-cream freezer: Pour the prepared mixture into the can of an ice-cream freezer; adjust the dasher, cover the can with its lid; put the can in the freezer bucket; put on the gear case so that the handle turns easily. Pack the bucket with one part rock salt to eight parts crushed ice. Churn the custard in a steady rhythm until the handle is very difficult to turn (at this point the mixture will have achieved its maximum density).

During the churning, add salt and ice as necessary, in the proportions given. Remove the gear case, the can lid, and the dasher; with a rubber spatula, clean the dasher, adding the drippings to the contents of the freezer can. Cover the can with aluminum foil and replace the lid. Allow the ice cream to stand for 2 hours, either in the freezer bucket or in the freezer compartment of the refrigerator.

In freezer trays: Pour the prepared mixture into deep freezer trays or another utensil and freeze it until it is solid for ½ inch around the edge. Transfer it to a mixing bowl and beat it vigorously until it is smooth. At this point add any solid special ingredients. Return the mixture to the freezing compartment until it is firm.

In an in-the-freezer freezer: There is available at modest cost an appliance that works electrically on the principle of the dasher-freezer; one puts it in the freezing compartment of the refrigerator. It is reliable for smooth ice creams but less effective for those with solid ingredients.

ALMOND ICE CREAM: In step one, to the cream when scalding it, add amaretto. In step two, to the hot custard add ½ cup toasted slivered almonds (page 4), crushed with a rolling pin. Complete the basic recipe as written.

IRISH COFFEE ICE CREAM: In step one, to the cream when scalding it, add Irish whiskey; use ½ cup sugar. In step two, to the hot custard add 2 tablespoons instant coffee powder; stir the mixture until the coffee is dissolved. Complete the basic recipe as written.

MINT ICE CREAM: In step one, to the cream when scalding it, add green crème de menthe. In step two, to the hot custard add ⅓ cup fine-chopped fresh mint leaves. Complete the basic recipe as written.

NESSELRODE ICE CREAM: In a mixing bowl, combine 1 cup candied mixed fruits and ½ cup dark rum; allow the fruit to macerate (more rum may be added as needed); in a saucepan, bring the fruit and its liquid just to the boil. In step one, use 1 cup light cream. In step two, to the hot custard add the macerated fruits and their liquid. In step three, add 1 teaspoon vanilla extract. Complete the basic recipe as written.

ORANGE ICE CREAM: In step one, to the cream when scalding it, add orange-flavored liqueur. In step two, to the hot custard add the grated rind of 1 large orange. Complete the basic recipe as written.

P e a r I c e C r e a m : In step one, to the cream when scalding it, add pear brandy (recommended: poire Williams). In step two, to the hot custard add the purée made from 5 large, very ripe pears, peeled and grated. Complete the basic recipe as written.

P e p p e r m i n t S t i c k I c e C r e a m : In step one, to the cream when scalding it, add white crème de menthe. Complete the basic recipe as written and start to freeze the ice cream. When the freezer crank offers resistance, or when the mixture in the freezer trays becomes mushy, stir in 1 cup peppermint candy sticks, crushed with a rolling pin. Continue to freeze the ice cream until it is set.

P r u n e I c e C r e a m : In a mixing bowl, combine ½ pound tenderized pitted prunes, chopped fine, and ½ cup brandy or dark rum; allow the fruit to macerate overnight; in a saucepan, bring the prunes and their liquid just to the boil. In step one, use 1 cup cream. In step two, to the hot custard add the prunes and their liquid. Complete the basic recipe as written.

P u m p k i n I c e C r e a m : In step one, use 1 cup cream and, when scalding it, add dark rum. In step two, to the hot custard add 1½ cups pumpkin purée seasoned with ½ teaspoon each ground allspice, ginger, and nutmeg, 1 teaspoon cinnamon, and the strained juice of 1 small lemon. In step three, add 1 teaspoon vanilla extract. Complete the basic recipe as written.

R a i s i n I c e C r e a m : In a mixing bowl, combine 1 (11-ounce) package of seedless raisins and 1 cup of dark rum; allow the fruit to macerate overnight. In a saucepan, bring the raisins and their liquid just to the boil. In step one, omit the alcoholic ingredient and use ¾ cup heavy cream. In step two, to the hot custard add the raisins and their liquid. In step three, add 1 teaspoon vanilla extract. Complete the basic recipe as written.

Strawberries Romanoff (FRANCE)

6 SERVINGS
PREPARATION: ABOUT 30 MINUTES
FREEZING TIME: 3 HOURS

Put a serving bowl in the freezer.

1 quart strawberries, hulled,   A few grains of salt
    rinsed, drained on   ¼ cup strained fresh
    absorbent paper, and   orange juice
    halved lengthwise   ⅓ cup orange-flavored
2 tablespoons superfine   liqueur
    granulated sugar

In a large mixing bowl, toss the strawberries with the sugar and salt and allow them to stand for 10 minutes. Add the orange juice and liqueur and, using a rubber spatula, toss them gently to blend the ingredients well.

1 cup heavy cream
1 pint rich vanilla ice cream

Whip the cream and set it aside. With a heavy fork, beat the ice cream until it is soft and light but not melted. Immediately fold in the whipped cream. Using a rubber spatula, fold the ice cream mixture into the strawberries. Transfer the dessert to the chilled serving bowl and freeze it for 3 hours.

Mousses

Apple Mousse

6 TO 8 SERVINGS
PREPARATION: ABOUT 30 MINUTES
CHILLING TIME: 6 HOURS

Lightly oil and chill a 6-cup ring mold or other mold.

Grated rind and strained juice of 1 large lemon
4 large tart apples, peeled

Into a mixing bowl containing the lemon rind and juice, grate the apples. Stir each addition to prevent its discoloring.

¼ cup apple juice
¼ cup Calvados *or* applejack
1 envelope unflavored gelatin

Combine the apple juice and Calvados. Over the mixture, sprinkle the gelatin and allow it to soften for 5 minutes. Over simmering water, dissolve the gelatin; stir it into the grated apple.

¾ cup sugar	2 or 3 drops almond
¼ teaspoon cinnamon	extract
½ teaspoon nutmeg	A few grains of salt

Into the apple mixture, stir the sugar and seasonings until the sugar is dissolved. Chill the mixture until it just begins to set.

1 cup heavy cream, whipped
Crème Anglaise (page 306) (optional)

With a rotary beater, whip the apple mixture until it is somewhat light. Fold in the whipped cream. Using a rubber spatula, transfer the mixture to the prepared mold. Chill the mousse for at least 6 hours, or until it is thoroughly set. To serve the dessert, unmold it onto a chilled serving platter and offer it with crème anglaise.

Fresh Fruit Mousse

6 TO 8 SERVINGS
PREPARATION AND COOKING: ABOUT 30 MINUTES
MACERATION TIME: 3 HOURS
CHILLING TIME: 6 HOURS

Lightly oil and chill an 8-cup mold.

1 cup cantaloupe balls	2 tablespoons superfine
1 cup honey dew balls	granulated sugar
1 cup seedless grapes,	¼ cup light rum
rinsed, dried on	
absorbent paper, and	
halved lengthwise	

In a mixing bowl, combine the fruits. Sprinkle them with the sugar and add the rum. Allow the mixture to macerate, refrigerated, for 3 hours.

1½ envelopes unflavored gelatin
¼ cup light rum

Sprinkle the gelatin over the rum; allow it to soften for 5 minutes.

4 egg yolks	A few grains of salt
⅔ cup sugar	1½ cups milk
½ teaspoon cornstarch	

In the top of a double boiler, lightly beat the egg yolks. Blend the sugar, cornstarch, and salt; add this mixture and the milk to the egg yolks. Over gently boiling water, cook the custard, stirring constantly, until it thickens and coats a metal spoon. Add the softened gelatin, stirring to dissolve it. Allow the custard to cool, and then chill it until it just begins to set.

Macerated fruit
4 egg whites, beaten until stiff but not dry
Crème Anglaise (page 306) (optional)

Drain the fruit through a sieve. With a rotary beater, briefly whip the egg yolk mixture. Beat in one-fifth of the egg white; fold in the remainder. Fold in the drained fruit. Using a rubber spatula, transfer the mixture to the prepared mold. Chill the mousse for at least 6 hours, or until it is thoroughly set. To serve the dessert, unmold it onto a chilled serving platter and offer it with crème anglaise.

Strawberry Mousse

6 TO 8 SERVINGS
PREPARATION: ABOUT 30 MINUTES
CHILLING TIME: 6 HOURS

Lightly oil and chill a 6-cup ring or other mold.

1 quart strawberries, hulled, rinsed, and drained

Set aside several strawberries for use as garnish. In the container of a food processor or blender, whirl the remainder until they are reduced to a smooth purée.

½ cup sugar
A few grains of salt
½ cup Sauternes
Puréed strawberries

In a mixing bowl, combine and blend the sugar, salt, wine, and strawberry purée. When the sugar is dissolved, chill the mixture.

 ½ cup boiling water
 2 envelopes unflavored gelatin, softened for 5 minutes in
      ½ cup cold water

Add the boiling water to the softened gelatin, stirring until the gelatin
is dissolved. Stir the gelatin into the contents of the mixing bowl. Chill
the mixture until it just begins to set.

 1 cup heavy cream, whipped
 Reserved whole strawberries
 Crème Anglaise (page 306) (optional)

With a rotary beater, briefly beat the strawberry mixture. Fold in the
whipped cream. Using a rubber spatula, transfer the mixture to the prepared dish. Chill the mousse for at least 6 hours, or until it is thoroughly
set. To serve the dessert, unmold it on a chilled serving platter, garnish
it with the reserved whole strawberries, and offer it with crème anglaise.

Soufflés

Basic Hot Dessert Soufflé

6 TO 8 SERVINGS
PREPARATION: ABOUT 30 MINUTES
COOKING: FOR A FIRM SOUFFLÉ, 30 MINUTES IN A 350° OVEN; FOR A CREAMY
   SOUFFLÉ, À LA FRANÇAISE, 20 TO 25 MINUTES IN A 375° OVEN.

*All the ingredients may be readied ahead and combined according to
directions at the time of cooking.*

Butter and sugar a 2-quart soufflé dish.

 3 tablespoons butter
 3 tablespoons flour

In a saucepan, heat the butter and in it, over gentle heat, cook the flour
for a few minutes. This mixture is called a roux.

 Special seasonings, as called for in the variations below

If a recipe calls for such special seasonings as ground spices, add them to
the roux; the butter in the roux facilitates smooth blending of the
seasonings.

¾ cup milk

Gradually add the milk, stirring constantly until the mixture is thickened and smooth. This mixture is called a béchamel.

½ cup sugar
A few grains of salt

Away from the heat, add the sugar and salt, stirring until they are dissolved. (The quantity of sugar will vary depending upon the sweetness of the prepared major ingredient.)

Prepared major ingredient, as called for in the variations below

Into the contents of the saucepan, blend the major ingredient.

4 egg yolks
Liquid seasoning, if called for

Beat in the egg yolks and seasoning.

4 or 5 egg whites, beaten until stiff but not dry

Beat in one-fifth of the egg white; fold in the remainder. Using a rubber spatula, transfer the mixture to the prepared dish. Bake the soufflé according to the directions given above, or until it is well puffed and golden.

Crème Anglaise (page 306) (optional)

Not obligatory, but very pleasant, especially if you bake the soufflé until firm.

Variations:

HOT ALMOND SOUFFLÉ: Toast (page 4) a 3½-ounce package of blanched slivered almonds; allow them to cool and then crush them with a rolling pin. Reserve them. In step five, reduce the sugar to ¼ cup. In step six, add ¼ cup amaretto. Following the addition of the egg yolks, stir in the crushed almonds. Complete the basic recipe as written.

HOT BANANA SOUFFLÉ: Into the roux stir ¼ teaspoon ground mace. After dissolving the sugar, stir in 2 large, *very* ripe bananas, peeled and puréed. With the egg yolks, add ¼ cup dark rum. Complete the basic recipe as written.

HOT DATE SOUFFLÉ: In 1 cup milk, cook ¾ cup fine-chopped pitted dates, covered, for 20 minutes, or until they are very tender. Allow the mixture to cool somewhat. In the container of a food processor, whirl it until it is smooth; reserve it. To the roux add a grating of nutmeg. Make the béchamel with the reserved date purée instead of the milk (it will be very thick). Reduce the sugar to ¼ cup. With the egg yolks, add ¼ cup dark rum and 1 teaspoon vanilla extract. Use 5 egg whites. Complete the basic recipe as written.

HOT HAZELNUT SOUFFLÉ: Reduce the sugar to ¼ cup. With the egg yolks, add ¼ cup Frangelico (hazelnut-flavored liqueur). When the mixture is well blended, stir in ½ cup hazelnuts, crushed with a rolling pin. Complete the basic recipe as written.

HOT MAPLE SOUFFLÉ: Reduce the milk to ½ cup and the sugar to ¼ cup. In step 3, add to the béchamel ⅓ cup maple syrup and ⅓ cup bourbon whiskey. Use 5 egg whites. Complete the basic recipe as written.

HOT ORANGE SOUFFLÉ I (Soufflé au Grand Marnier) (France): Make the roux with 4 tablespoons flour. Reduce the sugar to ⅓ cup; after dissolving it, stir in the grated rinds of 1 medium lemon and 1 medium orange. With the egg yolks, add ¼ cup strained fresh orange juice and ⅓ cup Grand Marnier. Use 5 egg whites. Complete the basic recipe as written.

HOT ORANGE SOUFFLÉ II: In place of the milk, use a 6-ounce can of frozen orange juice concentrate, fully thawed to room temperature. In step 3, add the grated rind of 1 medium orange. With the egg yolks, add ¼ cup orange-flavored liqueur (recommended: Triple Sec or curaçao). Complete the basic recipe as written.

Basic Chilled Dessert Soufflé

6 TO 8 SERVINGS
PREPARATION AND COOKING: ABOUT 30 MINUTES
CHILLING TIME: 6 HOURS

Lightly oil and chill a 2-quart soufflé dish, or furnish a 1½-quart soufflé dish with an oiled collar.

1½ cups milk
3 egg yolks

In the top of a double boiler, over direct heat, scald the milk. In a mixing bowl, beat the egg yolks. Pour the milk over the yolks in a steady stream, beating the mixture constantly. Return it to the top of the double boiler and set the pan over simmering water.

½ cup sugar
A few grains of salt

Add the sugar and salt. Cook the custard, stirring constantly, until it thickens and coats a metal spoon. Remove it from the heat.

1 envelope unflavored gelatin, softened for 5 minutes in ¼
   cup cold water
Liqueur or other alcoholic ingredient

Add the gelatin and the alcohol, stirring until the gelatin is dissolved.

Other ingredients or seasonings, as called for in the variations
   below

Stir in the major ingredients and seasonings. Transfer the mixture to a mixing bowl, allow it to cool, and then chill it until it just begins to set.

1 cup heavy cream, whipped
4 egg whites, beaten until stiff but not dry

With a rotary beater, beat the chilled mixture briefly to assure its smoothness. Fold in the whipped cream. Beat in one-fifth of the egg white; fold in the remainder. Using a rubber spatula, transfer the mixture to the prepared soufflé dish. Chill the soufflé for at least 6 hours, or until it is thoroughly set.

Crème Anglaise (page 306) (optional)

If you wish to offer a sauce, crème anglaise goes well with virtually every chilled soufflé. Other sauces that may appeal to you are suggested on pages 304–310.

CHILLED ALMOND SOUFFLÉ: Toast (page 4) a 3½-ounce package of blanched slivered almonds; allow them to cool and then crush them with a rolling pin. Reserve them. Reduce the sugar to ¼ cup. To the custard, together with the softened gelatin, add ¼ cup amaretto; when the gelatin is dissolved, stir in the crushed almonds. Complete the basic recipe as written.

CHILLED BRANDY ALEXANDER SOUFFLÉ: Reduce the milk to 1¼ cups; reduce the sugar to ¼ cup. To the custard, together with the softened gelatin, add ¼ cup *each* brandy and crème de cacao. Complete the basic recipe as written.

CHILLED SOUFFLÉ À LA CHARTREUSE VERTE: Reduce the sugar to ⅓ cupful. To the custard, together with the softened gelatin, add ¼ cup green chartreuse. Complete the basic recipe as written.

CHILLED CHOCOLATE-ORANGE SOUFFLÉ: Reduce the milk to 1¼ cups; in it, over simmering water, dissolve a 6-ounce package of semisweet chocolate bits. Reduce the sugar to ¼ cup. To the custard, together with the softened gelatin, add ¼ cup orange-flavored liqueur; when the gelatin is dissolved, stir in the fine-grated rind of 1 medium orange. Complete the basic recipe as written.

CHILLED COFFEE SOUFFLÉ: To the custard, together with the softened gelatin, add ¼ cup mocha-flavored liqueur (recommended: Kahlua) and 3 tablespoons instant coffee powder. Complete the basic recipe as written.

CHILLED EGGNOG SOUFFLÉ: To the custard, together with the softened gelatin, add ¼ cup bourbon whiskey and a generous grating of nutmeg. Complete the basic recipe as written.

CHILLED GINGER SOUFFLÉ: To the custard, together with the softened gelatin, add ½ cup light rum that has been ignited and allowed to burn out; when the gelatin is dissolved, stir in ½ cup fine-chopped crystallized ginger. Complete the basic recipe as written.

CHILLED SOUFFLÉ AU GRAND MARNIER: Increase the gelatin to 1½ envelopes (4½ teaspoons), softened in ½ cup cold water. To the custard, together with the softened gelatin, add ⅓ cup Grand Marnier and the fine-grated rind of 1 medium orange. Complete the basic recipe as written.

CHILLED HAZELNUT SOUFFLÉ: To the custard, together with the softened gelatin, add ¼ cup Frangelico (hazelnut-flavored liqueur); when the gelatin is dissolved, stir in ½ cup crushed hazelnuts. Complete the basic recipe as written.

CHILLED MAI-TAI SOUFFLÉ: Reduce the milk to 1 cup. To the custard, together with the softened gelatin, add ¼ cup strained lime juice, 2 tablespoons strained lemon juice, and 3 tablespoons *each* orange-flavored liqueur (recommended: Triple Sec), dark rum, and light rum. Complete the basic recipe as written.

CHILLED PEAR SOUFFLÉ: Drain a 16-ounce can of Bartlett pears, reserving the liquid. In the container of a food processor or blender, whirl the pears until they are reduced to a smooth purée. To the liquid from the pears, add milk to equal 1 cup to make the custard. Reduce the sugar to ¼ cup. To the custard, together with the softened gelatin and pear purée, add ¼ cup pear-flavored liqueur (recommended: poire Williams). Complete the basic recipe as written.

CHILLED RUM-FLAVORED SOUFFLÉ: In place of the milk, use light cream or half-and-half. Reduce the sugar to ⅓ cup and mix it with 2 teaspoons cornstarch. To the custard, together with the softened gelatin, add ⅓ cup dark rum and ½ teaspoon vanilla extract. Complete the basic recipe as written.

Soufflé au Marrons (Chilled Chestnut Soufflé) (FRANCE)

8 TO 10 SERVINGS
PREPARATION: ABOUT 40 MINUTES
CHILLING TIME: 6 HOURS

Lightly oil and chill a 2-quart soufflé dish, or furnish a 1½-quart soufflé dish with an oiled collar.

- 1 (17½-ounce) can of sweetened chestnut purée (available at specialty food shops)
- 2 cups milk
- 2 envelopes unflavored gelatin

In a saucepan, combine the chestnut purée and the milk; using a rotary beater, blend them until the mixture is smooth. Sprinkle the gelatin over the surface, and allow it to soften for 5 minutes. Over medium heat, bring the purée to the boil, stirring constantly until the gelatin is dissolved.

3 egg yolks
¼ cup dark rum
¾ teaspoon vanilla extract
A few grains of salt

Away from the heat, beat in the egg yolks and seasonings. Over gentle heat, cook the mixture, stirring constantly, until it is slightly thickened. Allow it to cool and then chill it until it just begins to set.

1 cup heavy cream, whipped
4 egg whites, beaten until stiff but not dry

With a rotary beater, beat the chilled mixture briefly to assure its smoothness. Fold in the whipped cream. Beat in one-fifth of the egg white; fold in the remainder. Using a rubber spatula, transfer the mixture to the prepared soufflé dish. Chill the soufflé for at least 6 hours, or until it is thoroughly set.

Crème Anglaise (page 306) (optional)

A delightful accompaniment, but not mandatory. You will find other sauces that may please you on pages 304–310.

Chilled Mincemeat Soufflé

6 TO 8 SERVINGS
PREPARATION AND COOKING: ABOUT 35 MINUTES
CHILLING TIME: 6 HOURS

Lightly oil and chill a 2-quart soufflé dish, or furnish a 1½-quart soufflé dish with an oiled collar.

1 (9-ounce) package dehydrated mincemeat
1½ cups milk

Into a saucepan, crumble the mincemeat. Add the milk, bring the mixture to the boil, and cook it, stirring, for 5 minutes. Allow it to cool somewhat.

3 egg yolks, beaten

Add the egg yolks and, over gentle heat, cook the mixture for a few minutes, stirring constantly; do not allow it to boil.

1 **envelope unflavored gelatin**
¼ **cup dark rum**

Soften the gelatin in the rum for 5 minutes; add it to the hot mixture, stirring until it is dissolved.

Grated rind and strained juice of 1 medium lemon

Stir in the lemon rind and juice. Transfer the mixture to a mixing bowl, allow it to cool, and chill it until it just begins to set.

1 **cup heavy cream, whipped**
4 **egg whites, beaten until stiff but not dry**

With a rotary beater, whip the chilled mixture briefly. Fold in the whipped cream. Beat in one-fifth of the egg white; fold in the remainder. Using a rubber spatula, transfer the mixture to the prepared soufflé dish. Chill the soufflé for at least 6 hours, or until it is thoroughly set.

Crème Anglaise (page 306) (optional)

Cakes

Almond-Brandy Torte

PREPARATION: ABOUT 20 MINUTES
COOKING: 30 MINUTES IN A 350° OVEN
REFRIGERATES

The cake may be iced—as tortes most frequently are—but I admit to a preference for it unadorned and unconfused by any additional flavor.

Butter and flour a deep 8-inch cake pan.

½ **pound blanched almonds**

In the container of a food processor equipped with the steel blade, whirl the almonds until they are ground very fine. Reserve the almond meal.

3 **eggs**	1 **cup fine dry bread**
1 **cup sugar**	**crumbs**
A few grains of salt	1 **cup brandy**
Grated rind of 2 large lemons	**Reserved almond meal**
1 **teaspoon mace**	

In a mixing bowl, beat together the eggs, sugar, and salt until the mixture is light. Stir in the lemon rind and mace. Stir in alternately, a small quantity at a time, the bread crumbs and brandy. Add the almond meal and continue to stir until the mixture is thoroughly blended.

Using a rubber spatula, transfer the batter to the prepared pan. Bake the torte at 350° for 30 minutes, or until a sharp knife inserted in the center comes out clean.

Applesauce Cake (UNITED STATES)

PREPARATION: ABOUT 30 MINUTES
COOKING: 1½ HOURS IN A 325° OVEN

This traditional recipe from Tennessee, a cousin of Kentucky Bourbon Cake (page 273), is easily made with store-bought applesauce.

Butter and flour a 9-inch spring-form pan.

8 tablespoons softened butter
1 cup sugar
2 eggs

In a mixing bowl, beat together the butter and sugar until the mixture is light. Beat in the eggs, one at a time.

2 cups flour	½ teaspoon mace
2 teaspoons baking soda	½ teaspoon salt
½ teaspoon allspice	¼ cup bourbon whiskey
½ teaspoon cinnamon	

Sift together the dry ingredients and add them, a small quantity at a time and alternating with the bourbon, to the liquid mixure.

1½ cups applesauce

Add the applesauce and continue to stir until the mixture is thoroughly blended.

Using a rubber spatula, transfer the batter to the prepared pan. Bake the applesauce cake at 325° for 1½ hours, or until a sharp knife inserted in the center comes out clean.

Baba au Rhum (FRANCE)

PREPARATION: ABOUT 25 MINUTES
COOKING: 30 MINUTES IN A 450° OVEN
REFRIGERATES

Traditionally, baba is made from yeast dough, but a very acceptable one may be prepared with baking powder, and with considerably less effort. In step three, you may add ½ cup currants, plumped in hot water, drained, and dried on absorbent paper.

Butter and flour a 5- or 6-cup ring mold or a deep 6-inch cake pan.

> 2 eggs
> ½ cup sugar
> ½ cup milk
> 3 tablespoons melted butter

In a mixing bowl, beat the eggs and sugar until the mixture is light. Beat in the milk and butter.

> ⅔ cup flour
> 1 teaspoon baking powder
> A few grains of salt

Sift together the dry ingredients and beat them into the liquid mixture. Using a rubber spatula, transfer the batter to the prepared pan. Bake the baba at 450° for 30 minutes, or until it is golden.

> Rum Syrup (page 309)

Allow the baba to cool briefly before unmolding it onto a serving plate. When it is lukewarm, saturate it with the rum syrup. Serve the baba warm with whipped cream.

Bourbon Cake (UNITED STATES)

PREPARATION: ABOUT 30 MINUTES
COOKING: 2½ HOURS IN A 275° OVEN
REFRIGERATES; FREEZES

A native of Kentucky, this rich cake is at its best, I feel, offered warm and garnished with whipped cream.

Butter a 9-inch tube pan.

  12 tablespoons softened butter
  1 cup sugar
  3 eggs

In a mixing bowl, beat together the butter and sugar until the mixture is light. Beat the eggs in one at a time.

2 cups flour	½ teaspoon ground cloves
1 teaspoon baking powder	1 teaspoon mace
1 teaspoon cinnamon	½ teaspoon salt

Sift together the dry ingredients and blend them into the butter mixture.

½ cup bourbon whiskey	bourbon whiskey and
4 tablespoons honey	drained
1 cup currants *or* golden raisins, plumped in	2 cups broken pecans

Add these four ingredients and stir the batter vigorously to blend it well. With a rubber spatula, transfer the batter to the prepared pan. Put the pan on a baking sheet and bake the bourbon cake at 275° for 2½ hours, or until it is golden and a sharp knife inserted in the center comes out clean.

  ¼ cup bourbon whiskey

Cool the cake for 10 minutes. Unmold it and wrap it in several thicknesses of cheesecloth. Sprinkle the cheesecloth with whiskey. Store the cake, tightly wrapped, in the refrigerator. (You may add more bourbon to the cheesecloth from time to time, just as one adds brandy to fruitcake.)

Note: The recipe may also be made with Scotch whisky; it will be slightly less sweet and have a pleasant, faintly smoky taste.

Brandy Snaps (ENGLAND)

YIELD: ABOUT 48
PREPARATION: ABOUT 15 MINUTES
COOKING: 12 MINUTES (PER BATCH) IN A 350° OVEN

Delicious served plain as an accompaniment to dessert creams or fruit; almost a dessert in themselves when filled with whipped cream flavored with ginger preserves.

> 1½ cups flour
> 1 tablespoon ginger
> ½ teaspoon nutmeg
> ¼ teaspoon salt

In a mixing bowl, sift together and blend the dry ingredients.

> 12 tablespoons hot melted butter
> 1 cup dark brown sugar, packed
> ½ cup molasses
> ¼ cup brandy

In a second mixing bowl, combine and blend these ingredients. Add this mixture to the flour, beating the batter to blend it thoroughly.

Drop the batter by the scant teaspoon, spaced 3 inches apart, onto a lightly buttered baking sheet. Bake about 6 brandy snaps at 300° for 10 to 12 minutes. Allow them to cool just enough to handle. With a spatula, lift them swiftly and roll each one around the handle of a wooden spoon. Withdraw the spoon from the "scroll" and allow the brandy snap to cool. If the snaps harden before you have rolled them, reheat them briefly. Repeat the baking and curling until the batter is used up. Store the brandy snaps in an airtight container.

Fruitcake

PREPARATION: ABOUT 45 MINUTES
COOKING: 2 HOURS IN A 275° OVEN
REFRIGERATES; FREEZES

The old-fashioned kind, which should mature for at least two weeks wrapped in a brandy-soaked cloth before being enjoyed—perhaps with Hard Sauce (page 308).

Line a 9 × 3-inch spring-form pan with buttered brown paper.

¼ pound blanched almonds
½ pound candied cherries, halved
½ pound citron, diced
1 (11-ounce) package of currants
½ pound pitted dates, chopped

½ pound dried figs, chopped
¼ pound candied lemon peel
¼ pound candied orange peel
1 (11-ounce) package of golden raisins
1 cup flour

In a large mixing bowl, combine and blend the fruits and flour.

¾ pound (3 sticks) softened butter
1½ cups (packed) light brown sugar
½ teaspoon salt
6 egg yolks

In a mixing bowl, combine and cream together the butter, sugar, and salt until the mixture is light and fluffy. Beat in the egg yolks.

2 cups flour
1 tablespoon each ground allspice, cinnamon, cloves, mace, and nutmeg
1½ teaspoons baking soda

In a mixing bowl, combine and sift together the dry ingredients.

½ cup brandy
Floured fruit
6 egg whites, beaten until stiff but not dry

To the butter mixture, add the dry ingredients and the brandy. When the batter is well blended, beat in the floured fruits. Fold in the egg whites.

Using a rubber spatula, transfer the batter to the prepared pan. Bake the fruitcake at 275° for 2 hours. Remove it from the oven and allow it to stand for 10 minutes. Remove the cake from the pan and peel off the paper.

When the cake is fully cooled, wrap it in a cloth that has been saturated with brandy. Then wrap the cake in foil. Allow the cake to ripen for at least 2 weeks; keep the cloth moist by adding more brandy from time to time.

Gingerbread

8 TO 10 SERVINGS
PREPARATION: ABOUT 20 MINUTES
COOKING: 35 MINUTES IN A 350° OVEN
REFRIGERATES; FREEZES

This old-fashioned recipe from my grandmother makes a very substantial gingerbread; it is especially good served with Lemon-Brandy Sauce (page 306). If you prefer not to use bacon fat, which gives a fine flavor, double the quantity of butter.

Butter a shallow baking pan, 9 × 9 inches square.

½ cup dark brown sugar, packed	4 tablespoons softened butter
4 tablespoons soft (not melted) bacon fat	1 egg, beaten
	1 cup dark molasses

In a mixing bowl, beat together until creamy the sugar, bacon fat, and butter. Add first the egg and then the molasses, blending thoroughly after each addition.

2½ cups flour	1 teaspoon cinnamon
1½ teaspoons baking soda	½ teaspoon ground cloves
2 teaspoons ginger	½ teaspoon salt

In a second mixing bowl, sift together the dry ingredients.

At this point you may stop and continue later.

¾ cup boiling water
⅓ cup dark rum

Into the dry ingredients, stir the molasses mixture. Combine the water and rum. Gradually add the liquid, beating the batter constantly to free it of lumps. Blend it for 3 minutes.

Spoon the batter into the prepared pan. Bake the gingberbread at 350°
for 35 minutes, or until a sharp knife inserted in the center comes out
clean. Allow it to cool slightly before turning it out of the pan onto a rack.

Orange Cake (UNITED STATES)

PREPARATION: ABOUT 30 MINUTES
COOKING: 50 MINUTES IN A 350° OVEN

This recipe from Florida is a delicious, fruity, uncomplicated cake.

Butter and flour a 9-inch tube pan.

> ¼ cup strained fresh orange juice
> ⅓ cup orange-flavored liqueur
> ½ cup sugar
> A few grains of salt

In a saucepan, combine the orange juice, liqueur, sugar, and salt. Heat
the mixture, stirring, until the sugar is dissolved. Allow the syrup to cool
and reserve it.

> ½ pound (2 sticks) softened butter
> 1 cup sugar
> 3 egg yolks

In a mixing bowl, cream together the butter and sugar until the mixture
is light and fluffy. Beat in the egg yolks one at a time.

> 2 cups flour
> 1½ teaspoons baking powder
> 1 teaspoon baking soda
> A few grains of salt

In a mixing bowl, sift together the dry ingredients.

At this point you may stop and continue later.

> 1 cup sour cream
> Grated rind of 2 medium oranges
> ½ cup chopped pecans (optional)
> 4 egg whites, beaten until stiff but not dry

Into the dry ingredients, beat alternately the butter-sugar mixture and the sour cream. When the batter is smooth, stir in the orange rind and pecans. Fold in the egg whites.

Using a rubber spatula, transfer the batter to the prepared pan. Bake the orange cake at 350° for 50 minutes, or until a sharp knife inserted in the center comes out clean.

Reserved orange syrup

Pour the syrup over the hot cake. Allow the cake to cool in the pan before removing it.

Pear Cake

PREPARATION: ABOUT 30 MINUTES
MACERATION TIME: 30 MINUTES
COOKING: 1 HOUR IN A 350° OVEN
REFRIGERATES

Butter a 9-inch baking dish or loaf pan.

4 firm ripe pears, peeled, cored, and cut into large dice
¼ cup orange-flavored liqueur
¼ cup sugar

In a mixing bowl, combine the pears, liqueur, and sugar. Stir the mixture to blend it well, and allow the pears to macerate for at least 30 minutes.

2 cups flour
¼ cup sugar
4 teaspoons baking powder
A few grains of salt

In a mixing bowl, sift together the dry ingredients.

3 eggs
¼ cup milk

In a mixing bowl, beat together the eggs and milk.

At this point you may stop and continue later.

4 tablespoons butter, melted and cooled to lukewarm
Macerated pear mixture

Add the butter to the milk and eggs. Combine the dry and liquid ingredients, beating them until the batter is smooth. Stir in the pear mixture.

Using a rubber spatula, transfer the batter to the prepared pan. Bake the pear cake at 350° for 1 hour, or until a sharp knife inserted in the center comes out clean. Allow the cake to cool for 5 minutes before turning it out of the dish onto a rack.

Tipsy Cake (ENGLAND)

6 SERVINGS
PREPARATION: ABOUT 20 MINUTES
STANDING TIME: 1 HOUR
COOKING (THE SAUCE): 10 MINUTES

"Tipsy cake," from the Spanish *bizcocho borracho*, "drunken cake," was actually brought to England by Philip II of Spain, Mary Tudor's husband. Philip deserted Mary, but left behind this dessert, which the English have made their own.

6 individual sponge cakes,
    split in half horizontally
¼ cup cream sherry *or* a
    combination of sweet
    sherry and brandy

Cinnamon
Crème Anglaise
    (page 306) made with
    sherry

In a serving dish, arrange the lower halves of the sponge cakes. Over them, drizzle the cream sherry; sprinkle them with cinnamon. Allow them to stand for 1 hour. Over them, spoon a bit of the crème anglaise. Replace the tops of the cakes and chill the dessert.

½ cup heavy cream, whipped
Lightly toasted crushed almonds (page 4)

When serving the dessert, garnish the individual portions with a spoonful of whipped cream and a sprinkling of toasted almonds.

Crêpes, Pastry, Tarts, and Pies

Crêpes

YIELD: ABOUT 18 CRÊPES
PREPARATION AND COOKING: ABOUT 1 HOUR
STANDING TIME: 2 HOURS
REFRIGERATES; FREEZES

In addition to being used in Crêpes Suzette (page 281), crêpes are an easy, delicious, and festive way of using leftovers.

1½ cups flour	¾ cup stale ale *or* beer
½ teaspoon salt	5 tablespoons butter,
2 eggs	melted
¾ cup milk	

In the container of a blender, combine the ingredients and, on medium speed, whirl them for 20 seconds, or until the mixture is completely blended and smooth. During the blending, clean the sides of the container with a rubber spatula. Allow the batter to rest for 2 hours.

Softened butter

Heat a 5- or 6-inch skillet or crêpe pan and butter it lightly with a pastry brush. Pour in sufficient batter barely to cover the bottom of the pan (about 3 tablespoons); rotate the pan to spread the batter evenly. Cook the crêpes as you would pancakes, first one side and then the other, turning them with a spatula.

To refrigerate or freeze the crêpes, separate them with pieces of wax paper to prevent their sticking together; wrap the stack in plastic wrap. Frozen crêpes will keep for as long as 6 months, and you may use a few at a time. Refreezing does not spoil them.

DESSERT CRÊPES: In step one, in place of the beer, use ¾ cup water; add ¼ cup powdered sugar, 1 teaspoon vanilla extract, and ¼ cup brandy *or* orange-flavored liqueur.

Crêpes Suzette (FRANCE)

6 SERVINGS
PREPARATION: ABOUT 15 MINUTES (THE PREPARATION TIME DOES NOT
   INCLUDE READYING THE CRÊPES)
COOKING: ABOUT 10 MINUTES

A truly gala dessert that can be finished in a chafing dish at table, making
the show part of the pleasure.

Dessert Crêpes for 6 persons (12 to 18 crêpes) (page 280)

Let the crêpes come to room temperature.

8 tablespoons softened
   butter
½ cup superfine granulated
   sugar
A few grains of salt

Grated rind and strained
   juice of 1 large orange
⅓ cup orange-flavored
   liqueur

In a small bowl, cream together the butter, sugar, and salt until the
mixture is light. Whip in the orange rind, juice, and liqueur. Reserve
the sauce.

Prepared sauce
Prepared crêpes
Superfine granulated sugar
¼ cup brandy mixed with ¼ cup orange-flavored liqueur,
   warmed

In a chafing dish, heat 3 tablespoons of the sauce. Add 6 crêpes, folded
in quarters. Heat them through, spooning the sauce over them; more
sauce may be added as necessary. When the sauce is syrupy and the
crêpes are hot, sprinkle them with sugar and a little of the warmed
liqueur mixture; ignite the spirits and let the flame die. (You may use
all orange-flavored liqueur if you prefer; the brandy cuts the sweetness.)
Repeat the process.

CRÊPES À LA CHARTREUSE: In step two, make the sauce
with 6 tablespoons butter, 3 tablespoons sugar, a few grains of salt,

the strained juice of 1 medium lemon, and ⅓ cup yellow chartreuse. Follow step three as written, using ⅓ cup yellow chartreuse in place of the brandy and orange-flavored liqueur (you will not need as much; the chartreuse is quite pungent).

Short Pastry for Quiches, Tarts, and Pastry Shells

YIELD: 2 (9-INCH) PASTRY SHELLS
PREPARATION: 15 MINUTES
COOKING (FOR RECIPES CALLING FOR BAKED PIE SHELLS): 12 MINUTES IN A
    450° OVEN
UNBAKED SHORT PASTRY REFRIGERATES AND FREEZES

    1¾ cups all-purpose sifted flour
    1¼ teaspoons salt

In a mixing bowl, combine and blend the flour and salt.

    ⅔ cup vegetable shortening *or* lard *or* ⅓ cup each lard and
        butter

Add the shortening to the flour. Using a blending fork or pastry blender, mix the ingredients until they form into even-sized bits, about the size of fresh peas. (Some cooks work with their fingers, very rapidly in order that the shortening not soften.)

    ⅓ cup ice water

Over the flour mixture, sprinkle the ice water by the tablespoonful, blending it in with a fork until just enough has been added to make possible patting the dough into a light ball. (You may not need all the water.) Handle the dough as little as possible; do not knead it. Wrap it in wax paper or foil and chill it for 1 hour.

On a lightly floured surface, place the chilled dough. Flatten the ball and with a rolling pin roll it outward from the center as evenly as possible to assure that the baked pastry will be the same thickness throughout. (Lift the pastry occasionally as you roll it, to assure that it is not sticking; add a light sprinkling of flour to the surface if the dough tends to adhere to it.)

Fit the dough into the pan and trim around the edges. Make a ball of the remaining dough and return it to the refrigerator or freezer for later use.

To bake the pie shell, prick the dough in several places with the tines of a fork (or set another pie pan inside it to hold its shape). Bake the shell at 450° for 12 minutes, or until it is golden brown.

Apple Tart (Tarte aux Pommes) (FRANCE)

6 TO 8 SERVINGS

PREPARATION AND COOKING: ABOUT 30 MINUTES (THE PREPARATION TIME DOES NOT INCLUDE READYING THE PASTRY)

A recipe from Normandy, France's apple country.

1 (9-inch) pie shell

Bake the pie shell (see above).

6 large tart apples, peeled, cut into eighths, the core removed	**¼ cup Calvados *or* applejack**
3 tablespoons butter	**½ teaspoon cinnamon**
3½ tablespoons sugar	**A few grains of salt**

In a saucepan, combine these six ingredients and, over moderate heat, cook the apples, stirring them gently, for about 8 minutes, or until they are tender but still hold their shape.

¼ cup Calvados *or* applejack
2½ tablespoons sugar

Arrange the apples in the pie shell. In a small saucepan, combine the Calvados and sugar. Warm the liquor, stirring; ignite it and pour over the apples.

Whipped cream *or* thickened cream (page 6)

Serve the tart hot, accompanied by the cream.

Variations:

Brandy or orange-flavored liqueur may be substituted for the Calvados.

Not French, but a very good tart: Do not bake the pie shell. In a mixing bowl, toss together the apple segments, sugar, cinnamon, and salt, and add 1 tablespoonful flour; omit the butter and Calvados. Arrange the apple in the pastry shell. Turn a pie plate upside down on top of the uncooked tart. Bake the tart at 425° for 8 minutes; remove the pie plate, reduce the heat to 325°, and continue to bake the dessert 30 to 35 minutes longer, or until the apples are tender. Then follow steps three and four of the recipe as written. This is a particularly effective way to make an apple tart from juicy apples.

Bourbon Pie (UNITED STATES)

6 TO 8 SERVINGS

PREPARATION AND COOKING: ABOUT 20 MINUTES (THE PREPARATION TIME DOES NOT INCLUDE READYING THE PASTRY)

CHILLING TIME: 6 HOURS

A traditional recipe from Kentucky.

> 1 (9-inch) pie shell

Bake the pie shell (page 283).

> 1 envelope unflavored gelatin, softened for 5 minutes in ¼ cup cold water

Over simmering water, dissolve the gelatin.

> 5 egg yolks   ⅓ cup bourbon whiskey
> ¾ cup sugar   Prepared gelatin
> A few grains of salt

In the top of a double boiler, beat the egg yolks, sugar, and salt until the mixture is smooth and lemon-colored. Add the bourbon and gelatin. Over simmering water, cook the custard until it thickens and coats a metal spoon. Allow it to cool and then chill it until it just begins to set.

> 2 cups heavy cream, whipped
> ½ ounce unsweetened chocolate, grated

With a rotary beater, briefly beat the custard to assure its smoothness. Fold in the whipped cream. With a rubber spatula, transfer the mixture to the prepared pastry shell. Chill the pie for at least 6 hours, or until it is thoroughly set. Garnish it with grated chocolate.

Mincemeat (UNITED STATES)

YIELD: ABOUT 3 QUARTS (SUFFICIENT FOR 3 MEDIUM OR 2 LARGE PIES)
PREPARATION: ABOUT 30 MINUTES
STANDING TIME: 3 WEEKS
REFRIGERATES

This mincemeat, from my great-great-grandmother's handwritten recipe book of the 1840s, is more stalwart than the cooked variety.

2 pounds lean roast beef, chopped fine	1½ cups sugar
½ pound beef suet, grated	½ teaspoon salt
2 cups currants	1 teaspoon allspice
2 cups dark seedless raisins	1½ teaspoons cinnamon
2 cups golden raisins	½ teaspoon ground cloves
6 cups chopped peeled tart apple	½ teaspoon mace

In a mixing bowl, combine and blend these ingredients.

   2 cups brandy
   1 cup dry red wine (recommended: a hearty Burgundy)

Add the brandy and wine; stir the mixture well. Because the liquid is absorbed while the mincemeat stands, covered, add as necessary ¼ cup at a time mixed brandy and wine in a 2-to-1 ratio.

Mince Pie (UNITED STATES)

6 TO 8 SERVINGS
PREPARATION: ABOUT 20 MINUTES (THE PREPARATION TIME DOES NOT
   INCLUDE READYING THE MINCEMEAT OR THE PASTRY)
COOKING: 40 MINUTES IN A 450°/350° OVEN

Our mince pie, a shortening of "minced meat pie," derives from Henry VIII's Christmas pudding. Originally Henry's pudding, which weighed

240 pounds, was rectangular (presumably the shape of the baby Jesus' manger), but following Henry's break with the Catholic Church, the shape was changed to round in an effort to avoid any connection with popery.

> **Pastry for a two-crust, 9-inch pie (page 282)**
> **3 cups Mincemeat (page 285)**

In a 9-inch pie pan, arrange the bottom crust so that it just overlaps the rim of the pan. Fill it with enough mincemeat to come level with the edge of the pan. Add the top crust, and seal it by pressing the two crusts together with the tines of a fork. Set the pie pan on a baking sheet and bake the pie at 450° for 10 minutes. Lower the heat to 350° and continue baking 30 minutes longer, or until the top is brown. Serve the pie warm.

You may, if you wish, warm a little brandy, ignite it, and pour it over the top of the pie. Offer the dessert while the brandy is still flaming.

Pear Tart

6 TO 8 SERVINGS
PREPARATION AND COOKING: ABOUT 40 MINUTES (THE PREPARATION TIME
    DOES NOT INCLUDE READYING THE PASTRY)
CHILLING TIME: 6 HOURS

> **1 (9-inch) pie shell**

Bake the pie shell (page 283).

> **1 cup dry white wine (recommended: Chablis)**
> **¼ cup sugar**
> **A pinch of ginger**
> **A few grains of salt**

In a saucepan, combine these four ingredients. Bring the liquid to the boil, reduce the heat, and simmer the mixture for 3 minutes.

> **4 firm, ripe pears (Anjou or Comice are good choices), peeled,**
> **quartered lengthwise, and cored**

In the simmering wine, poach the pear quarters for 10 minutes, or until they are just tender. Remove and reserve them. Over high heat, reduce the wine mixture to ½ cup.

1 tablespoon cornstarch
1 cup heavy cream

Blend the cornstarch into a little of the cream until smooth. Add it and the remaining cream to the saucepan, stirring until the mixture is thickened and smooth.

3 egg yolks   Reserved pear quarters
3 tablespoons sugar   Ground ginger
½ teaspoon almond
    extract

In a small mixing bowl, combine the egg yolks, sugar, and almond extract. Beat the mixture until it is lemon-colored, and then add it to the contents of the saucepan. Over gentle heat, cook the mixture, stirring constantly, until it thickens; do not allow it to boil. Cool the custard. With a rubber spatula, spread it evenly over the pie shell. Arrange the pear quarters over the custard. Dust them with a sprinkling of ginger. Chill the pear tart for at least 6 hours, or until it is thoroughly set.

Pumpkin Chiffon Pie

6 TO 8 SERVINGS
PREPARATION AND COOKING: ABOUT 40 MINUTES (THE PREPARATION TIME
    DOES NOT INCLUDE READYING THE PASTRY)
CHILLING TIME: 6 HOURS

1 (9-inch) pie shell

Bake the pie shell (page 283).

1 envelope unflavored   ½ cup water
    gelatin   3 egg yolks
⅓ cup sugar   ½ cup orange-flavored
½ teaspoon ground ginger   liqueur
½ teaspoon salt

In the top of a double boiler, combine and sift together the gelatin, sugar, ginger, and salt. Add the water. Beat in the egg yolks one at a time. Stir in the liqueur. Over simmering water, cook the mixture, stirring, until the gelatin and sugar are dissolved and the custard coats a metal spoon.

1¼ cups canned pumpkin purée

Into the custard, stir the pumpkin purée. Allow the mixture to cool, and then chill it until it just begins to set.

3 egg whites
⅓ cup sugar
½ cup heavy cream, whipped
3 tablespoons fine-chopped candied ginger

In a mixing bowl, beat the egg whites, adding the sugar gradually, until they are very stiff. With a rotary beater, briefly beat the pumpkin mixture to assure its smoothness. Into it, fold the whipped cream. Beat in one-fifth of the egg white; fold in the remainder. With a rubber spatula, transfer the filling to the pastry shell. Chill the pie for at least 6 hours, or until it is thoroughly set. Garnish it with candied ginger.

Sauces

Of the countless sauces that can be made with wines and spirits, I have arbitrarily selected a few—those that I find tasty, reasonably easy to make, and serviceable in a number of different culinary contexts.

We begin with béchamel sauce, the progenitor of all flour-based sauces, and I write about it at some length because I think you will find it a useful base upon which to build your own inventions.

Then we address ourselves to the various sauces for meats, fish, vegetables, and desserts. A few of them are of my creation. None of them are very time-consuming or finicky in their preparation.

To start on your own creative path, the next time you make giblet gravy for roast fowl or turkey, boil the giblets, neck, and wing tips in a combination of water and white wine *or* dry vermouth; use the liquid, with a little Madeira, Marsala, or sherry added, to thin the pan juice–flour mixture to the desired consistency. Giblet gravy was never like this!

Savory Sauces

Béchamel Sauce

One recalls from one's childhood, or at least I do, an anemic mixture of butter, flour, and milk. My grandmother called it "cream sauce," albeit at our house cream never came near it; it resembled library paste in both appearance and texture, and was always plopped precariously on boiled asparagus. Sometimes it was served with baked potatoes. However, white sauce was—and is—capable of sophisticated variations of flavor and consistency and is most versatile.

Usually called béchamel (after a steward to Louis XIV), it is generally assumed to be of French origin (surely the simplest member of the lengthy canon of French sauces!), but its genesis is also claimed by the Greeks, who had a thriving colony in the area that is now Marseilles. No matter; regardless of who invented this basic and classic sauce, it continues to be eminently useful.

There are four grades of béchamel, each with its particular use. Save for the quantity of milk added to the roux, they are all made alike. The amount of liquid used determines the consistency and hence the function of the sauce. The four grades of béchamel are:

    I: a thin pouring sauce, often the base for cream soups
    II: a thick pouring sauce, often used to dress vegetables
    III: a coating sauce, used to cover meats, fish, and vegetables
    IV: panada, the base for the soufflés offered in this book

The cooking technique, the same for all four:

In a saucepan, melt the butter.

Add the flour and, over gentle heat, cook the mixture (roux) for a few minutes, to eliminate the raw taste and grainy texture of the flour. Stir in salt and white pepper to taste, and perhaps a grating of nutmeg.

Gradually add the milk and cook the mixture, stirring constantly, until it is thickened and smooth.

The quantities are:

      I: for a thin pouring sauce
        2 tablespoons butter
        2 tablespoons flour
        3 cups milk
     II: for a thick pouring sauce
        2 tablespoons butter
        2 tablespoons flour
        2 cups milk
    III: for a coating sauce
        2 tablespoons butter
        2 tablespoons flour
        1 to 1¼ cups milk

IV: for a panada
    4 tablespoons butter
    4 tablespoons flour
    1 cup milk

There are several variations of béchamel sauce, all of them easy, all of them pleasant. Perhaps the most famous and useful is Mornay (named for a sixteenth-century French statesman and Huguenot leader), which you will find below, along with other variations. Before going on to them, however, let me add that if you use any liquid other than milk or light cream in making the béchamel, you will have made a velouté (who said French cuisine was not complicated?). Nonetheless, a velouté is an equally useful sauce and may be made (employing the same quantities as of milk) with:

Beef or chicken stock *or* canned broth
Fish stock or clam broth
Vegetable broth
The liquid from preparing mushrooms for use in cooking (page 5)
A combination of dry white wine and a broth of your choice

To the completed sauce, béchamel or velouté, and their variants, may be added Madeira, Marsala, or dry sherry, to taste. Over gentle heat, simmer the sauce, stirring it, for a few minutes to cook out the "edgy" alcohol of the wine.

Herewith are a few variations, usually made with béchamel sauce, but often applied to velouté as well. To each cup of prepared sauce, add the ingredients for the sauce of your choice:

AURORE: 2 tablespoons tomato purée and 1 additional tablespoon butter (for poultry, fish and seafood, vegetables).

CHEESE: ½ cup grated Muenster cheese and 1 teaspoon Worcestershire sauce (for poultry, veal scallops, fish and seafood, vegetables).

DILL: 1 teaspoon dried dill (or more, to taste) *or* 1 tablespoon fresh-snipped dill and 1 teaspoon strained lemon juice (for poultry, fish, vegetables).

HORSERADISH: 2 tablespoons (or more, to taste) prepared horseradish (for fish, vegetables).

MORNAY: 2 tablespoons grated Swiss cheese, 2 tablespoons grated Parmesan cheese, 2 additional tablespoons butter, and, if desired, 1 egg yolk and ¼ cup heavy cream (do not allow the sauce to boil) (for broiled meats, poultry, fish, vegetables).

MUSTARD: 1 tablespoon Dijon mustard (for broiled meats, poultry, fish, vegetables).

PARSLEY: ¼ cup fine-chopped parsley and 1 teaspoon strained lemon juice (for poultry, fish and seafood, vegetables).

SOUBISE (named for Charles, Prince de Soubise, an eighteenth-century French marshal): ½ cup fine-chopped onion, cooked until translucent in 2 tablespoons butter (for poultry, fish, vegetables).

Beurre Blanc (White Butter) (FRANCE)

FOR BROILED OR SAUTÉED MEATS AND FOR FISH
YIELD: ABOUT 1 CUP
PREPARATION AND COOKING: ABOUT 20 MINUTES

¼ cup white wine
  (recommended:
  Chablis)
¼ cup white wine vinegar
3 shallots, peeled and
  chopped fine,

or 4 scallions (white
  part only), trimmed
  and chopped fine
½ teaspoon salt
¼ teaspoon white pepper

In a saucepan, combine these five ingredients. Bring the liquid to the boil, reduce the heat, and simmer the mixture, uncovered, until the liquid is nearly evaporated.

½ pound (2 sticks) softened butter
Strained lemon juice

Into the contents of the saucepan, beat the butter one tablespoon at a time. Season the mixture to taste with lemon juice. Strain the white butter, pressing the solids to extract their flavor.

Beurre Rouge (Red Butter) (FRANCE)

FOR BROILED OR SAUTÉED MEATS AND FOR FISH
YIELD: ABOUT 1½ CUPS
PREPARATION AND COOKING: ABOUT 20 MINUTES

1 cup dry red wine
  (recommended: a
  hearty Burgundy)
2 tablespoons red wine
  vinegar
1 small garlic clove, peeled
  and chopped fine

3 shallots, peeled and
  chopped fine, or 4
  scallions (white part
  only), trimmed and
  chopped fine
½ teaspoon salt
¼ teaspoon white pepper

In a saucepan, combine these six ingredients. Bring the liquid to the boil, reduce the heat, and simmer the mixture, uncovered, until it is reduced to ⅓ cup.

½ pound (2 sticks) softened butter

Into the contents of the saucepan, beat the butter one tablespoon at a time. Strain the red butter, pressing the solids to extract their flavor.

Bordelaise Sauce

FOR GRILLED MEATS
YIELD: ABOUT 2 CUPS
PREPARATION AND COOKING: ABOUT 40 MINUTES

2 tablespoons butter
1 thin slice of a
  medium-sized onion
2 tablespoons flour
A pinch of sugar

½ teaspoon salt
Fresh-grated pepper
1 (10½-ounce) can of
  beef bouillon

In a saucepan, heat the butter and in it, over gentle heat, cook the onion until the butter is browned. Discard the onion. Add the flour and seasonings and cook the mixture, stirring, for a few minutes. Gradually add the beef bouillon, stirring constantly until the mixture is thickened and smooth. Set it aside and reserve it.

> 2 tablespoons butter
> 2 tablespoons fine-chopped scallion
> ¾ cup dry red wine (recommended: Beaujolais *or* Gamay Beaujolais)

In a saucepan, heat the butter and in it cook the scallion, white part only, until it is translucent. Add the wine, bring the liquid to the boil, and reduce it, uncovered, by half.

> Reserved bouillon mixture
> 2 tablespoons strained fresh lemon juice
> ¼ cup fine-chopped parsley
> Salt
>
> A few grains of cayenne pepper
> ¾ cup fine-sliced mushrooms, sautéed in 2 tablespoons butter (optional)

Into the wine, stir the reserved bouillon mixture, the lemon juice, and the parsley. Season the sauce to taste with salt and cayenne pepper. Stir in the mushrooms.

Brandy-Wine Sauce

FOR FISH

YIELD: ABOUT 3 CUPS

PREPARATION AND COOKING: ABOUT 20 MINUTES

> 4 tablespoons butter
> 2 medium garlic cloves, peeled and chopped fine
> 3 shallots, peeled and chopped fine, *or* 4 scallions (white part only), trimmed and chopped fine
> ¼ cup brandy
>
> 2 cups white Burgundy
> Beurre manié (page 4) made of 2 tablespoons each softened butter and flour
> ¼ cup heavy cream *or* thickened cream (page 6)
> Salt
> Fresh-ground white pepper

In a saucepan, heat the butter, and in it cook the garlic and shallot until translucent. Add the brandy, ignite it, and allow the flame to die. Add the wine. Add the beurre manié and cook the mixture, stirring, until it is thickened and smooth. Stir in the cream and season the sauce to taste with salt and pepper.

A little Worcestershire sauce and fine-chopped parsley may also be added to the completed sauce.

Brown Sauce (Sauce Espagnole) (FRANCE)

FOR MEATS AND GAME
YIELD: ABOUT 2¼ CUPS
PREPARATION: ABOUT 15 MINUTES
COOKING: 30 MINUTES

Together with béchamel and velouté, perhaps one of the most important French sauces because of its variety of uses and number of guises.

4 tablespoons butter	and chopped fine
1 medium carrot, scraped and chopped fine	4 parsley sprigs
	1 bay leaf, crumbled
1 medium onion, peeled	2½ tablespoons flour

In a saucepan, heat the butter and in it cook the carrot, onion, parsley, and bay leaf until the onion is translucent. Stir in the flour, and continue to cook the mixture until it is golden brown.

1 cup dry red wine (recommended: Mâcon or Gamay
   Beaujolais)
1½ cups beef stock or canned beef bouillon
Salt
Pepper

Add the wine, stirring until the mixture is thickened and smooth. Stir in the beef stock. Season the sauce to taste with salt and pepper. Simmer it, covered, for 30 minutes.

3 tablespoons tomato paste

Add the tomato paste, stirring to blend the mixture well; simmer the sauce for 10 minutes longer.

Variations:

MADEIRA SAUCE: To 1 cup brown sauce, add ¼ cup dry Madeira; simmer the mixture, stirring, for about 5 minutes.

MARCHAND DE VINS SAUCE: In ⅓ cup butter, sauté 2 bunches of scallions (white part only), trimmed and chopped fine, and ½ pound mushrooms, trimmed and chopped fine; when the mushrooms are limp, add 1½ cups of the same dry red wine used to make the brown sauce; reduce the liquid by half. Add 1 cup brown sauce and 1 tablespoon strained lemon juice, stirring to blend the mixture well.

SAUCE ROBERT: In 2 tablespoons of butter, sauté 1 large onion, peeled and chopped fine, until golden. Add 1 cup dry white wine and reduce the mixture to ½ cup. Add 1 cup brown sauce, ¼ teaspoon sugar, and 1½ teaspoons dry mustard blended until smooth with a little water. Simmer the sauce, uncovered, for 15 minutes.

Cherry Sauce (POLAND)

FOR FISH
YIELD: ABOUT 3 CUPS
PREPARATION AND COOKING: ABOUT 10 MINUTES

    1 (1-pound) can of pitted sour cherries

Drain the cherry liquid into a large measuring cup; add enough water to make 1⅔ cups. Reserve the cherries.

3 tablespoons butter	Cherry liquid
3 tablespoons sugar	2 tablespoons cornstarch
¼ teaspoon cinnamon	mixed with ¼ cup
¼ teaspoon ground cloves	cold water
1 cup dry red wine	Reserved cherries
(recommended: a	Salt
hearty Burgundy)	Fresh-ground pepper

In a saucepan, combine the butter, sugar, seasonings, wine, and cherry liquid. Bring the mixture to the boil. Add the cornstarch, stirring constantly until the sauce is thickened and smooth. Stir in the cherries and adjust the seasoning to taste with salt and pepper.

Clam Sauce (ITALY)

FOR PASTA
6 SERVINGS
PREPARATION: ABOUT 35 MINUTES (IF YOU USE FRESH CLAMS, WHICH ARE
    WORTH THE ADDITIONAL EFFORT)
COOKING: 15 MINUTES

> 4 dozen littleneck clams, or 3 (6½-ounce) cans of chopped
>   clams

If using fresh clams, steam them open, chop them coarse, and reserve their liquid. If using canned clams, drain them and reserve their liquid.

> ½ cup olive oil
> 2 large garlic cloves, peeled and chopped fine
> 1 medium onion, peeled and chopped fine
> ½ medium green pepper, seeded and diced

In a saucepan, heat the olive oil and in it cook the garlic, onion, and pepper until the onion is translucent.

> Reserved clam liquid
> ½ cup dry white wine
>   (recommended:
>   Orvieto *secco* or
>   Chardonnay)
>
> ½ cup fine-chopped
>   parsley
> 1 bay leaf
> ¼ teaspoon dried thyme
> ½ teaspoon salt
> Fresh-ground pepper

To the contents of the saucepan, add these ingredients. Bring the liquid to the boil, reduce the heat, and simmer the mixture, covered, for 15 minutes.

> Reserved clams

Add the clams and just heat them through. Do not overcook the clams, or they will be tough and rubbery.

Variation:

R E D W I N E C L A M S A U C E : In a saucepan, combine 1 garlic clove, peeled and put through a press, ⅓ cup olive oil, 1 medium onion, peeled and chopped, 4 tablespoons tomato paste, ¾ teaspoon dried basil, ½ teaspoon dried oregano, the reserved clam liquid, ½ cup dry red wine (recommended: Barbera *or* Zinfandel), ½ teaspoon salt, and fresh-ground pepper to taste. Bring the mixture to the boil, reduce the heat, and simmer it, covered, for 15 minutes. To the contents of the saucepan, add 12 large mushrooms, trimmed and sliced thin; continue to simmer the mixture, covered, for 5 minutes longer. Stir in the reserved clams and heat them through.

Cumberland Sauce (ENGLAND)

FOR ROAST MEATS AND GAME

YIELD: ABOUT 2 CUPS

PREPARATION AND COOKING: ABOUT 20 MINUTES

This very old English sauce is a traditional accompaniment to cold meats.

½ cup red currant jelly	juice of 1 large orange
1 small onion, peeled and chopped	¾ teaspoon ginger
Grated rind and strained	1 teaspoon dry mustard
juice of 1 medium lemon	2 teaspoons cornstarch
Grated rind and strained	1 cup tawny port
	A few grains of salt

In the container of a blender, combine the ingredients and whirl them for about 15 seconds, or until the mixture is smooth. Pour the sauce into a saucepan and bring it to the boil, stirring until it is somewhat thickened and smooth. Over gentle heat, simmer it for 5 minutes. Allow it to cool before serving it at room temperature, or chilled, if you prefer.

Juniper Berry Sauce (POLAND)

FOR HAM OR GAME
YIELD: ABOUT 1½ CUPS
PREPARATION AND COOKING: ABOUT 25 MINUTES

2 tablespoons butter
2 tablespoons flour
1 cup beef stock *or* canned
   beef bouillon
½ cup Madeira

1½ teaspoons juniper
   berries, crushed
Salt
Fresh-ground pepper

In a saucepan, heat the butter and in it, over gentle heat, cook the flour
for a few minutes. Add the beef stock and Madeira, stirring constantly
until the mixture is thickened and smooth. Stir in the juniper berries,
and season the sauce to taste with salt and pepper. Simmer it, uncovered,
for 10 minutes.

A Marinade for Game

MARINATING TIME: 18 TO 24 HOURS

This marinade, of Italian origin, is excellent not only for game meats, but
also for beef, lamb, and pork.

1 large carrot, scraped and
   sliced thin
1 large celery rib, with the
   leaves, chopped fine
2 medium garlic cloves, peeled
   and put through a press
1 large onion, peeled and
   chopped fine
2 bay leaves, crumbled

2 cloves, bruised
1 teaspoon dried rosemary,
   bruised
1 teaspoon rubbed sage
1 teaspoon salt
8 peppercorns, bruised
¼ cup olive oil
¼ cup red wine vinegar
2½ cups Madeira

Combine and blend all the ingredients. Put the meat in a deep dish or
bowl. Pour the marinade over it. Allow the meat to marinate in the refrigerator for 18 to 24 hours, turning it occasionally. Drain the meat and
broil or roast it. Strain the marinade to make sauce, thickened with a
little flour.

Mustard Sauce

FOR MEATS, POULTRY, AND FISH
YIELD: ABOUT ¾ CUP
PREPARATION AND COOKING: ABOUT 15 MINUTES

1 tablespoon butter
3 scallions (white part only),
    trimmed and chopped fine
¼ cup dry white wine
    (recommended:
    Chablis)

1 tablespoon Dijon
    mustard
¼ cup heavy cream

In a saucepan, heat the butter and in it cook the scallion until translucent. Add the wine and boil the mixture for about half a minute. Stir in the mustard and cream.

Newburg Sauce

FOR HOT FISH AND SEAFOOD
YIELD: ABOUT 2¼ CUPS
PREPARATION AND COOKING: ABOUT 15 MINUTES

The story of how this famous sauce was named is fairly well known, but amusing enough to warrant repeating: In posh mid-nineteenth-century New York City, a steady client of the elegant Delmonico's Restaurant was the newly rich Mr. Wenburg, who swaggeringly exhibited his affluence and importance. When his display became more than the proprietors of the establishment could bear, Mr. Wenburg was asked not to return. But the sauce especially created for him had become so popular that it could not be banished. Sauce Wenburg became overnight the Newburg sauce we enjoy today.

2 tablespoons butter
2½ tablespoons flour
½ teaspoon dry mustard
½ teaspoon paprika

(preferably sweet
    Hungarian)
A few grains of cayenne
    pepper

In the top of a double boiler over direct heat, heat the butter and in it gently cook the flour for a few minutes. Stir in the seasonings and blend the mixture well.

> 2 cups light cream
> 2 egg yolks
> ¼ cup dry sherry *or* 2 tablespoons each dry sherry and brandy
> Salt

Gradually add the cream, stirring constantly until the mixture is thickened and smooth. Away from the heat, whisk in the egg yolks and sherry. Season the sauce to taste with salt. Reheat it over simmering, not boiling, water.

Rouille (Potato and Garlic Sauce) (FRANCE)

FOR FISH SOUPS AND STEWS (DO NOT USE WITH CREAMED DISHES)
YIELD: ABOUT 1½ CUPS
PREPARATION: ABOUT 40 MINUTES (INCLUDES COOKING THE POTATO)

Although this sauce is not made with wine or spirits, I include it because it is a very special accompaniment to fish soups and stews.

> 2 egg yolks
> 4 large garlic cloves, peeled and chopped coarse
> 1 medium potato, boiled for 25 minutes or until very tender,
>   peeled and chopped coarse

In the container of a food processor equipped with the steel blade, combine the egg yolks, garlic, and potato. Whirl the ingredients until the mixture is smooth.

> ¾ cup fine olive oil
> Strained juice of 1 medium lemon
> ½ teaspoon salt
> ¼ teaspoon white pepper

With the motor running, add the olive oil in a thin steady stream. Add the lemon juice, salt, and pepper. Transfer the sauce to a serving dish or, if you wish to heat it later, to the top of a double boiler, in which it can be brought to serving temperature over simmering water.

Salsa Stracotto (Long-Cooked Sauce) (ITALY)

FOR PASTA
4 SERVINGS
PREPARATION: ABOUT 30 MINUTES
COOKING: 3 HOURS
REFRIGERATES; FREEZES

4 tablespoons butter	1 large garlic clove, peeled
4 tablespoons olive oil	and chopped fine
1 medium carrot, scraped	1 large onion, peeled and
and chopped fine	chopped fine
1 large celery rib, trimmed	½ cup fine-chopped parsley
and chopped fine	

In a saucepan, heat the butter and olive oil and in it cook the vegetables, stirring, for 5 minutes.

1 pound lean chuck, cut into small dice
½ cup Marsala
1 (8-ounce) can of tomato sauce
Grated rind of 1 small lemon

To the contents of the saucepan, add these ingredients. Over the lowest possible heat, simmer the sauce, covered, for 3 hours.

¼ pound mushrooms, trimmed and sliced thin
Salt
Fresh-ground pepper

Add the mushrooms and continue to simmer the sauce, uncovered, for 5 minutes, or until the mushrooms are limp. Season the sauce to taste with salt and pepper.

Sauce Provençale (Rayte) (FRANCE)

FOR POULTRY AND FISH
YIELD: ABOUT 6 CUPS
PREPARATION AND COOKING: ABOUT 1 HOUR

4 tablespoons butter
4 tablespoons olive oil
3 medium onions, peeled
    and chopped
3 large garlic cloves, peeled
    and chopped fine
1 (28-ounce) can of
    Italian tomatoes,
    chopped coarse

1 bay leaf
¼ teaspoon fennel seed
1 teaspoon dried rosemary
2 cups dry red wine
    (recommended: a
    Côte du Rhône *or*
    Pinot Noir)
1 (6-ounce) can of tomato
    paste

In a saucepan, heat the butter and olive oil and in it cook the onion and garlic until translucent. Add the tomatoes, seasonings, wine, and tomato paste. Over moderate heat, cook the mixture, uncovered, until it thickens slightly (about 15 minutes).

½ cup pine nuts
    (pignolias) (optional)
2 tablespoons capers

1 cup pitted ripe olives,
    halved lengthwise
Salt
Fresh-ground pepper

To the contents of the saucepan, add the pine nuts, capers, and olives. Season the sauce to taste with salt and pepper. Over gentle heat, simmer it, covered, for 30 minutes.

Sauterne Sauce

FOR FISH
YIELD: ABOUT 1½ CUPS
PREPARATION AND COOKING: 15 MINUTES

1 cup dry sauterne
4 egg yolks
1 teaspoon white wine
    vinegar

1 teaspoon sugar
A few grains of salt

In the top of a double boiler, combine and, with a rotary beater, thoroughly blend the ingredients. Over simmering water, cook the mixture, stirring constantly, until it thickens and coats a metal spoon; do not allow it to boil. Transfer the sauce to a serving dish and offer it at once.

Vinaigrette Sauce

FOR SALADS AND COLD VEGETABLES
YIELD: ABOUT 1½ CUPS
PREPARATION: ABOUT 5 MINUTES

The sauce is most flavorful when used at room temperature.

1 small garlic clove, peeled
  and put through a press
  (optional)
1 teaspoon Dijon mustard
¼ cup dry vermouth
Strained juice of ½ small
  lemon

2 tablespoons white wine
  vinegar
½ teaspoon sugar
1 teaspoon salt
½ teaspoon white pepper
1 cup fine olive oil

In a container with a tight-fitting lid, combine all of the ingredients except the olive oil. Shake vigorously to dissolve the sugar and salt. Add the olive oil and shake again to blend well.

Dessert Sauces

Apricot Sauce

FOR CAKE, ICE CREAM, AND PUDDINGS
YIELD: ABOUT 2½ CUPS
PREPARATION AND COOKING: ABOUT 45 MINUTES
REFRIGERATES

1 cup tenderized pitted
  apricots
¼ cup sugar
1½ cups water

½ teaspoon cinnamon
¼ teaspoon mace
A pinch of salt

In a saucepan, combine these six ingredients. Bring the water to the boil, reduce the heat, and simmer the apricots, covered, for 30 minutes, or until they are very tender. Remove the cover and allow the mixture to cool.

⅓ cup Southern Comfort

In the container of a food processor or blender, combine the apricots and Southern Comfort. Whirl the mixture until it is smooth. Transfer the sauce to a covered jar and store it in the refrigerator. The sauce may be served hot or chilled.

Brandy Butter (ENGLISH)

FOR PLUM PUDDING
YIELD: ABOUT 1¾ CUPS
PREPARATION: ABOUT 10 MINUTES

8 tablespoons butter, at room temperature	A few grains of salt
1 cup superfine granulated sugar	½ cup brandy
	1 teaspoon vanilla extract

In a mixing bowl, combine the ingredients and, using a rotary beater, whip the mixture until it is smooth. Chill it before offering it with hot plum pudding.

CUMBERLAND BUTTER (not to be confused with Cumberland Sauce, page 298): In place of superfine granulated sugar, use 1 cup light brown sugar; in place of the brandy, use ½ cup light rum; add a generous grating of nutmeg. Complete the recipe as written, and offer the sauce with hot puddings.

Brandy Sauce

FOR PUDDINGS
YIELD: ABOUT 1¼ CUPS
PREPARATION AND COOKING: ABOUT 15 MINUTES

This recipe is adapted from *Mrs. Beeton's Book of Household Management*, which was written at the zenith of the Victorian era.

6 tablespoons butter	A few grains of salt
⅓ cup sugar	½ cup Madeira
¼ cup brandy	

In a saucepan, combine the butter, sugar, 2 tablespoons of the brandy, and the salt. Over gentle heat, warm the mixture, stirring, until the sugar is melted. Add the remaining brandy and the Madeira; stir the sauce to blend it well.

Lemon-Brandy Sauce

FOR CAKES
YIELD: ABOUT 1½ CUPS
PREPARATION: ABOUT 10 MINUTES

⅔ cup brandy   ⅔ cup honey
¼ cup strained lemon juice   A few grains of salt
½ teaspoon ginger

In a container with a tight-fitting lid, combine the ingredients and shake vigorously to blend well.

Crème Anglaise (Custard Sauce)

FOR DESSERT CREAMS, PUDDINGS, AND SOUFFLÉS
YIELD: ABOUT 2½ CUPS
PREPARATION AND COOKING: ABOUT 20 MINUTES

This sauce will keep under refrigeration for 3 days. When making it, have all the ingredients ready at room temperature.

⅔ cup sugar
½ teaspoon cornstarch
4 egg yolks, lightly beaten
A few grains of salt

Sift together the sugar and cornstarch. In the top of a double boiler, combine the sugar, egg yolks, and salt.

2 cups milk, scalded and slightly cooled

Into the contents of the double boiler, stir the milk. Over simmering water, cook the custard, stirring, until it thickens and coats a metal spoon.

1 teaspoon vanilla extract

Allow the sauce to cool slightly before stirring in the vanilla.

Variations:

CRÈME ANGLAISE À L'ORANGE: Reduce the milk to 1¾ cups and add to the thickened custard ¼ cup orange-flavored liqueur and the grated rind of 1 medium orange; omit the vanilla.

CRÈME ANGLAISE WITH PORT WINE: Reduce the milk to 1½ cups and add to the thickened custard ½ cup white port; omit the vanilla.

Crème anglaise may be made with a variety of liqueurs; merely reduce the quantity of milk by the amount of liqueur you use—usually ¼ cup is sufficient for a delicately flavored dessert sauce. Omit the vanilla (I include it in the basic recipe for use with a heavily liquored dessert that would not be complemented by a liqueur-flavored sauce). Some liqueurs you should try: amaretto, crème de cacao, yellow chartreuse, mocha- or coffee-flavored liqueur, cream sherry, dark rum.

If, while you are preparing crème anglaise, the sauce curdles, transfer the mixture to the container of a blender and whirl it until it is smooth. This will make the sauce thinner, but the flavor will be the same.

Grand Marnier Sauce (FRANCE)

FOR SOUFFLÉS
YIELD: ABOUT 1½ CUPS
PREPARATION: ABOUT 15 MINUTES
CHILLING TIME: 2 HOURS

1 egg yolk
1¼ cups confectioners' sugar
A few grains of salt
¼ cup Grand Marnier *or* other orange-flavored liqueur
¾ cup heavy cream, whipped to soft peaks

In a mixing bowl, beat the egg yolk until light. Gradually add the sugar and salt, beating the mixture constantly. Beat in the liqueur. Fold in the whipped cream. With a rubber spatula, transfer the sauce to a chilled serving bowl, and refrigerate it for at least 2 hours.

Hard Sauce

FOR HOT PUDDINGS AND FRUITCAKES
YIELD: ABOUT 2 CUPS
PREPARATION: ABOUT 20 MINUTES

½ pound (2 sticks) butter,
   at room temperature
2 cups sifted
   confectioners' sugar

A few grains of salt
1 teaspoon vanilla extract
¼ cup brandy

In a mixing bowl, cream together until light the butter, sugar, and salt. Beat in the vanilla and brandy. With a rubber spatula, transfer the sauce to a serving bowl, and chill it slightly (so that individual spoonfuls hold their shape).

Variation:

Dark rum may be substituted for the brandy.

Orange Sauce

FOR CAKES, CREAMS, PUDDINGS
YIELD: 1 CUP
PREPARATION AND COOKING: ABOUT 20 MINUTES

1 cup strained fresh
   orange juice
Grated rind of 1 medium
   orange

¼ cup sugar
1 tablespoon cornstarch
A few grains of salt

In the container of a blender, whirl these five ingredients at medium speed until the mixture is homogenous.

2 tablespoons softened butter
⅓ cup orange-flavored liqueur

In a saucepan, over moderate heat, cook the orange juice mixture, stirring constantly, until it is thickened and smooth. Stir in the butter and then the liqueur. The sauce may be served warm or chilled.

Raisin Sauce

VERY GOOD WITH VANILLA ICE CREAM
YIELD: ABOUT 1½ CUPS
PREPARATION AND COOKING: ABOUT 20 MINUTES

> ½ cup seedless raisins
> ¾ cup water

In a saucepan, combine the raisins and water. Bring the liquid to the boil, reduce the heat, and simmer the raisins, uncovered, for 5 minutes, or until they are plumped.

> ¼ cup currant jelly
> 2 tablespoons softened butter

Add the jelly and butter, stirring until both are melted.

> 2 teaspoons cornstarch, mixed until smooth with ¼ cup cold
>   water
> A few grains of salt
> ⅓ cup dark rum

Add the cornstarch and cook the mixture, stirring constantly, until the sauce is thickened and smooth. Stir in the salt and rum.

Rum Syrup

FOR CAKES AND PUDDINGS—AND SURELY FOR BABA AU RHUM (PAGE 272)
YIELD: ABOUT 2 CUPS
PREPARATION AND COOKING: ABOUT 40 MINUTES

> 1 cup sugar
> A few grains of salt
> 1½ cups water
> ½ cup dark rum

In a saucepan, combine the sugar, salt, and water. Bring the liquid to the boil, reduce the heat to moderate, and simmer the mixture, uncovered, for 30 minutes. Stir in the rum. Pour the hot syrup over fresh-baked babas, or allow it to cool for use as a dessert sauce.

Whiskey Sauce (UNITED STATES)

FOR PUDDINGS
YIELD: ABOUT 2 CUPS
PREPARATION AND COOKING: ABOUT 20 MINUTES

8 tablespoons butter	A few grains of salt
1 egg	½ cup bourbon whiskey
1 cup sugar	

In the top of a double boiler over simmering water, melt the butter. In a mixing bowl, blend the egg, sugar, and salt. Add the egg mixture to the butter, stirring until the sugar is dissolved; do not allow it to boil. Cool the sauce to room temperature and stir in the bourbon.

White Wine Custard

FOR CAKES, PUDDINGS, AND FRESH FRUIT
YIELD: ABOUT 3 CUPS
PREPARATION AND COOKING: ABOUT 20 MINUTES

2 cups dry white wine (recommended: Muscadet or Chablis)	4 eggs
	½ cup sugar
½ cup water	A few grains of salt

In the top of a double boiler, combine the ingredients and, with a rotary beater, blend them thoroughly. Set the pan over simmering water (the water should not touch the pan), and cook the mixture, stirring constantly, until it thickens and coats a metal spoon. Serve the sauce hot or chilled.

Breads

Breads made with ale or beer or spirits tend to be substantial, hearty fare. My favorites are bock beer bread, on the one hand, and muffins (which are very light), on the other. Waffles (page 318), of course, are not really bread, and, eaten as they are in Belgium, become more nearly a dessert; I find them a pleasant ending to a light meal.

Bock Beer Bread (GERMANY)

YIELD: 2 8-INCH LOAVES
PREPARATION: ABOUT 20 MINUTES
RISING TIME: ABOUT 2 HOURS
BAKING: 35 MINUTES IN A 375° OVEN

Bock beer, at one time a springtime drink, is now available most of the year. However, any dark beer will work nicely.

Butter two 8-inch loaf pans.

    1 cup bock beer
    2 envelopes of dry yeast
    4 tablespoons dark brown
        sugar
    1 teaspoon salt

    1 egg, beaten
    4 tablespoons butter,
        melted and slightly
        cooled

In a saucepan, heat the beer to lukewarm, and pour it into a mixing bowl. Over the beer, sprinkle the yeast and allow it to dissolve. Add the sugar, salt, and egg, stirring to dissolve the sugar. Add the butter.

3½ cups unbleached flour
½ cup wheat germ

Stir in half the flour and the wheat germ. Add the remaining flour. Turn the dough onto a floured surface and knead it, adding flour as necessary, until it is elastic and satiny (about 10 minutes). Put the dough ball in a warm buttered bowl, cover it with a damp cloth, and put it in a warm, sheltered place. Allow the dough to rise until it is doubled in bulk (about 1½ hours).

Divide the dough in half; mold each half into a loaf shape and set the loaves in the prepared pans. Allow the dough to rise a second time (about 30 minutes), and when it reaches just over the top of the pan, bake the bread on the center rack of the oven at 375° for 35 minutes, or until it sounds hollow when tapped on top. Allow the loaves to cool for a few minutes before turning them out of the pan to cool fully on a rack.

Variation:

PORTUGUESE BEER BREAD: In step two, use 1½ cups lukewarm beer; omit the brown sugar; use 2 tablespoons white sugar, 1 tablespoon salt; omit the egg; in place of the butter, use vegetable oil; add ½ cup scalded milk, cooled to lukewarm. In step three, use 4½ cups unbleached flour and 1½ cups whole-wheat flour; follow the recipe up to the point of baking the bread. Put a pan of hot water on the lower rack of the oven; bake the bread on the center rack at 500° for 15 minutes; lower the heat to 400° and continue to bake the loaves for 15 minutes longer, or until they are a deep brown and sound hollow when tapped on top.

Date-Nut Bread

YIELD: 1 (9-INCH) LOAF
PREPARATION: ABOUT 25 MINUTES
BAKING: 50 MINUTES IN A 350° OVEN

Butter a 9-inch loaf pan.

1 cup fine-chopped dates
½ cup sugar
½ teaspoon salt
4 tablespoons softened
   butter

⅔ cup boiling water
¼ cup dark rum *or*
   Marsala

In a mixing bowl, combine these six ingredients, stirring until the sugar dissolves and the butter melts. Allow the mixture to cool.

1 egg, beaten

Stir in the egg.

1¾ cups unbleached flour
1 teaspoon baking soda
½ cup chopped nuts

In a mixing bowl, sift together the dry ingredients.

At this point you may stop and continue later.

Into the liquid mixture, beat the dry ingredients. When the batter is well blended, transfer it to the prepared pan. Bake the date-nut bread at 350° for 50 minutes, or until a sharp knife inserted at the center comes out clean.

Variation:

FIG BREAD: In step two, use 1 cup dried figs, chopped fine, instead of the dates. Follow step three as written. In step four, add to the dry ingredients ½ teaspoon ground ginger, the grated rind of 1 medium orange, and 1 teaspoon baking powder. Complete the recipe as written.

Muffins

YIELD: 12 MUFFINS
PREPARATION: ABOUT 10 TO 15 MINUTES (DEPENDING UPON WHICH KIND YOU MAKE)
BAKING: 15 MINUTES IN A 400° OVEN
REFRIGERATES; FREEZES

Butter 12 muffin cups.

　　2 cups unbleached flour
　　1 tablespoon baking powder
　　2 tablespoons sugar
　　½ teaspoon salt

In a mixing bowl, sift together the dry ingredients.

　　1 egg
　　¾ cup milk
　　¼ cup liquor, as called for in the variations below
　　4 tablespoons butter, melted and cooled slightly

In a mixing bowl, using a rotary beater, blend the liquid ingredients.

At this point you may stop and continue later.

To the dry ingredients, add the liquid, stirring just enough to moisten the flour. Fill the prepared muffin cups two-thirds full. Bake the muffins at 400° for 15 minutes, or until they are well risen and lightly browned.

Variations:

APPLE MUFFINS: In step two, add ½ teaspoon cinnamon. In step three, add 1 large apple, peeled, cored, and grated; for the liquor, use dark rum. Complete the basic recipe as written.

BANANA MUFFINS: In step one, add ½ teaspoon ground coriander. In step three, add 1 very ripe banana, peeled and mashed with a fork until smooth; for the liquor, use rum *or* bourbon whiskey. Complete the basic recipe as written.

BLUEBERRY MUFFINS: In step one, increase the sugar to ¼ cup. In step three, toss 1 cup blueberries, stemmed, rinsed, and well drained, with ¼ cup of the flour; add the grated rind of 1 small orange; for the liquor, use orange-flavored liqueur. Complete the basic recipe as written.

CORN MEAL MUFFINS: In step one, use ¾ cup corn meal and 1¼ cups flour; omit the sugar. In step three, add ¼ cup maple sryup; for the liquor, use bourbon whiskey *or* Southern Comfort. Complete the basic recipe as written.

DATE MUFFINS: In step one, use dark brown sugar in place of white. In step three, add ⅔ cup fine-chopped dates; for the liquor, use dark rum. Complete the basic recipe as written.

OATMEAL MUFFINS: In step one, in place of 1 cup of the flour, use 1 cup quick-cooking oatmeal. In step three, for the liquor, use bourbon whiskey *or* Southern Comfort. Complete the basic recipe as written.

ORANGE MUFFINS: Follow step one as written. In step three, add the grated rind of 1 large orange; for the liquor, use orange-flavored liqueur; into the top of each unbaked muffin press a small sugar cube soaked in orange-flavored liqueur. Complete the basic recipe as written.

RAISIN MUFFINS: Follow step one as written. In step three, add ½ cup seedless raisins *or* currants; for the liquor, use dark rum *or* Southern Comfort. Complete the basic recipe as written.

WHEAT GERM MUFFINS: In step one, in place of 1 cup of the flour, use 1 cup wheat germ; increase the baking powder to 4 teaspoons and the sugar to 4 tablespoons. In step three, use 2 eggs, 1 cup milk, 5 tablespoons butter; for the liquor, use dark rum *or* bourbon whiskey. (This recipe will require a few minutes longer to bake.) Complete the basic recipe as written.

WHOLE-WHEAT AND ORANGE MUFFINS: In step one, use whole-wheat flour; increase the sugar to 3 tablespoons. In step three, use 2 eggs; add the grated rind of 1 large orange; for the liquor, use orange-flavored liqueur; add ½ teaspoon orange extract. Complete the basic recipe as written.

Squash Rolls

YIELD: ABOUT 24 CLOVERLEAF ROLLS
PREPARATION: ABOUT 30 MINUTES
RISING TIME: ABOUT 2 HOURS
BAKING: 20 MINUTES IN A 400° OVEN

The recipe may be made with cooked, mashed carrots or with canned pumpkin purée replacing the squash.

Butter 24 muffin cups.

1 envelope of dry yeast
¼ cup lukewarm water

In a small mixing bowl, combine the yeast and water; allow the yeast to dissolve.

¾ cup milk, scalded and
   cooled to lukewarm
⅓ cup bourbon whiskey *or*
   dark rum
1 (12-ounce) package of
   frozen cooked winter
   squash, fully thawed
   to room temperature

Grated rind of 1 lemon
   or orange
⅓ cup dark brown sugar
½ teaspoon salt
6 tablespoons butter,
   melted and cooled to
   lukewarm

In a mixing bowl, combine and blend the milk, bourbon, squash, lemon rind, sugar, salt, and butter.

Reserved yeast
4½ cups unbleached flour

To the squash mixture, add the reserved yeast and 2 cups of the flour. Beat the mixture well. Gradually beat in additional flour until the dough is stiff enough to knead. Turn it onto a floured surface and knead it until it is elastic and satiny (about 10 minutes). Put the dough in a buttered bowl, set the bowl in a sheltered warm place, and allow the dough to rise until doubled in bulk (about 1 hour).

Melted butter

Punch down the dough. In each buttered muffin cup, arrange 3 small balls of the dough, about the size of walnuts. Cover the muffin tins and allow the dough to rise again until doubled in bulk, about 45 minutes. Bake the squash rolls at 400° for 20 minutes, or until they are golden. While they are still hot, brush them with melted butter.

Vörtlimpor (Christmas Bread) (SWEDEN)

YIELD: 1 (9-INCH) LOAF
PREPARATION: ABOUT 25 MINUTES
RISING TIME: ABOUT 3 HOURS
BAKING: 45 MINUTES, STARTING IN AN UNHEATED OVEN

Butter a 9-inch loaf pan.

> 1 envelope of dry yeast
> ¼ cup lukewarm water
> 3 tablespoons dark brown sugar

In a small bowl, combine the yeast, water, and sugar; allow the mixture to stand until it is frothy. Reserve it.

> 1½ cups unbleached flour
> 1 teaspoon salt
> 1 tablespoon anise seed
>
> 1 teaspoon powdered fennel
> Grated rind of 1 large orange

In a large mixing bowl, sift together these five ingredients.

> 1½ cups beer *or* ale
> 2 tablespoons softened butter
> ⅓ cup molasses
> Reserved yeast mixture

In a saucepan, combine the beer, butter, and molasses; heat the mixture just long enough to melt the butter.

Make a well in the flour mixture. Into it, pour the beer and yeast mixtures. Beat the batter until it is smooth. Set the mixing bowl in a larger bowl of quite warm water, cover it, and allow the mixture to rise for 1 hour.

> 2 cups rye flour

Beat in the rye flour; the dough should be light and elastic (if necessary, add a little lukewarm water). Beat the dough for 5 minutes; return the mixing bowl to the pan of very warm water; cover the dough and allow it to rise until doubled in bulk (about 1 hour).

Punch the dough down, and spoon it into the prepared pan. Put the pan in warm water, cover the dough, and allow it to rise for 1 hour.

Set the loaf pan on the middle rack of a cold oven. Turn on the oven to 375° and bake the bread for 15 minutes; reduce the heat to 325° and bake the bread for 30 minutes longer, or until it sounds hollow when tapped on top. Allow it to cool slightly before turning it out of the pan to cool fully on a rack.

Beer Waffles (BELGIUM)

YIELD: ABOUT 15 WAFFLES
PREPARATION: ABOUT 15 MINUTES
STANDING TIME: 2 HOURS
BAKING: ABOUT 2 MINUTES

Gaufres (waffles) are as ubiquitous in Brussels as crêpes are in Paris; they are sold on street corners, garnished with various jams, or with thickened cream (page 6) and natural (or brown) sugar—which is the way I like them best.

3 cups light beer	½ teaspoon vanilla extract
2 eggs	½ teaspoon salt
½ cup cooking oil	3½ cups flour
Grated rind of 1 large lemon	

In a deep mixing bowl, using a rotary beater, blend the beer, eggs, and oil. Add the lemon rind, vanilla, and salt and blend the mixture briefly once again. Add the flour and beat the batter until it is smooth. Allow it to stand at room temperature for about 2 hours; it will rise slightly, for the beer acts as a leavening agent.

Softened butter

Using a pastry brush, spread a little butter evenly on the waffle iron (top and bottom). Spread a little of the batter over the bottom (waffles will not cook crisp if you are too generous with the batter). Cook them as you would a breakfast waffle, for about 2 minutes; they will brown quickly. Serve them as soon as they come off the iron, piping hot, garnished as suggested above.

If desired, you may prepare a sauce for the waffles: In a mixing bowl, combine and blend until the sugar is dissolved 1 cup sour cream at room temperature, 3 tablespoons each dark brown and granulated sugar, a few grains of salt, and ¼ cup either dark rum *or* orange-flavored liqueur.

Beverages

This selection of beverages prepared with wines or spirits is in no way exhaustive; several books could be written on this topic alone. I have chosen drinks, both hot and cold, that serve a variety of purposes: traditional drinks, long drinks, holiday drinks, end-of-meal drinks. Effort has been made to keep their preparation as simple as possible so that offering them to family and friends will be easy and pleasurable.

Bishop (England)

10 TO 12 SERVINGS
PREPARATION: ABOUT 40 MINUTES
COOKING: 30 MINUTES IN A 400° OVEN
MACERATING: SEVERAL DAYS

A bishop, named for its red color, is a pleasantly spiced port wine with an orange flavor. Dating from the Middle Ages, it was perhaps brought to England from Holland by Dutch sailors. The ecclesiastical name was an English innovation: archbishops were made with claret, cardinals with champagne, and popes with Burgundy. In colonial America, a "farmer's bishop" was made with rum and cider (see page 320).

3 medium oranges, each stuck with 12 cloves

In a baking pan, arrange the oranges and roast them at 400° for 30 minutes.

319

½ cup sugar
Zest of 1 medium lemon
A few grains of salt
Roasted oranges

1 bottle of ruby port,
   heated very hot but
   not boiling

In a container with a tight-fitting lid, put the first four ingredients. Add the hot port. Cover the container and allow it to stand at room temperature for several days.

Wine mixture with oranges
2 bottles of ruby Port
Fresh-grated nutmeg

In an enamel saucepan or casserole, combine the spiced wine, the oranges, and the additional port. Heat the mixture until it is very hot; do not allow it to boil. Discard the lemon zest. Transfer the oranges to a heated serving bowl and over them pour the wine. Serve the bishop in heated mugs garnished with a sprinkling of nutmeg.

Farmer's Bishop (AMERICA)

ABOUT 25 SERVINGS
PREPARATION: 1 HOUR
COOKING: 30 MINUTES IN A 400° OVEN

6 medium oranges, each stuck with 12 cloves

In a baking pan, arrange the oranges and roast them at 400° for 30 minutes.

1 cup sugar
A few grains of salt
1 quart dark rum
Roasted oranges

In an enamel saucepan or casserole, combine these four ingredients. Over gentle heat, cook the mixture until the sugar is dissolved.

At this point you may stop and continue later. (The contents of the saucepan may be cooled and stored, tightly covered, at room temperature —I have kept the mixture for as long as four years.)

8 cups cider, warmed
Ground cinnamon
Fresh-grated nutmeg

Pour the cider into a large heated bowl and add the oranges. Warm and ignite the rum and, after the flame dies, pour it over the oranges. Offer the farmer's bishop in heated mugs garnished with a sprinkling of cinnamon and nutmeg. (The oranges may be used again; simply cover them with rum and store them as suggested above.)

Café Brûlot

YIELD: 6 SERVINGS

PREPARATION AND COOKING: ABOUT 12 MINUTES

The *ne plus ultra* of after-dinner demitasses, sometimes called café au diable.

1 (2-inch) piece of
    cinnamon stick
6 whole cloves
1 (4-inch) piece of orange
    zest

¾ cup cognac
3 cups hot strong coffee
6 lumps of sugar

In a saucepan, combine the seasonings and cognac. Warm the liqueur, ignite it, and allow it to burn out. Add the coffee and, over the lowest possible heat, barely simmer the mixture, covered, for 5 to 7 minutes, to release the flavor of the seasonings. In each of six demitasse cups, put a lump of sugar. Pour in the coffee mixture.

Russian Coffee (Cafe à la Russe)

6 SERVINGS

PREPARATION AND COOKING: ABOUT 10 MINUTES (THE PREPARATION TIME
DOES NOT INCLUDE MAKING THE COFFEE)

¾ cup boiling water
1 ounce semisweet
   chocolate
4 teaspoons sugar
A few grains of salt
3 cups hot strong coffee
½ cup heavy cream,
   scalded

¼ cup brandy
   (recommended: a
   very dry cognac of
   good quality)
¼ cup crème de cacao
Cinnamon
Nutmeg

In a double boiler, combine the boiling water, chocolate, sugar, and salt;
over simmering water, melt the chocolate, stirring. Add the coffee, cream,
brandy, and crème de cacao. Stir the mixture to blend it well, and offer
it dusted lightly with cinnamon and nutmeg.

Candeel (NETHERLANDS)

6 SERVINGS

PREPARATION AND COOKING: ABOUT 20 MINUTES

There is a tradition of offering this beverage to a young mother recently
delivered when she invites the neighbors in to see her baby. Candeel
cups, no longer made even in Holland, are much sought after by antique
collectors.

4 eggs
1 cup sugar
A few grains of salt
Grated rind and strained
   juice of 1 medium lemon

1 bottle of dry white wine
   (recommended:
   Chardonnay)
Cinnamon

In a saucepan, combine and beat the eggs, sugar, and salt until the mixture is light. Stir in the lemon rind and juice. Add the wine and, over

gentle heat, warm the mixture, stirring constantly; do not allow it to boil. Serve the candeel in punch cups, garnished with a sprinkling of cinnamon.

Eggnog

YIELD: ABOUT 2½ QUARTS
PREPARATION: ABOUT 25 MINUTES
CHILLING: 4 HOURS

This recipe from Mississippi yields a very rich, thick eggnog that can be eaten with a spoon. If desired, it may be thinned (see below).

6 egg yolks, beaten until thick	1½ teaspoons vanilla extract (optional)
½ cup sugar	1 cup bourbon whiskey
A pinch of salt	½ cup dark rum

To the egg yolks, add the sugar, salt, and vanilla, stirring to blend the mixture. Stir in the bourbon and rum. Transfer the mixture to a punch bowl.

6 egg whites, beaten until they stand in soft peaks
4 cups heavy cream, beaten until frothy but not stiff
Fresh-grated nutmeg

Fold in the egg white and then the cream. Sprinkle the surface with nutmeg. Chill the eggnog for at least 4 hours. When serving the drink, garnish each portion with an additional sprinkling of nutmeg.

A less calorie-explosive and thinner eggnog can be made with light cream or even half-and-half: in this case, the yield will be less, for much of the suggested 2½-quart amount is pure air.

Escayon au Vin (FRANCE)

8 SERVINGS

PREPARATION AND COOKING: ABOUT 20 MINUTES

A sort of zabaglione, this very old recipe is mentioned by the folklorist poet Autron de Coudray; it was formerly used, like mead (see page 328), to ease the inhibitions of young newlyweds.

6 eggs	1 bottle of dry red wine
½ cup sugar	(recommended:
A few grains of salt	Pinot Noir)
	½ teaspoon vanilla extract

In the top of a double boiler, combine and beat the eggs, sugar, and salt until the mixture is light. Add the wine and vanilla extract; over simmering water, heat the drink, stirring constantly; do not allow it to boil. Serve it in warmed punch cups.

Fish House Punch (UNITED STATES)

ABOUT 50 PUNCH-CUP SERVINGS

PREPARATION: ABOUT 20 MINUTES

Known to Washington and Lafayette, this drink is said to have first been made at the Fish House, an inn located on the wharves of pre-Revolutionary Philadelphia.

¾ pound sugar	2 bottles of dark rum
A few grains of salt	(4/5 quart)
8 cups water	⅓ cup apricot *or* peach-
4 cups strained fresh	flavored liqueur
lemon juice	A block of ice
1 bottle of brandy	
(4/5 quart)	

In a large punch bowl, combine the sugar, salt, water, and lemon juice; stir the mixture until the sugar is dissolved. Add the brandy, rum, and liqueur, stirring to blend the punch well. Add the block of ice and ladle the punch over it.

Glögg (SWEDEN)

20 PUNCH-CUP SERVINGS
PREPARATION AND COOKING: ABOUT 30 MINUTES
STANDING TIME: 24 HOURS

A traditional Christmas-season drink.

 3 whole cardamom seeds, bruised
 1 (3-inch) piece of cinnamon stick
 8 cloves
 Zest of 1 medium orange

Tie these seasonings loosely in cheesecloth.

 1⅓ cups water
 ¼ cup blanched almonds
 ½ cup golden raisins

 1 bottle of dry red wine
  (recommended:
  Cabernet Sauvignon)
 1 bottle of ruby port
 2 cups brandy

In a large saucepan, combine the spice bag and water; bring the liquid to the boil, reduce the heat, and simmer the seasonings, covered, for 10 minutes. Add the almonds and raisins and continue to simmer the mixture for 10 minutes longer. Add the red wine, port, and brandy. Bring the mixture quickly to the boil, remove it from the heat, and allow it to stand, covered, for 24 hours.

 Sugar to taste
 A few grains of salt

Season the glögg to taste with sugar and salt; serve it in warmed punch cups, garnished with a few of the almonds and raisins.

Glühwein (AUSTRIA)

8 TO 10 SERVINGS
PREPARATION AND COOKING: ABOUT 25 MINUTES

2 bottles of dry white wine
  (recommended:
  Riesling or Sylvaner)
1 cup water
1 cup golden raisins
¼ cup sugar
A few grains of salt

2 (3-inch) pieces of
  cinnamon stick
1½ tablespoons
  cardamom seeds,
  bruised
1 teaspoon whole cloves

In a saucepan, combine the ingredients. Over high heat, bring the mixture rapidly to the boil; immediately reduce the heat and simmer the glühwein gently, uncovered, for 10 minutes. Strain the mixture into a warmed pitcher before serving it.

Irish Coffee

1 SERVING
PREPARATION: ABOUT 10 MINUTES (THE PREPARATION TIME DOES NOT
  INCLUDE MAKING THE COFFEE)

Irish whiskey

Into each warmed mug, pour 1 or 2 ounces of whiskey.

Sugar

Add sugar to taste.

Strong hot coffee

Add the coffee, not all the way to the top of the mug.

Sweetened whipped cream

To each mug, add a generous dollop of whipped cream. And . . . *Erin go bragh!*

Krambambali (GERMANY)

YIELD: ABOUT 3 QUARTS
PREPARATION AND COOKING: ABOUT 20 MINUTES

A traditional Bavarian Christmas punch.

4 cups dry red wine
   (recommended:
   Pinot Noir)
4 cups ruby port
1 cup (packed) dark
   brown sugar

A few grains of salt
2 (3-inch) pieces of
   cinnamon stick
6 cloves

In a large saucepan, combine the ingredients; bring the liquid to the boil, stirring to dissolve the sugar. Pour the mixture into a heatproof bowl.

1 pound sugar cubes
1 cup brandy

Put the sugar cubes in a coarse sieve and over them pour ½ cup of the brandy. In a coarse sieve held over the heatproof bowl, ignite the sugar cubes. As the flame dies, add, a little at a time, the remaining brandy. When the flame disappears entirely, add the contents of the sieve to the bowl.

1 bottle of champagne, at room temperature

Add the champagne and gently stir the krambambali to blend it well. Serve it in warmed punch cups.

Maibowle (GERMANY)

12 SERVINGS
PREPARATION: ABOUT 25 MINUTES
MACERATION TIME: OVERNIGHT

The celebrated May wine from Bavaria.

6 to 8 sprigs fresh woodruff,
rinsed, shaken dry, and
bruised
½ cup brandy

1 bottle of dry white wine
(recommended:
Rhine wine *or* Mosel)
½ cup sugar
A few grains of salt

In a crockery or stainless steel bowl, combine these five ingredients. Allow the mixture to stand, covered and refrigerated, overnight.

Block of ice
2 bottles of wine, as above
1 bottle of champagne
Strawberries, hulled, rinsed, and drained

Put the ice in a punch bowl. Over it, strain the wine mixture; discard the woodruff. Add the additional wine and the champagne, stirring gently to blend the mixture. On top of the maibowle float the strawberries, and when serving the drink, put a strawberry in each punch cup.

Mead (England)

YIELD: ABOUT 2½ QUARTS
PREPARATION: 25 MINUTES

This recipe does not call for a wine or alcohol, but gives you the fun of making your own.

Mead, the oldest known of Anglo-Saxon alcoholic drinks, plays an important role in the English epic poem *Beowulf*, in which the "meadheall" was the principal place of meeting and drinking—rather heavily, one might add. In the Middle Ages and up through the Tudor era, mead was given to young newlyweds, married because of family interests but not necessarily amorously inclined. As mead is reasonably intoxicating, inhibitions were released by drinking it. And because honey was the principal ingredient of the mead drunk by the couples during their first month of marriage, we derive from their custom our "honeymoon." Mead, like many liqueurs in France, became the province of monks; for this reason, following the dissolution of the monasteries by Henry VIII, mead making—as well as the then-thriving production of English wines —gradually ended.

The following recipe calls for dry yeast, unknown in medieval England, where mead was started in the same wooden tub used for bread making or apple mashing, two excellent sources of natural yeast.

   8 cups water
   2 cups honey
   1 cup dark brown sugar
   A few grains of salt

In a large saucepan, combine these four ingredients. Heat the mixture, stirring to dissolve the sugar, and then bring it to the boil.

   Zest and strained juice of 1 medium lemon
   12 whole cloves
   2 walnut-sized pieces fresh ginger, sliced and bruised
   1 teaspoon crumbled rosemary

While the liquid is coming to the boil, combine these ingredients in an earthenware crock or large glass container. Add the boiling liquid. Cover the crock and allow the mixture to cool to lukewarm.

   1 envelope of dry yeast

Over the surface of the lukewarm liquid, sprinkle the yeast. Tie a double thickness of cheesecloth over the crock and allow it to stand for 2 weeks, until the fermentation stops hissing. Strain the mead through a paper coffee filter. Bottle the mead and cork it securely. Allow it to stand in a cool place for at least 6 weeks. It will be tastier and fuller-bodied if aged for 6 months.

Milk Punch

4 TO 6 SERVINGS
PREPARATION: ABOUT 15 MINUTES

The time-honored formula from Louisiana.

   3 cups milk   A few grains of salt
   1 cup light cream   1 cup bourbon whiskey
   ⅓ cup sugar   Nutmeg

In a pitcher, combine the first four ingredients, stirring them to dissolve the sugar. (It is difficult, these days, to find light cream; I find that 1 part heavy cream plus 2 parts half-and-half works well.) When the sugar is dissolved, add the bourbon, stirring to blend the mixture. Serve the milk punch over ice, garnished with a sprinkling of nutmeg.

Variation:

Although bourbon is traditional, the punch may also be made with rye or scotch, which will yield a somewhat less sweet drink.

Mulled Cider

8 SERVINGS
PREPARATION AND COOKING: ABOUT 15 MINUTES

5 cups cider	5 cloves
1 (3-inch) piece of cinnamon stick	Zest of 1 small orange
	A few grains of salt

In a saucepan, combine these five ingredients, bring the mixture to the boil, reduce the heat, and simmer the cider for 10 minutes.

¾ cup applejack
¾ cup dark rum

Stir in the applejack and rum. Bring the mixture nearly to the boil and serve it in heated mugs.

Mulled Wine

12 SERVINGS
PREPARATION AND COOKING: ABOUT 15 MINUTES

A very old recipe for this traditional drink.

2 (3-inch) pieces of cinnamon stick	4 tablespoons sugar
½ teaspoon whole cloves	A few grains of salt
6 black peppercorns	2 bottles of red Burgundy
	1 cup brandy

In a saucepan, combine all the ingredients except the brandy. Bring the liquid to the boil, reduce the heat, and simmer the wine, uncovered, for 5 minutes. Add the brandy, bring the mulled wine nearly to the boil, and serve it in heated mugs.

Variation:

The following, quite different, recipe for mulled wine (6 servings) yields a sweeter and milder drink.

2 (3-inch) pieces of cinnamon stick	1 small orange, sliced
6 cloves	⅓ cup sugar
1 small lemon, sliced	A few grains of salt
	⅓ cup water

In a large saucepan, combine these ingredients and heat the mixture, stirring to dissolve the sugar.

6 cups red Burgundy

Add the wine, bring the mixture nearly to the boil, and strain it into heated mugs.

Hot Buttered Rum

1 SERVING

PREPARATION AND COOKING: ABOUT 10 MINUTES

1 cup milk	¼ cup rum
¼ teaspoon cinnamon	1 tablespoon softened
1½ teaspoons sugar	butter
A few grains of salt	Nutmeg

In a saucepan, heat the milk; do not allow it to boil. In a warmed mug, combine and blend the cinnamon, sugar, and salt. Add the rum and butter. Pour in the hot milk. Garnish the buttered rum with a sprinkling of nutmeg.

Syllabub (ENGLAND)

10 TO 12 SERVINGS
PREPARATION: ABOUT 15 MINUTES
CHILLING TIME: OVERNIGHT

This old English drink derives its names from Sille, once an area of the Champagne country in France (the town of Sillery is there today), and "bub," Tudor slang for any bubbly drink. A variation on the beverage similar to Italian zabaglione may be served as a dessert.

1½ cups dry white wine
1½ cups Madeira or sweet
    sherry
Grated rind and strained
    juice of 1 lemon
Grated rind and strained
    juice of 1 orange
¼ teaspoon nutmeg or
    mace

1 teaspoon orange-flower
    water (optional)
A pinch of crumbled
    rosemary
½ cup superfine
    granulated sugar
A few grains of salt

In a mixing bowl, combine the ingredients, stirring until the sugar is dissolved. Refrigerate the mixture, covered, overnight.

At this point you may stop and continue later. (The wine mixture will only improve with aging.)

**4 cups heavy cream, beaten until very frothy and thick but
    not yet "whipped"**

When ready to serve, whip together the wine mixture and cream. Transfer the syllabub to a chilled serving bowl and offer it in chilled glasses.

Variation:

SYLLABUB AS A DESSERT CREAM: Combine ½ cup Madeira, ½ cup sweet sherry, the strained juice of 1 medium lemon, the strained juice of ½ medium orange, ½ teaspoon nutmeg or mace, ¼ cup superfine granulated sugar, and a few grains of salt. Stir the mixture until the sugar is dissolved. Chill it thoroughly. Whip 2 cups heavy cream until it stands in soft (not stiff) peaks. Into the cream, whip the wine mixture. Transfer the syllabub to chilled dessert glasses and serve it immediately. Makes 6 servings.

Posset

6 TO 8 SERVINGS

PREPARATION AND COOKING: ABOUT 20 MINUTES

This is another old English drink, similar to syllabub; it too may be served as a dessert. The fact that Lady Macbeth says of Duncan's chamberlains,

> I have drugg'd their possets,
> That death and nature do contend about them,
> Whether they live or die . . .

should not put you off; posset is very tasty.

> 6 eggs
> 3 tablespoons sugar
> A few grains of salt

In the container of an electric blender, combine these three ingredients and whirl them on high speed for 15 seconds, or until the mixture is creamy.

> 2 cups heavy cream
> 1 cup Madeira *or* sweet
>   sherry *or* (for an ale
>   posset) 1 cup stale ale

> ¼ teaspoon cinnamon
> ¼ teaspoon ground cloves
> ¼ teaspoon grated
>   nutmeg

To the contents of the blender, add the cream, wine, and seasonings; whirl the mixture briefly to blend it. Pour it into the top of a double boiler and, over simmering water, cook it, stirring constantly, until it is thickened. Serve the posset in heated mugs as a beverage, or in warmed dessert glasses as a dessert.

Wassail (ENGLAND)

10 TO 12 SERVINGS
PREPARATION: ABOUT 45 MINUTES
COOKING: 30 MINUTES IN A 400° OVEN

Wassail is a Christmas beverage closely associated with the traditions of Henry VIII's "merrie England." Made of hot ale and sack, a spiced sweet sherry, it was served in a large loving cup passed among the guests. The drink was garnished with twelve roasted crab apples, each stuck with three cloves, representing the twelve apostles and the holy trinity. Lesser folk drank wassail from an earthenware bowl in which the clove-stuck apples bobbed about, to which were added pieces of toasted bread. When saturated, these sank to the bottom, so that those persons drinking the last of the wassail were said to "drink a toast." The word *wassail* comes from the Middle English *Waes haeil*, "Be well!"

> **12 crab apples, each stuck with 3 cloves**
> **Dark brown sugar**

Put the crab apples in a baking dish, sprinkle them with a little brown sugar, and add enough water to the bottom of the dish to keep them from sticking. Roast them at 400° for 30 minutes.

> **12 cups ale**   **2 walnut-sized pieces**
> **1 bottle of sweet sherry**   **ginger root, sliced and**
> **2 (3-inch) pieces of**   **bruised**
> **cinnamon stick**   **½ teaspoon mace**
>   **A few grains of salt**

In an enamel saucepan or casserole, combine these six ingredients. Bring the mixture to the boil, reduce the heat, and simmer it for 10 minutes.

At this point you may stop and continue later.

> **6 eggs, separated**

In a mixing bowl, beat the egg yolks until they are thick. In a second bowl beat the whites until they are stiff but not dry.

Remove the ale mixture from the heat. Fold the egg whites into the yolks and, in a thin stream, pour 1 cup of the hot liquid into the egg mixture, beating constantly. Then add the egg mixture to the remaining hot ale, stirring. Pour the wassail into a heated bowl; add the hot crab apples, and if you wish, a piece or two of dry toast.

Variation:

GOSSIP'S CUP: Very like wassail but less complicated to prepare, this was apparently drunk year round. In an enamel saucepan, combine and bring just to the simmer (do not boil) 3 (12-ounce) cans of stale ale, ⅓ cup cognac, the zest of 1 medium lemon, ¼ teaspoon ground ginger, and ¼ teaspoon grated nutmeg. Season the drink to taste with dark brown sugar. Makes 4 to 6 servings.

A Lexicon of Wines and Spirits

Wine is the naturally fermented juice pressed from ripe grapes. When the grape is crushed, the yeast that grows naturally on its skin ferments its sugars to produce alcohol, which in turn preserves the wine. The principal wine-grape family is Vitis vinifera, native to the Old World and later brought to the New, where more than 150 varieties are now grown commercially. In America, a native grape, Vitis labrusca, is also used to make a few wines.

Nearly all wine-grape juice is virtually colorless. The hue of the wine comes from the skins. Red wine is fermented with the skins of the grape; their natural pigment colors the wine. White wine is made from the fermented juice alone, drawn from the grapes immediately after pressing. Rosé wines are made by allowing the juice to ferment with the dark grape skins for a short time only.

Fermentation in wooden cooperage may require a few days or as long as a few weeks, and produces wine of 10 to 14 percent acohol content by volume. The wine is then aged, a much slower process and a carefully controlled one, to bring out its smoothness, mellowness, and bouquet. Next, one wine may be blended with another to assure uniformity. Finally, it may be filtered and then bottled.

The lore and technique of wine making boast a long and interesting bibliography. Unfortunately, lack of space here precludes any detailed account of this fascinating subject.

This lexicon of wines and spirits is arranged in alphabetical order.

AKVAVIT: The Scandinavian spelling of *aquavit* (L. *aqua vitae*, water of life). A strong, dry, clear liquor distilled from grain or potato mash and flavored, generally, with caraway seed. Served ice-cold and drunk neat as an apéritif, it is also sometimes used in cooking.

ALE: Like beer, an alcoholic beverage made from fermented malt and cereal and flavored with hops. It is usually heavier and somewhat more bitter than beer.

AMARETTO: A pungent, sweet liqueur made from bitter almonds. Native to Italy, it is also produced domestically; the imported is smoother and mellower. Because of its pronounced flavor, a small quantity goes a long way. It is a delightful complement to fresh fruit.

ANISE-FLAVORED LIQUEURS: As apéritifs, alcohols flavored with anise are usually drunk diluted with water—which makes them turn milky with a pale green caste. Anise, a member of the carrot family, has a faint taste of licorice. See also *Pastis, Pernod.*

APPLEJACK: An American brandy distilled from fermented cider. See also *Brandy, Calvados.*

ARMAGNAC: A fine French brandy (see page 339), drier than cognac (page 341), named for the hilly region of Gascony in the southwest of France, where it is made. Sometimes called the *eau-de-vie de la Gascogne,* the country of at least one of the three musketeers (d'Artagnan), it was first known in the sixteenth century, and has since been aged, as it was then, in handmade casks of local oak.

BARBERA: A hearty Italian red wine named for the grape from which it is pressed and ready for use shortly after it has been bottled. Barbera is popular in Italy as an accompaniment to roast meats.

BEAUJOLAIS: A dry red wine, full-bodied and smooth, that is at its best when young; *le beaujolais nouveau* is, in France, near-cause of an autumn gastronomic celebration. Both the wine and the district, the hilly section of southern Beaujolais, derive their names from a village in the foothills.

BEER: A mildly alcoholic beverage made from malted barley and other cereals and flavored with hops. Beer and ale (above) are popular cooking liquids in Flanders.

BENEDICTINE: A liqueur distilled from a fine cognac (page 341) and flavored with herbs, fruit peels, and aromatic plants. First made in the sixteenth century by the monks of the Benedictine Abbey of Fécamp, France, it is still made there, but no longer by the religious brotherhood. Its formula continues to be a closely guarded secret.

BOCK BEER: A heavy, dark, sweet beer, originally made in winter for use in spring, but now generally available year round.

BORDEAUX: Wines, both red and white, from the southwestern region of France. Médoc and Sauternes are the Bordeaux named in this book but others merit your attention, both as complements to cooking and as enjoyable table wines: Graves, St. Emilion, St. Julien, Pomerol, and Margaux, to name but a few. Since before the time of Pepys (who refers to them), red wines from the Bordeaux have been known in England, where they were called "claret," from *clairet,* a French word describing their clear luminous color.

BOURBON: A whiskey distilled from corn or partly from corn. Straight bourbon is distilled from mash containing not less than 51 percent corn; blended bourbon contains not less than 51 percent straight bourbon. The name derives from Bourbon County, Kentucky, where it was first made. It is a sweeter-tasting whiskey than Canadian, Scotch, and rye.

BRANDY: A liquor distilled from wine rather than grain and usually aged in wood. Cognac and Armagnac (pages 341 and 338) are among the finest brandies. Brandies are also made from fermented fruit juices (Calvados from apple, for example). In America, only the pure distillate of grape wine may be labeled "brandy"; when other fruits are used in making brandy, the product must be so designated: "apricot brandy," "peach brandy." The name derives from the Dutch *brandewijn,* literally "burnt wine."

BURGUNDY: Red or white wine named for the region in eastern France where it is made. Burgundies are among the finest of French wines, and include such famous names as Chablis, Meursault, Beaujolais, and Chardonnay, among others (see pages 340, 343, 338, and 340).

CABERNET SAUVIGNON: A dry red California wine, full-bodied and fruity, named for the grape from which it is pressed, which in France is the principal red wine grape of Bordeaux.

CALVADOS: Similar to but considerably drier than domestic applejack, Calvados is the Norman brandy made from cider. First mentioned in writing in 1553 by a gentleman farmer who was one of many making it, Calvados later received royal protection, and its standards of manufacture were dictated by decree. The name Calvados as applied to the brandy goes back to the nineteenth century. Actually, it was the name of a vessel in the Spanish armada—*El Calvador*—that sank on the rocks of the Norman coast. The name of the ship in its Gallicized form was given to these reefs and then came to be applied to the *département* where the wreck occurred.

CANADIAN WHISKY: Traditionally spelled without the "e," Canadian whisky is a blend of rye, corn, wheat, and sometimes barley malt. It is lighter, milder, and drier than American rye and bourbon whiskies.

CASSIS: A sweet black-currant liqueur used in mixed drinks and on desserts. Also called crème de cassis.

CHABLIS: A crisp, straw-colored, dry white Burgundy, made in and near the village of Chablis in north central France. Domestic Chablis are often labeled "Chardonnay," or "Pinot Chardonnay." A very useful wine in cooking. (When in doubt about a dry white wine, I use it.) And one of the world's most imitated!—So I advise you to find one that suits your culinary purposes and drinking tastes, and then stay with it.

CHAMPAGNE: Perhaps the world's most renowned wine. Clear and sparkling, white or light pink, it is made in the Champagne region of northcast France, with sugar and wine syrup added to the original pressing in the final stages of aging. The degree of sweetness or dryness depends upon the amount of sugar added, *brut* being the driest, *sec* being second in "crackle."

CHARDONNAY: A major white wine grape grown in both France and California. One of the grapes used in champagne, it produces a fine white table wine, often called Pinot Chardonnay. (See also *Chablis.*)

CHARTREUSE: An aromatic herbal liqueur with a brandy base made by Carthusian monks in the monastery of La Grande Chartreuse near Grenoble. The green variety is colored with chlorophyll and is stronger, drier, and more aromatic than the yellow, which is colored with saffron.

Both are flavored with hyssop, angelica, balm, cinnamon, and other seasonings. The formula is a closely guarded secret.

Chenin Blanc: A serviceable domestic dry white wine named for the grape from which it is pressed, which lends itself well to use in the kitchen. If Chenin Blanc is suggested in a recipe but is, for some reason difficult to find, Chablis is an entirely satisfactory substitute.

Claret: The English name for red Bordeaux (page 339).

Cognac: With Armagnac (page 338), the finest French brandy. Made in or nearby the town of Cognac in the Charente region of western France. The name is sometimes applied, erroneously, to brandy in general. (See also *Brandy*.)

Cointreau: The trade name of a fine, colorless, orange-flavored liqueur.

Corn whiskey: See *Bourbon*, page 339.

Crème de menthe: A sweet, faintly syrupy liqueur flavored strongly with mint. Available in either green or white (colorless); there is little or no difference in taste.

Curaçao: An orange-flavored liqueur first made in Holland from the dried peel of bitter oranges brought from the island of Curaçao. Now manufactured in various places, it is always the product of bitter oranges. Excellent for use in the kitchen.

Frangelico: The trade name for an Italian liqueur made from hazelnuts. According to legend, a seventeenth-century hermit, affectionately called Frangelico, lived largely on the earth's bounty and from it created various drinks. This one, at first made from wild hazelnuts and flavored with flowers and berries, is the only one to survive, and bears his name in memoriam. Frangelico is mild-tasting, but with a distinctive and pleasant nutty flavor.

Gamay Beaujolais: A substantial domestic dry red varietal wine and an excellent substitute for French wine in such dishes as *boeuf bourguignon*.

GENEVA: Another name for Holland gin (below), the English form of the Dutch *jenever*, deriving from the French *genièvre*, juniper. Geneva is heavy in body, highly flavorful, and is usually drunk neat and very cold as an apéritif.

GIN: A liquor distilled from various grains that can be drunk without aging. It is a clear and potent alcohol, usually flavored with juniper berries and sometimes with added herbs (see *Geneva*).

GRAND MARNIER: The choicest of the orange-flavored liqueurs, the French product (Grand Marnier is a trade name) is based on cognac and is recommended for kitchen use, especially when the liqueur is not to be too thoroughly cooked, for it is the smoothest and most delicate of its genre.

GRENACHE ROSÉ: A varietal California rosé wine that substitutes nicely for more costly imports.

IRISH WHISKEY: The national whiskey of Ireland, made from cereal mash, chiefly barley.

KIRSCHWASSER (*kirsch*): A brandy distilled from the fermented juice of cherries and flavored with crushed cherry pits. Produced in France, Switzerland, Alsace, and the Black Forest region of Germany.

LAGER: A beer stored for sedimentation and carbonated by its own carbon dioxide. Most American beers are lager beers, but the full term is rarely used today. The name derives from the German *lager*, meaning storehouse.

MÂCON: Named for a town in the Mâconnais, the southern part of Burgundy. Red Mâcon, while not the finest of table wines, is considered admirable for cooking by many French housewives. The most celebrated white Mâcon, Puilly-Fuissé, is presently very popular in America.

MADEIRA: A fortified wine from the Portuguese island of the same name. Perhaps the most famous Madeira is the sweet, dark malmsey. Sercial, on the other hand, is dry and pale. Madeira is served as an apéritif or dessert wine, and is also a boon to the cook. See also *Port*.

MARSALA: A fortified Italian wine named for a city in Sicily, it is somewhat like Madeira. Rich and sweet, it is used in the preparation of desserts and certain meat dishes. Dry Marsala is used as an apéritif. (See also *Port*.)

MÉDOC: A red wine named for an area in the Bordeaux region of France. Some of the best (and mostly costly) Bordeaux is produced in this section. For our purposes, however, an inexpensive Médoc can lend lightness and a delicate bouquet to dishes prepared with it.

MEURSAULT: A village in the Burgundy region of France gives its name to this fine white wine. Meursault reds are generally not very distinguished.

MOCHA-FLAVORED LIQUEUR: Originally a fine coffee from Arabia, *mocha* now usually refers to a flavor combining coffee and chocolate. Kahlua is a representative brand of this liqueur.

MOSEL (*Moselle*): A delicate, light, dry white wine pressed from the grapes grown in the Mosel River Valley, which runs through France, Luxembourg, and western Germany. Very good both in the kitchen and at table.

MUSCADET: A dry white wine named for the grape from which it is pressed in the lower Loire Valley of France. Especially admired by French cooks in the preparation of fish and seafood dishes, it is good when new, with a light, tart flavor.

MUSCATEL: A rich, sweet dessert wine, colored gold to amber, made from the Muscat grape. In Europe, it may be red or white or sparkling. In America, however, it is amber-colored and still.

NEUCHÂTEL: A pale, dry white wine produced in the Lake Neuchâtel area of Switzerland. In its native habitat it is slightly sparkling (*mousseux*); that exported is a still wine. In America, it is not very easily found and can be expensive; if you are in doubt, use Chablis.

ORANGE-FLAVORED LIQUEURS: See *Cointreau, Curaçao, Grand Marnier, Triple Sec*.

PASTIS: A licorice-flavored French apéritif. When drunk with water (as it usually is), it becomes milky. Used sparingly, it gives a refreshing taste to many vegetables. See also *Pernod.*

PEAR-FLAVORED LIQUEUR: See *Poire Williams.*

PERNOD: A yellowish anise-flavored liqueur somewhat similar to absinthe, but without the toxic effects of the wormwood with which absinthe is made. When mixed with water, it turns cloudy. Pernod is a trade name deriving from the family who first made it. It is the most popular and perhaps the smoothest of the anise-flavored pastis family.

PILSNER: A fine light lager named for the city of Pilsen in Czechoslovakia. The name has been borrowed worldwide to describe the best of lager beers.

PINOT BLANC: A variety of white grape used in France to produce many Burgundy wines and now used in California to produce the wine to which it has given its name.

PINOT NOIR: The purple grape from which the finest red Burgundies are made in France. It is also used in making champagne. In California, it produces a red wine to which it has given its name.

POIRE WILLIAMS: A Swiss eau-de-vie made from Williams (or Bartlett) pears.

PORT: A sweet, fortified dessert wine. The red is very dark and fruity; the tawny is a tan color and softer and mellower; and the white, which is not highly esteemed by wine lovers, is useful in the kitchen when no color is desired. Port may take fifty years to age. Originally made (and the finest still is) in the Douro Valley of Portugal, it is now also produced domestically. Its name derives from Oporto, a city in Portugal.

Port is the typical fortified wine. To make the wine sweet, very ripe grapes are pressed, and the juice is allowed to ferment until the alcohol is at least 15 percent. Then the pressed grapes and their juice are combined with brandy, raising the alcohol level to the point at which fermentation ceases. Half the grape sugar remains in the wine, which is, in consequence, strong and sweet.

R H I N E W I N E : Made from grapes grown in the area of the Rhine River. There are only a few (and not very good) red Rhine wines, but the white ones are light and refreshing. Rhine wine is also produced domestically.

R I E S L I N G : A small white grape from the Rhine Valley that has given its name to the wine made from it. Riesling is one of the best Rhine wines (see above), very popular in Alsace-Lorraine, and now successfully produced domestically.

R I O J A : An area between Burgos and Madrid which produces the finest red wines of Spain some of them comparable to the French wines of the Médoc. Less expensive than similar French wines, they are the products of plantings made by French wine growers who came to Spain after the scourge of the vine louse in the late 1800s.

R O S É D'A N J O U : Sometimes called "the wine of thirsty people." Its color comes (as does that of red wine) from the skins of the black grapes from which it is pressed. For rosé wine, fewer skins are left in the fermenting juice and are allowed to remain for less time—else one would end up with a red wine. Tavel is the leading French *vin rosé*, but rosé d'Anjou is less expensive. (See also *Grenache Rosé*.)

R U M : A liquor distilled from sugar cane syrup or molasses. Both dark and light rums are products of blending. The dark is heavier-bodied than the light and is used in tall drinks and, generally, in more prepared dishes than is the light. Light rum is used in cocktails and in dishes where no color is desired.

S A U T E R N E S : A French white dessert wine from the Bordeaux district, rich gold in color and varyingly sweet in taste. It is made from Semillon, Sauvignon Blanc, and Muscadelle grapes, picked late so that they are overripe and thus at the height of their sweetness.

New York state sauterne (no capital or final "s") is a dry white table wine.

S A U V I G N O N B L A N C : In California, a fine white wine named for the grape from which it is pressed. In France, the grape is used in Bordeaux to make Graves, Sauternes (see above), Pouilly-Fumé, and Sancerre.

SCOTCH WHISKY (no "e" in Scotland!): A liquor made by blending malt and grain whiskies. Scotch has a characteristically smoky taste, deriving from the peat used to heat and dry the sprouted malted barley from which the whisky is principally made.

SHERRY: A fortified wine ranging in color from pale gold to yellow brown and from dry and light to sweet and very robust (cream sherry). Made in Spain mainly from the Palomino grape in the district near Jerez (formerly Xerez), near Cadiz. See also *Port*.

SLIVOVITZ: A dry plum brandy made in Yugoslavia, Hungary, and the Balkans from the fruit of plum trees at least twenty years old. The liquor is distilled twice, with the addition, after a year's aging, of fresh plums. The name derives from the Serbo-Croatian word for plum.

SOAVE: One of the best Italian dry white wines, produced in the area surrounding the town of Soave, east of Verona. The name of the town means "sweet" or "gentle." Perhaps Soave is to Italy what Chablis is to France.

SOUTHERN COMFORT: Quite probably the only native American liqueur, and surely the oldest, this combination of bourbon whiskey, peach nectar, and herbs comes from New Orleans and/or St. Louis (the exact place of its birth is uncertain). Relatively dry for a liqueur, Southern Comfort is really a flavored whiskey, although its texture is considerably denser than that of most spirits.

STOUT: A strong, dark English or Irish ale with a distinctive malt and hops flavor.

SYLVANER: A white grape that has given its name to the wine pressed from it. Originally from Germany, but now widely found in Austria, the Italian Tyrol, Alsace-Lorraine, and California. The name derives from the Latin *Sylvanus*, the Roman god of trees and forests.

TOKAY: A white dessert wine from Hungary. Some Tokays are dry and are useful in cooking, especially Hungarian dishes; for the most part, however, Tokay is sweet.

Torres Vina Sol: A dry white Spanish wine produced by the Torres family near the town of Villafranca del Panadés.

Triple Sec: A strong, colorless, orange-flavored liqueur that tends to have more of an "edge" than either curaçao or, surely, Grand Marnier. Useful in cooking.

Verdicchio: An Italian dry white wine made from the Verdicchio grape in five or six villages in the Castelli di Jesi district of the Appenine foothills. Rather like Soave (page 346).

Vermouth: Not a true wine, but having a white wine base, this apéritif is flavored with aromatic herbs and spices. Dry (French) vermouth is pale, whereas sweet (Italian) vermouth is dark. Both varieties are produced in France and Italy, as well as in the United States.

Vodka: A colorless, ordorless, and virtually tasteless alcohol native to Russia, where it was first made from a fermented mash of rye or wheat. Now it is made throughout the world from other cereals, as well as from potatoes. Like gin, vodka is not aged, but unlike gin, it contains no flavor additives.

Whiskey: A liquor aged in wood and obtained by distilling the fermented mash of grain (rye, barley, corn, wheat). In the United States and Ireland, *whiskey* is now commonly spelled with an "e," whereas in Canada and Scotland, the "e" is omitted. See *Bourbon, Canadian, Irish,* and *Scotch* whiskies.

Zinfandel: A grape widely produced in California, it yields a good-quality red wine of the same name. The origin of the name is uncertain; the European source of its importation to the United States is also unclear. Sometimes Zinfandel is called the "Beaujolais of California," and it is, indeed, an excellent comrade in the kitchen.

Index

Robert Ackart

Robert Ackart has had three careers: first as a teacher of college English, then as an operatic stage director in Europe and America, and now as the author of ten books on food and cooking. He makes his home in Katonah, New York, where, in a large paneled, eat-in kitchen with open hearth, he evolves recipes, cooks, and writes. When not busy in the kitchen or with village civic work, Mr. Ackart enjoys sailing, music, reading, and traveling—a source of many ideas for his books.